SUPER SIKH

LOVES ELVIS. HATES BAD GUYS.

CREATED BY:
EILEEN KAUR ALDEN
SUPREET SINGH MANCHANDA

COVER & ART BY:
AMIT TAYAL

ADAPTED BY:
ADRIAN REYNOLDS
EILEEN KAUR ALDEN

Super Sikh, Volume 1
Copyright © 2019 by Fearless Media Ventures.

Rosarium Publishing
P.O. Box 544
Greenbelt, MD 20768-0544

www.rosariumpublishing.com

Printed in Canada

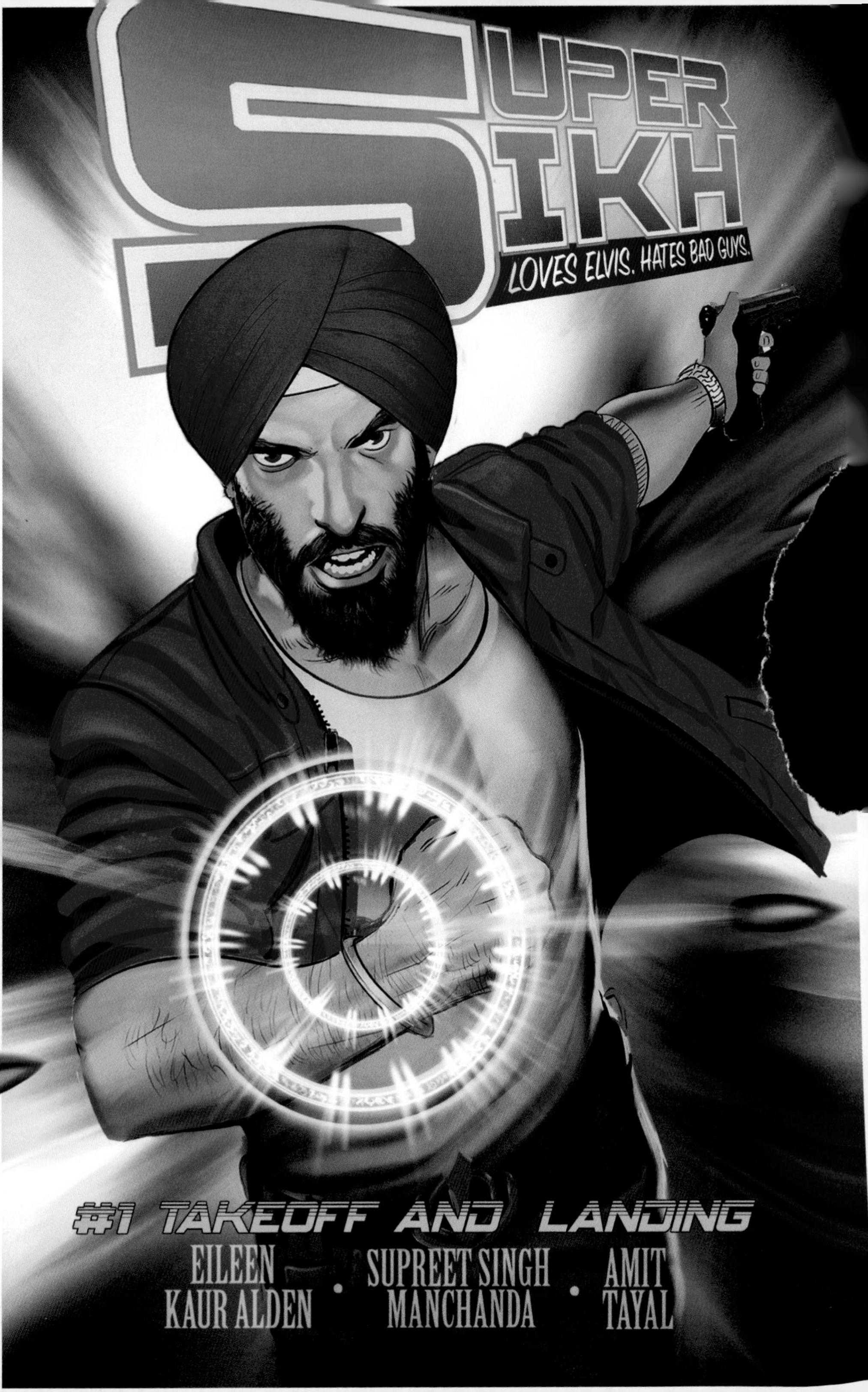
SUPER SIKH
LOVES ELVIS. HATES BAD GUYS.
#1 TAKEOFF AND LANDING
EILEEN KAUR ALDEN • SUPREET SINGH MANCHANDA • AMIT TAYAL

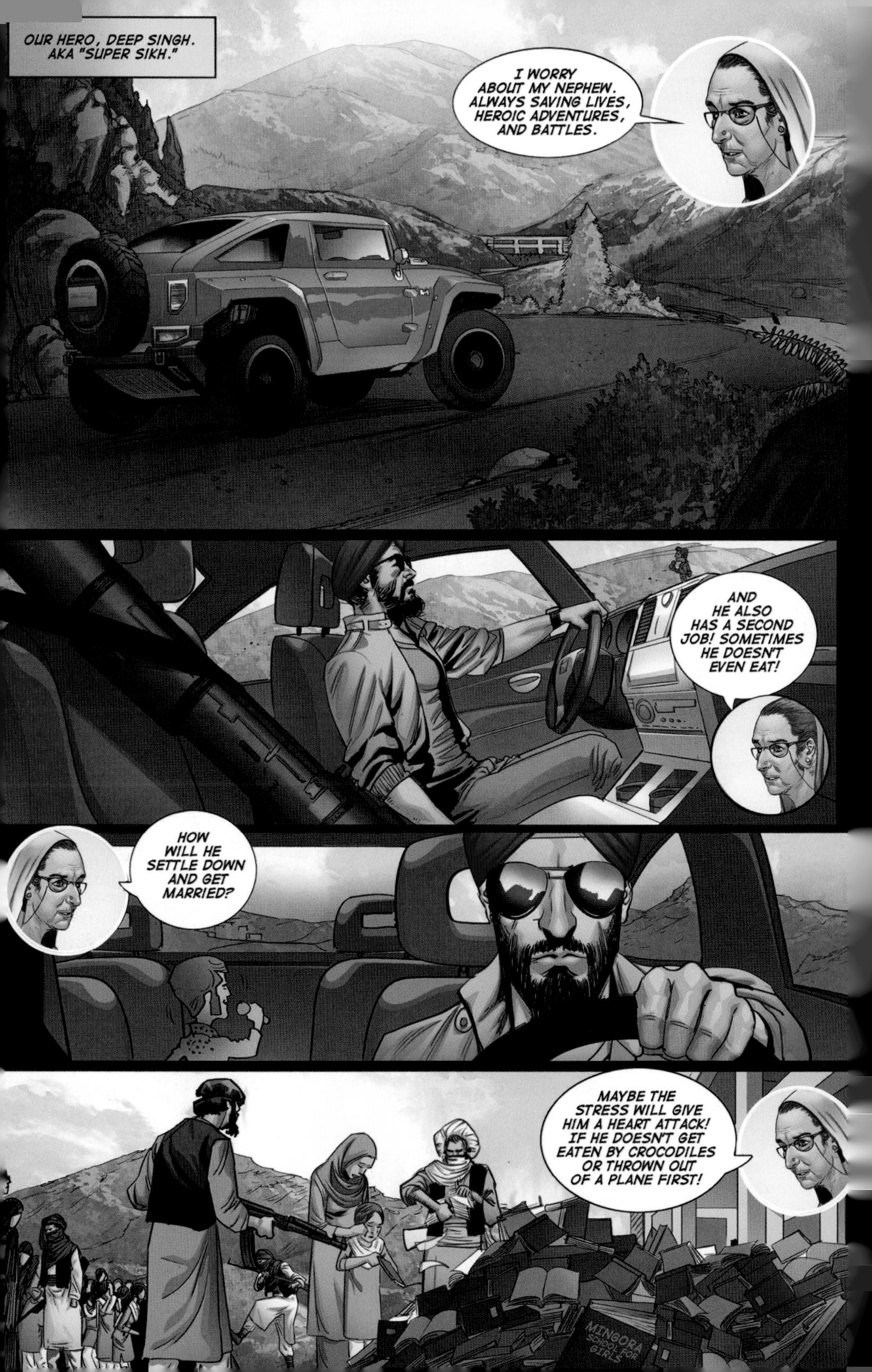
OUR HERO, DEEP SINGH. AKA "SUPER SIKH."
I WORRY ABOUT MY NEPHEW. ALWAYS SAVING LIVES, HEROIC ADVENTURES, AND BATTLES.
AND HE ALSO HAS A SECOND JOB! SOMETIMES HE DOESN'T EVEN EAT!
HOW WILL HE SETTLE DOWN AND GET MARRIED?
MAYBE THE STRESS WILL GIVE HIM A HEART ATTACK! IF HE DOESN'T GET EATEN BY CROCODILES OR THROWN OUT OF A PLANE FIRST!
MINGORA SCHOOL FOR GIRLS

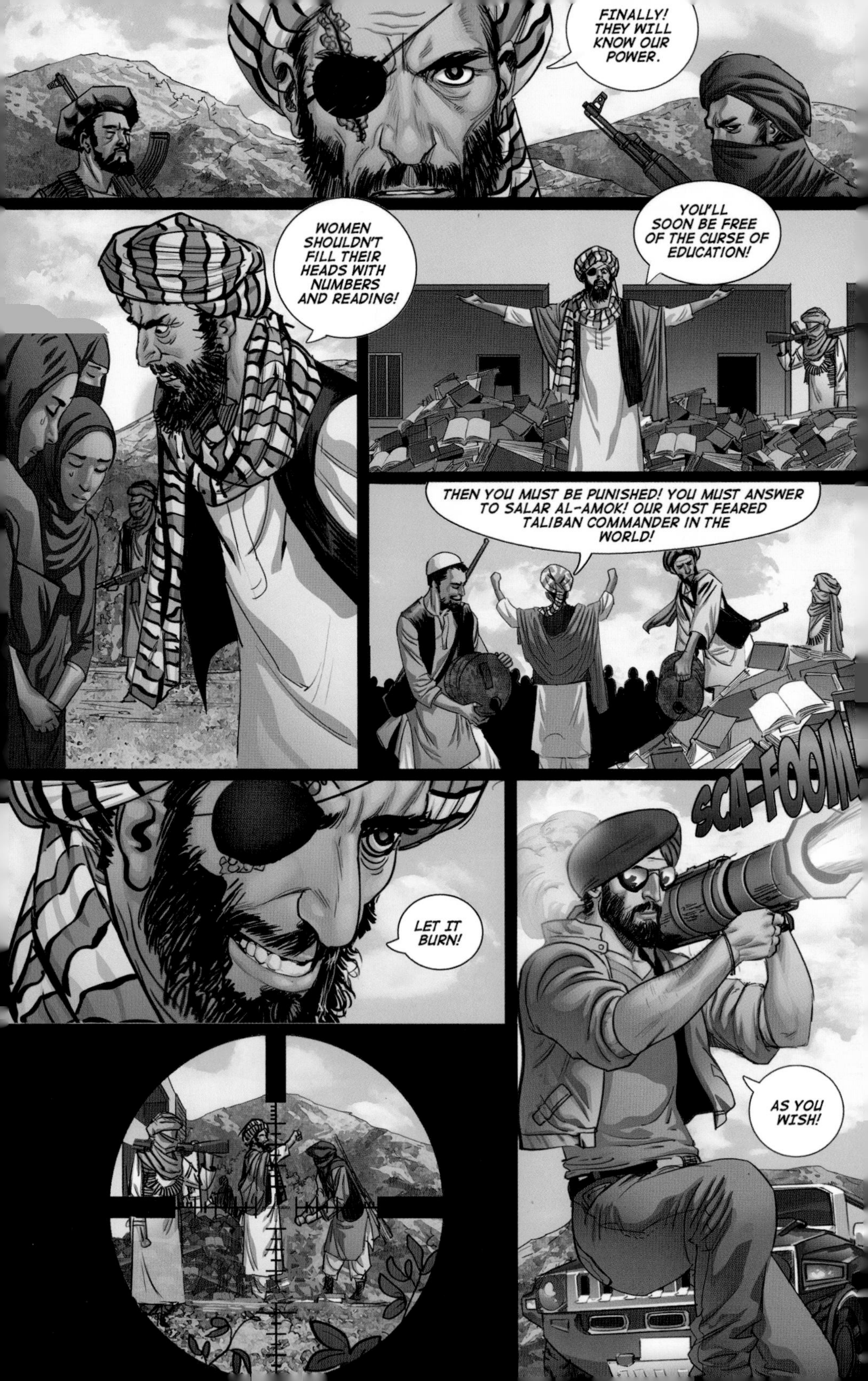
FINALLY! THEY WILL KNOW OUR POWER.
WOMEN SHOULDN'T FILL THEIR HEADS WITH NUMBERS AND READING!
YOU'LL SOON BE FREE OF THE CURSE OF EDUCATION!
THEN YOU MUST BE PUNISHED! YOU MUST ANSWER TO SALAR AL-AMOK! OUR MOST FEARED TALIBAN COMMANDER IN THE WORLD!
LET IT BURN!
SCA-FOOM!
AS YOU WISH!

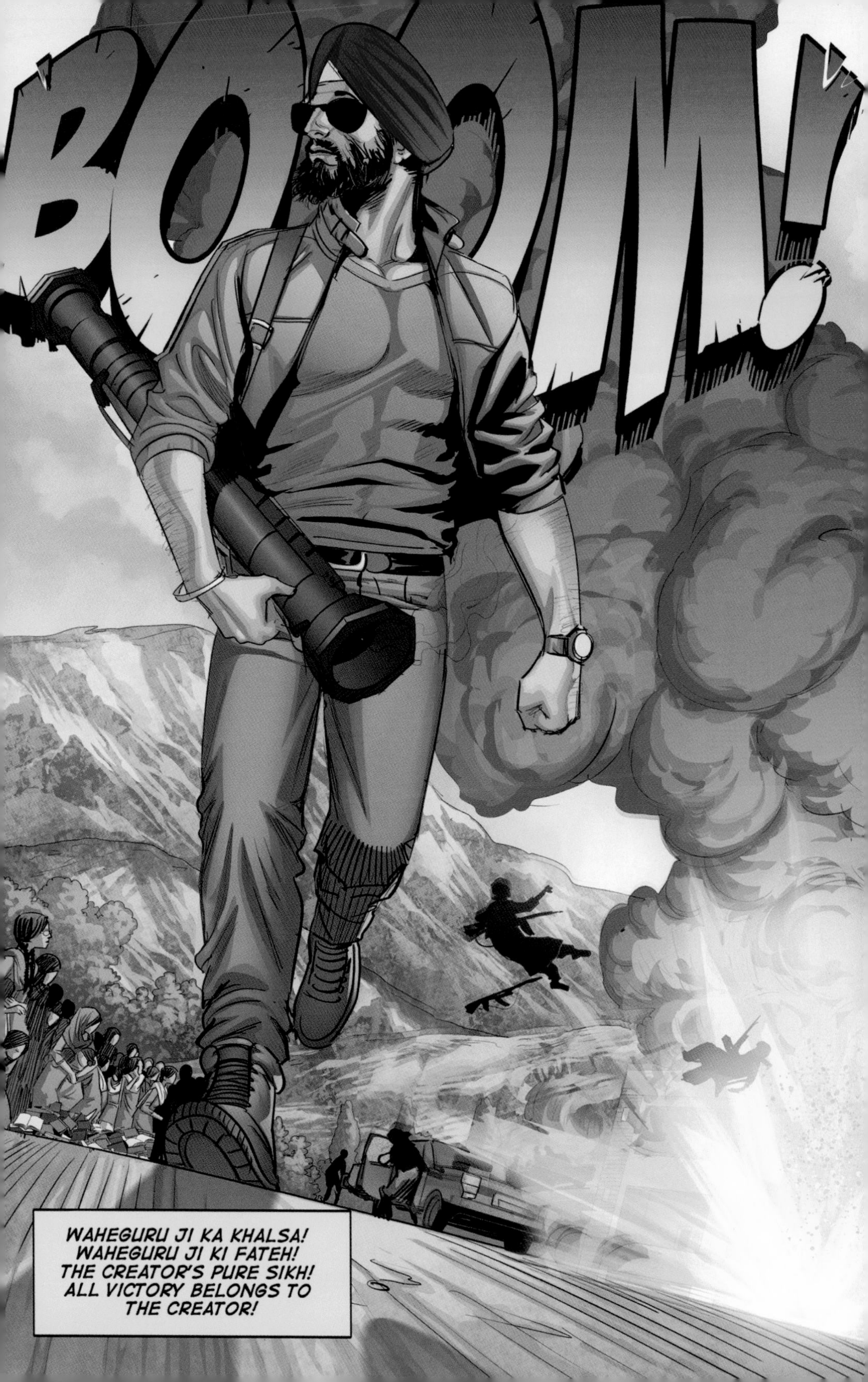
BOOM!
WAHEGURU JI KA KHALSA!
WAHEGURU JI KI FATEH!
THE CREATOR'S PURE SIKH!
ALL VICTORY BELONGS TO
THE CREATOR!

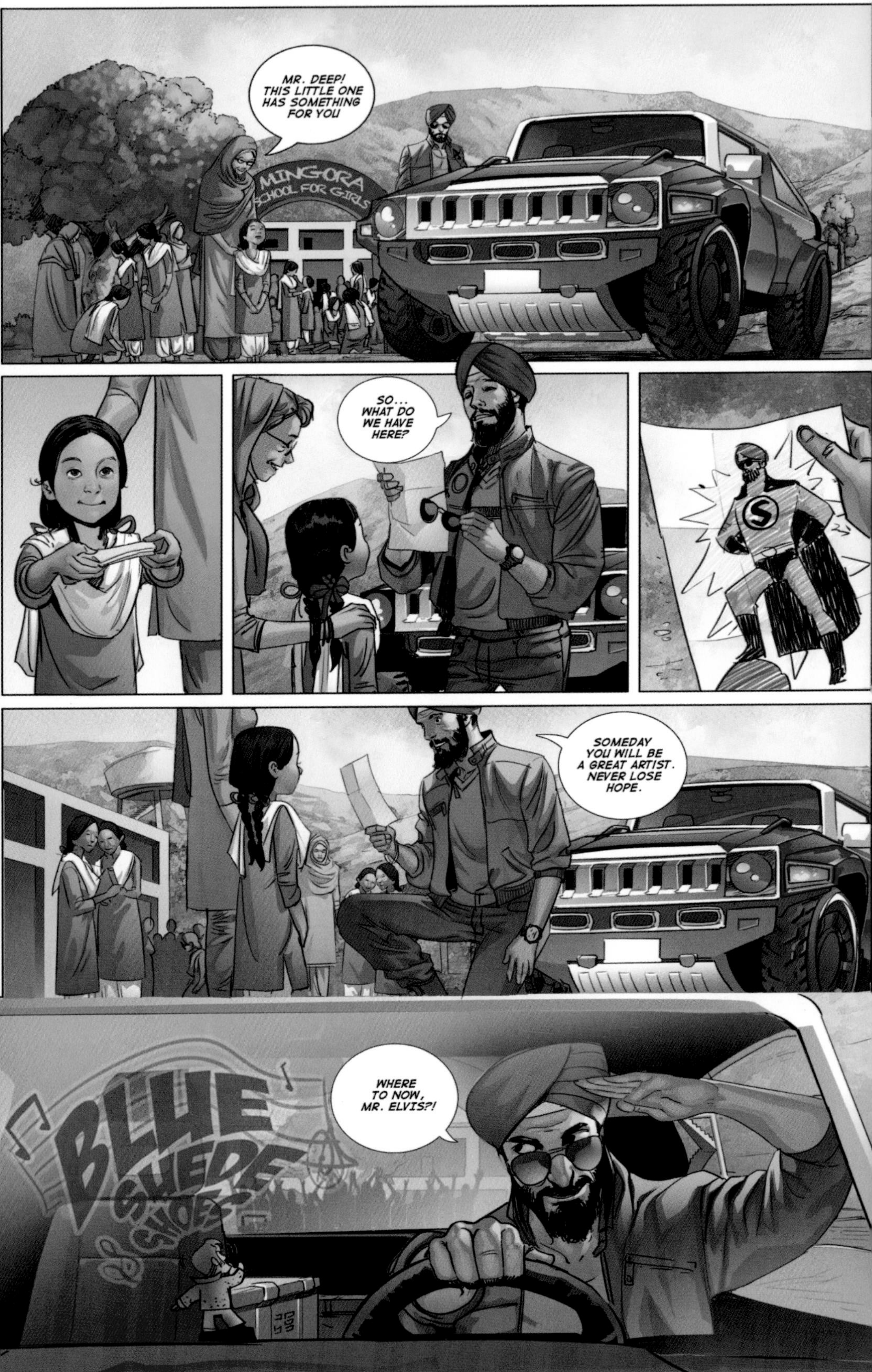
MR. DEEP! THIS LITTLE ONE HAS SOMETHING FOR YOU
MING-ORA SCHOOL FOR GIRLS
SO... WHAT DO WE HAVE HERE?
S
SOMEDAY YOU WILL BE A GREAT ARTIST. NEVER LOSE HOPE.
BLUE SUEDE
WHERE TO NOW, MR. ELVIS?!

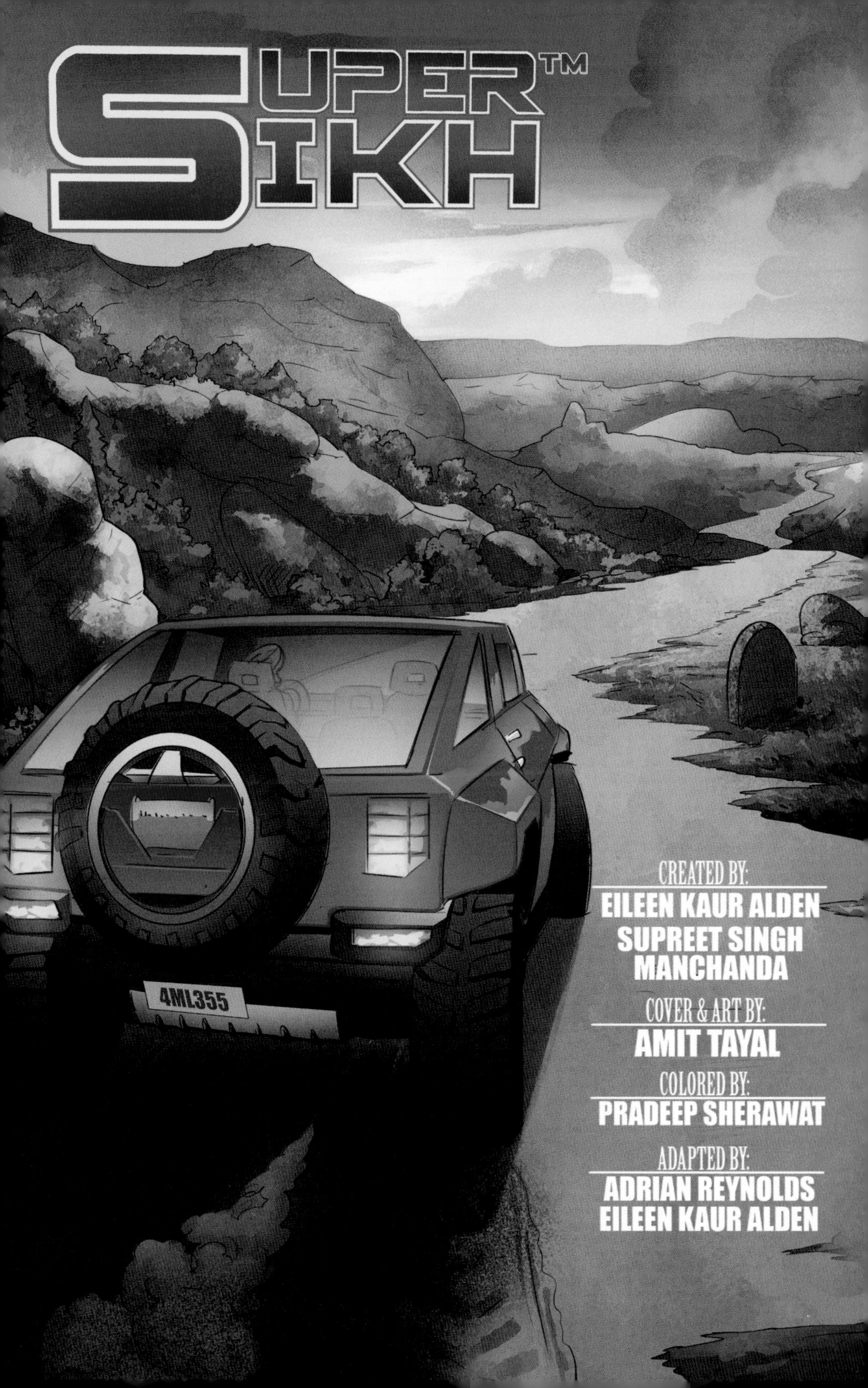
SUPER SIKH™
4ML355
CREATED BY:
EILEEN KAUR ALDEN
SUPREET SINGH MANCHANDA
COVER & ART BY:
AMIT TAYAL
COLORED BY:
PRADEEP SHERAWAT
ADAPTED BY:
ADRIAN REYNOLDS
EILEEN KAUR ALDEN

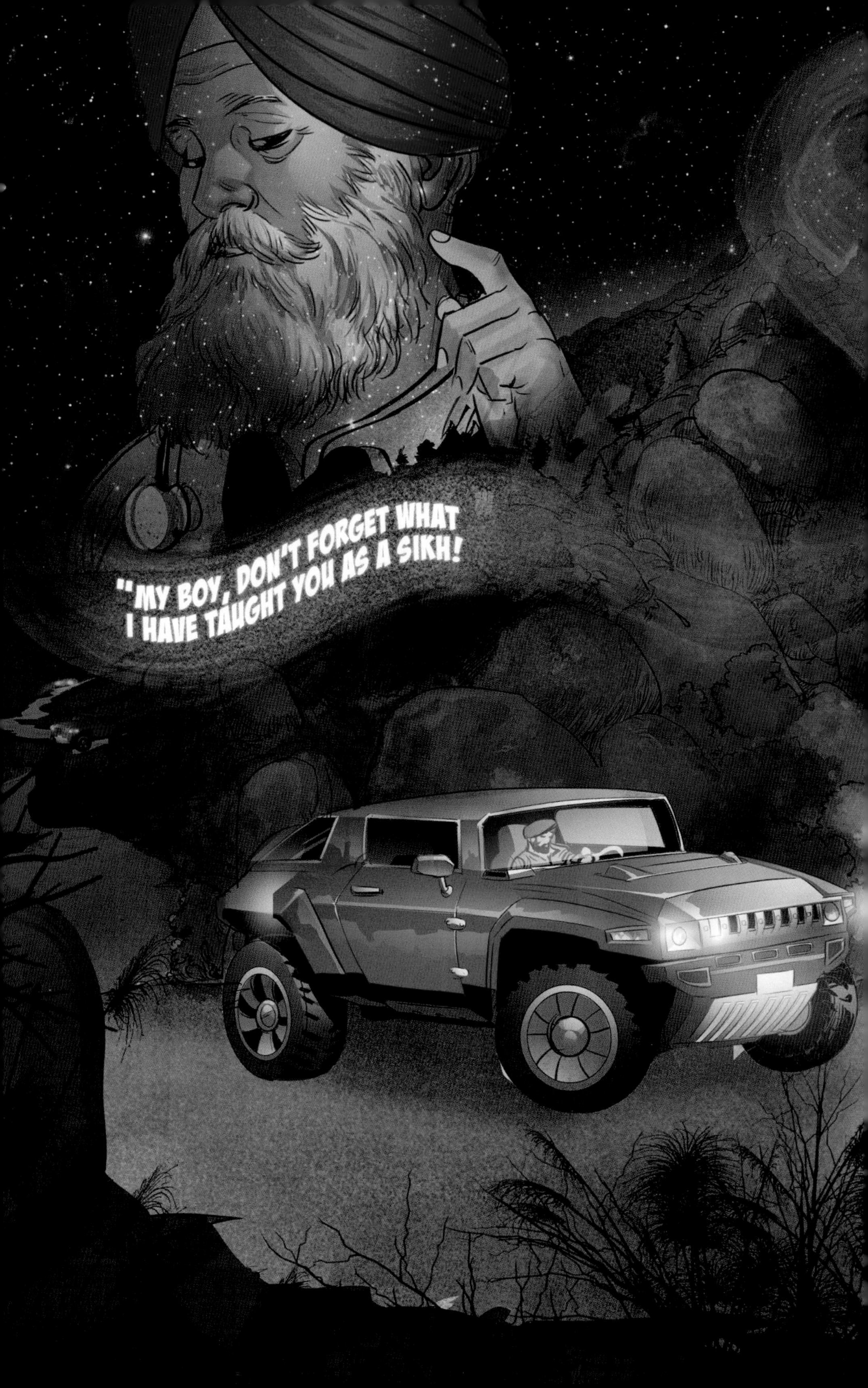
"MY BOY, DON'T FORGET WHAT I HAVE TAUGHT YOU AS A SIKH!

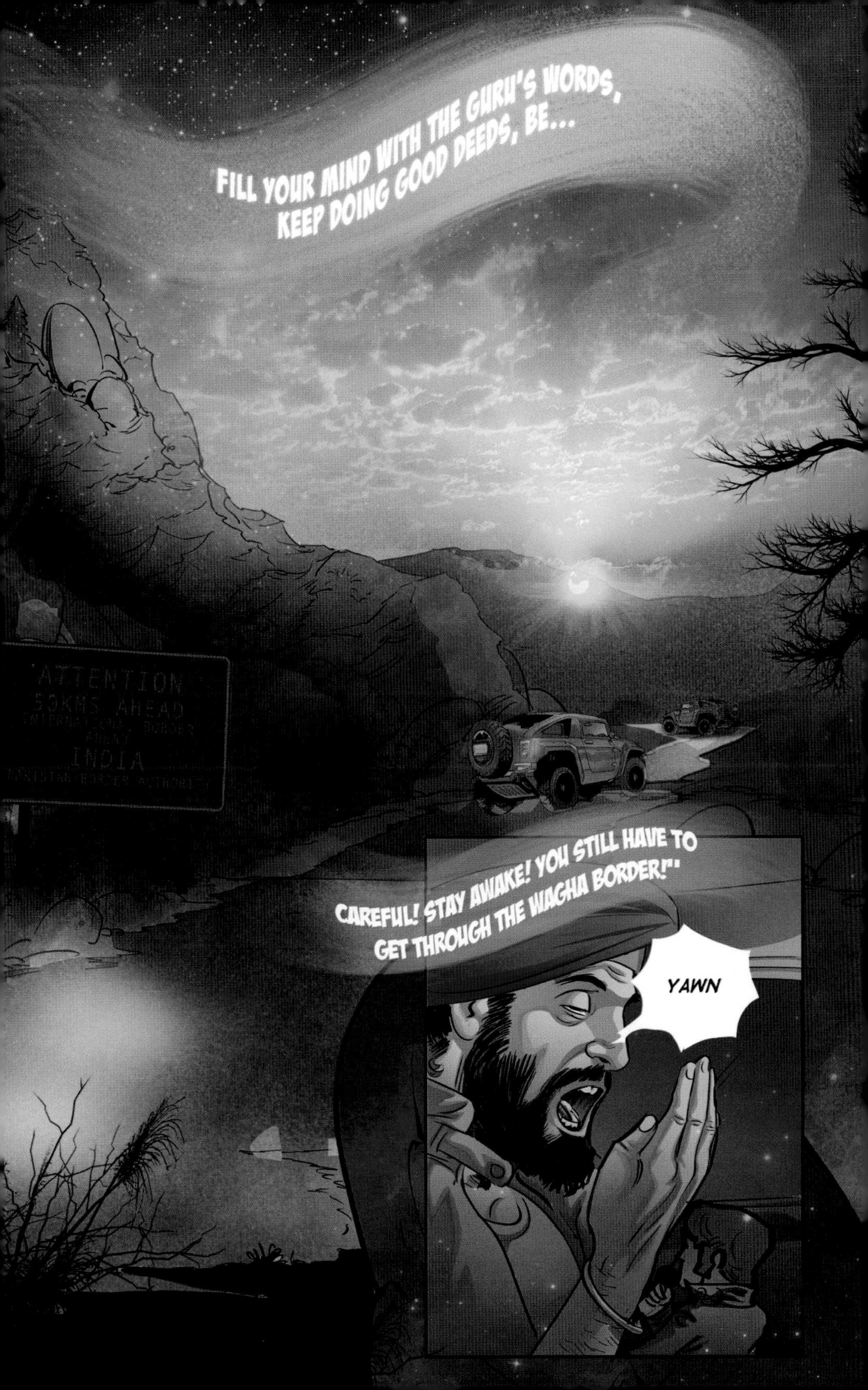
FILL YOUR MIND WITH THE GURU'S WORDS, KEEP DOING GOOD DEEDS, BE...
ATTENTION
50KMS AHEAD
INDIA
CAREFUL! STAY AWAKE! YOU STILL HAVE TO GET THROUGH THE WAGHA BORDER!"
YAWN

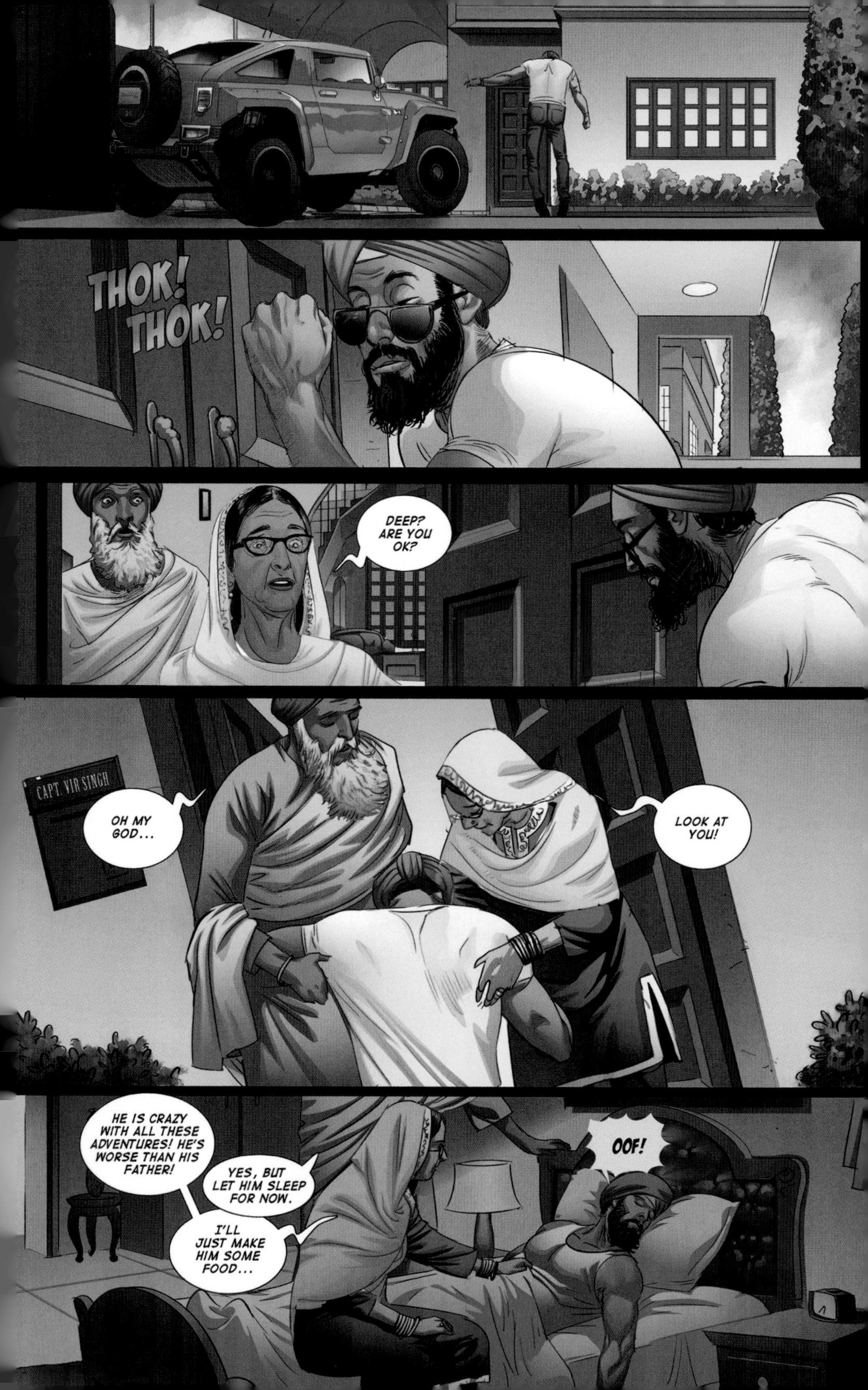
THOK! THOK!
DEEP? ARE YOU OK?
CAPT. VIR SINGH
OH MY GOD...
LOOK AT YOU!
HE IS CRAZY WITH ALL THESE ADVENTURES! HE'S WORSE THAN HIS FATHER!
YES, BUT LET HIM SLEEP FOR NOW.
I'LL JUST MAKE HIM SOME FOOD...
OOF!

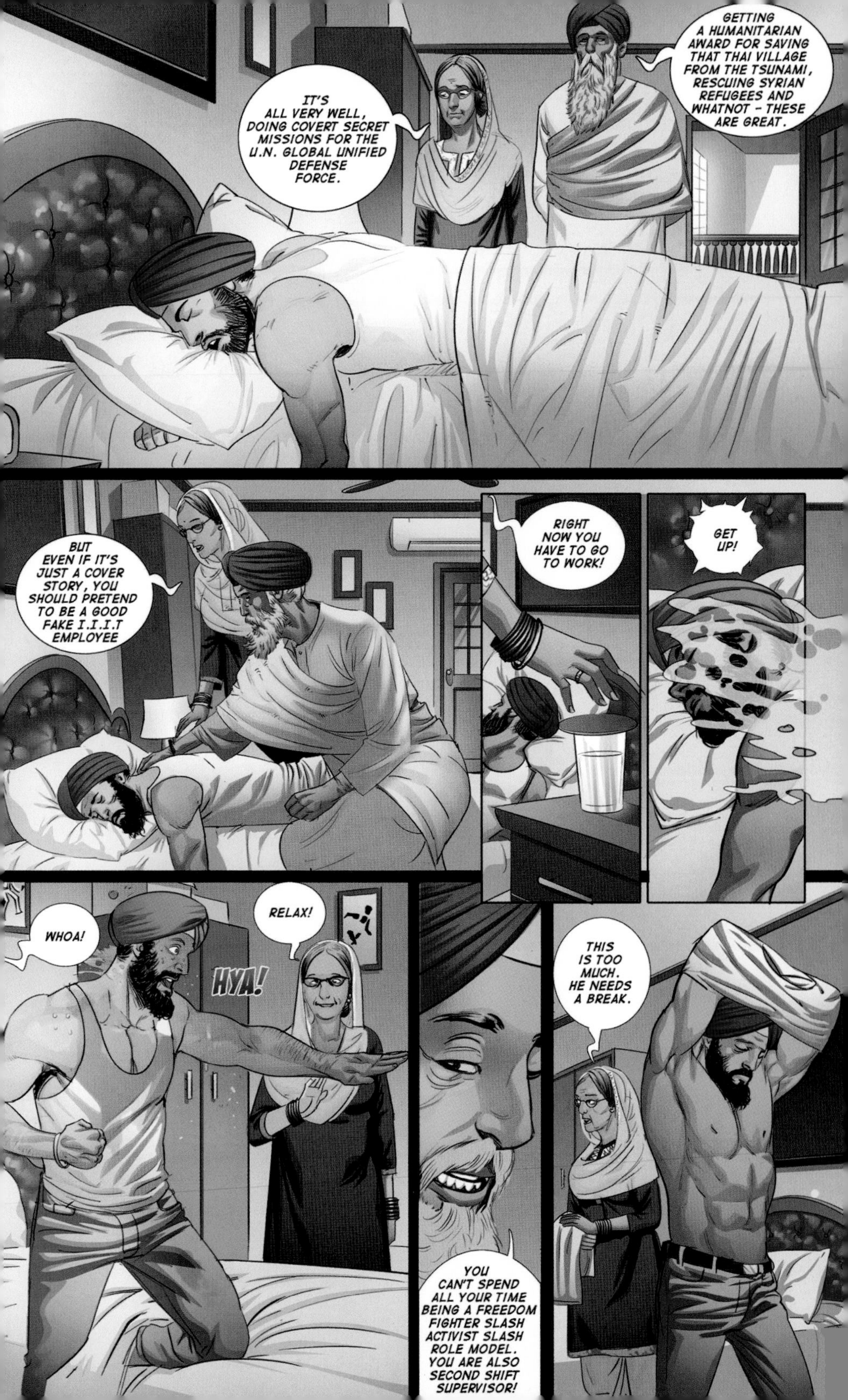
IT'S ALL VERY WELL, DOING COVERT SECRET MISSIONS FOR THE U.N. GLOBAL UNIFIED DEFENSE FORCE.
GETTING A HUMANITARIAN AWARD FOR SAVING THAT THAI VILLAGE FROM THE TSUNAMI, RESCUING SYRIAN REFUGEES AND WHATNOT - THESE ARE GREAT.
BUT EVEN IF IT'S JUST A COVER STORY, YOU SHOULD PRETEND TO BE A GOOD FAKE I.I.I.T EMPLOYEE
RIGHT NOW YOU HAVE TO GO TO WORK!
GET UP!
WHOA!
RELAX!
HYA!
YOU CAN'T SPEND ALL YOUR TIME BEING A FREEDOM FIGHTER SLASH ACTIVIST SLASH ROLE MODEL. YOU ARE ALSO SECOND SHIFT SUPERVISOR!
THIS IS TOO MUCH. HE NEEDS A BREAK.

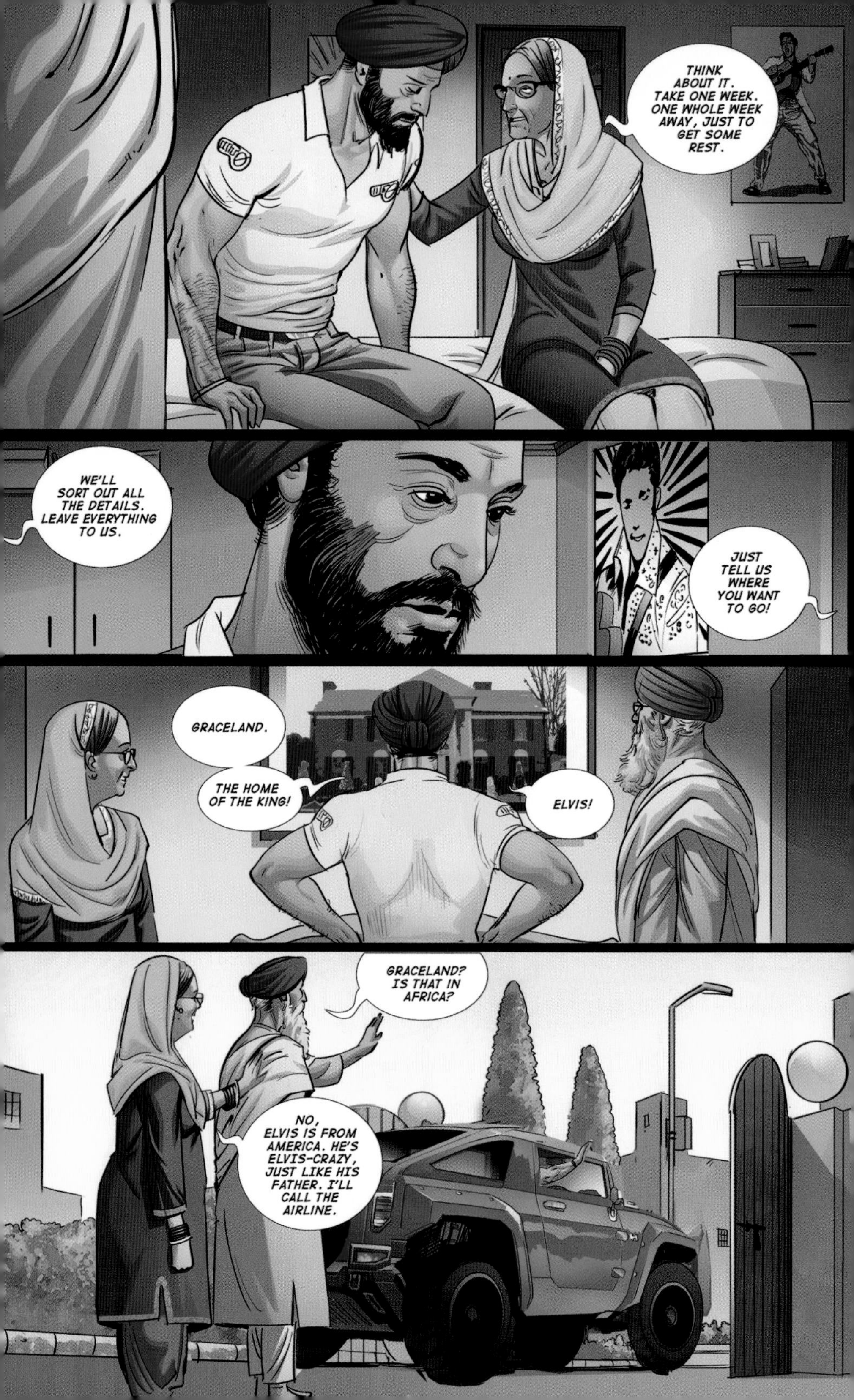
THINK ABOUT IT. TAKE ONE WEEK. ONE WHOLE WEEK AWAY, JUST TO GET SOME REST.
WE'LL SORT OUT ALL THE DETAILS. LEAVE EVERYTHING TO US.
JUST TELL US WHERE YOU WANT TO GO!
GRACELAND.
THE HOME OF THE KING!
ELVIS!
GRACELAND? IS THAT IN AFRICA?
NO, ELVIS IS FROM AMERICA. HE'S ELVIS-CRAZY, JUST LIKE HIS FATHER. I'LL CALL THE AIRLINE.

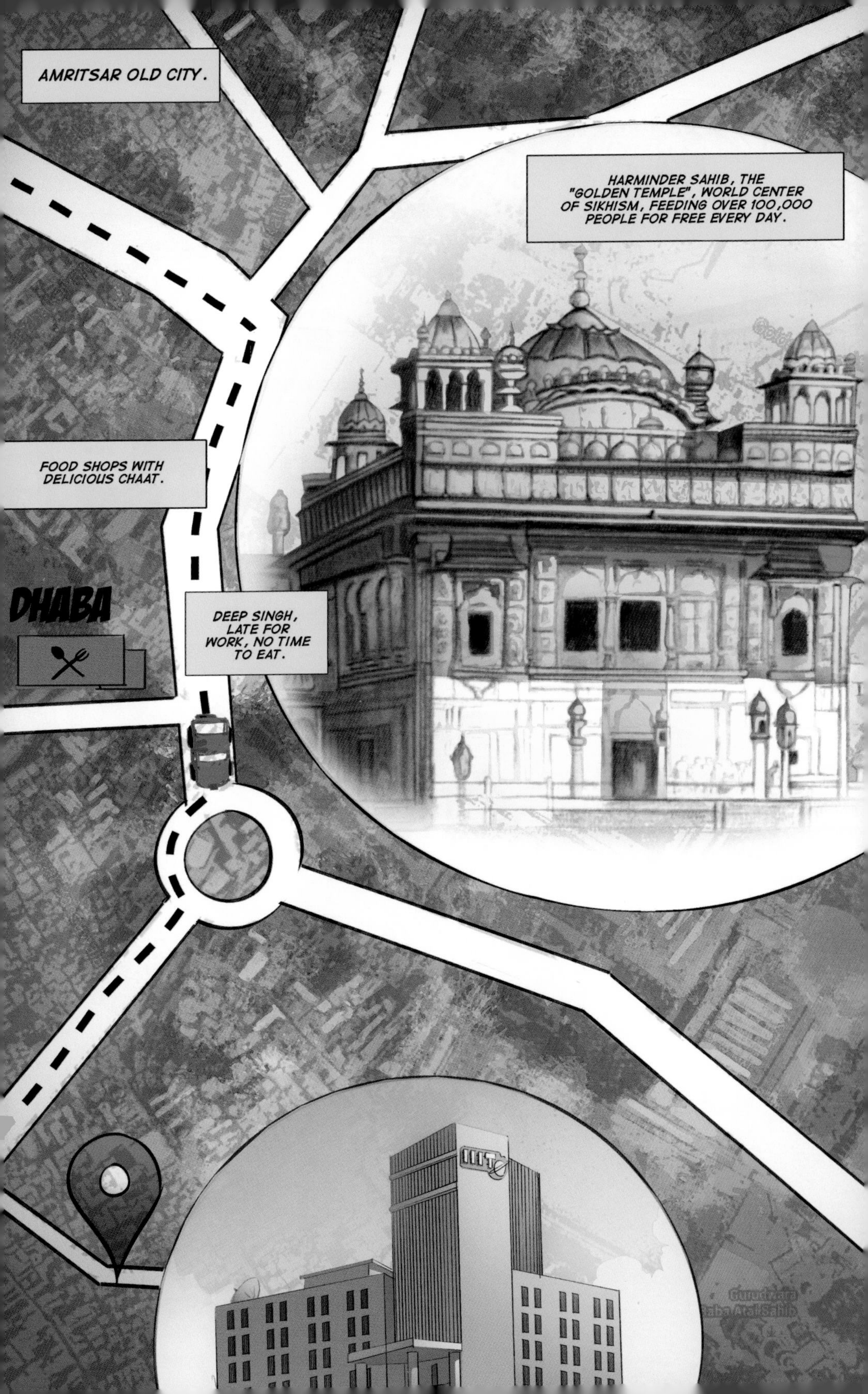
AMRITSAR OLD CITY.
HARMINDER SAHIB, THE "GOLDEN TEMPLE", WORLD CENTER OF SIKHISM, FEEDING OVER 100,000 PEOPLE FOR FREE EVERY DAY.
FOOD SHOPS WITH DELICIOUS CHAAT.
DHABA
DEEP SINGH, LATE FOR WORK, NO TIME TO EAT.
IIIT

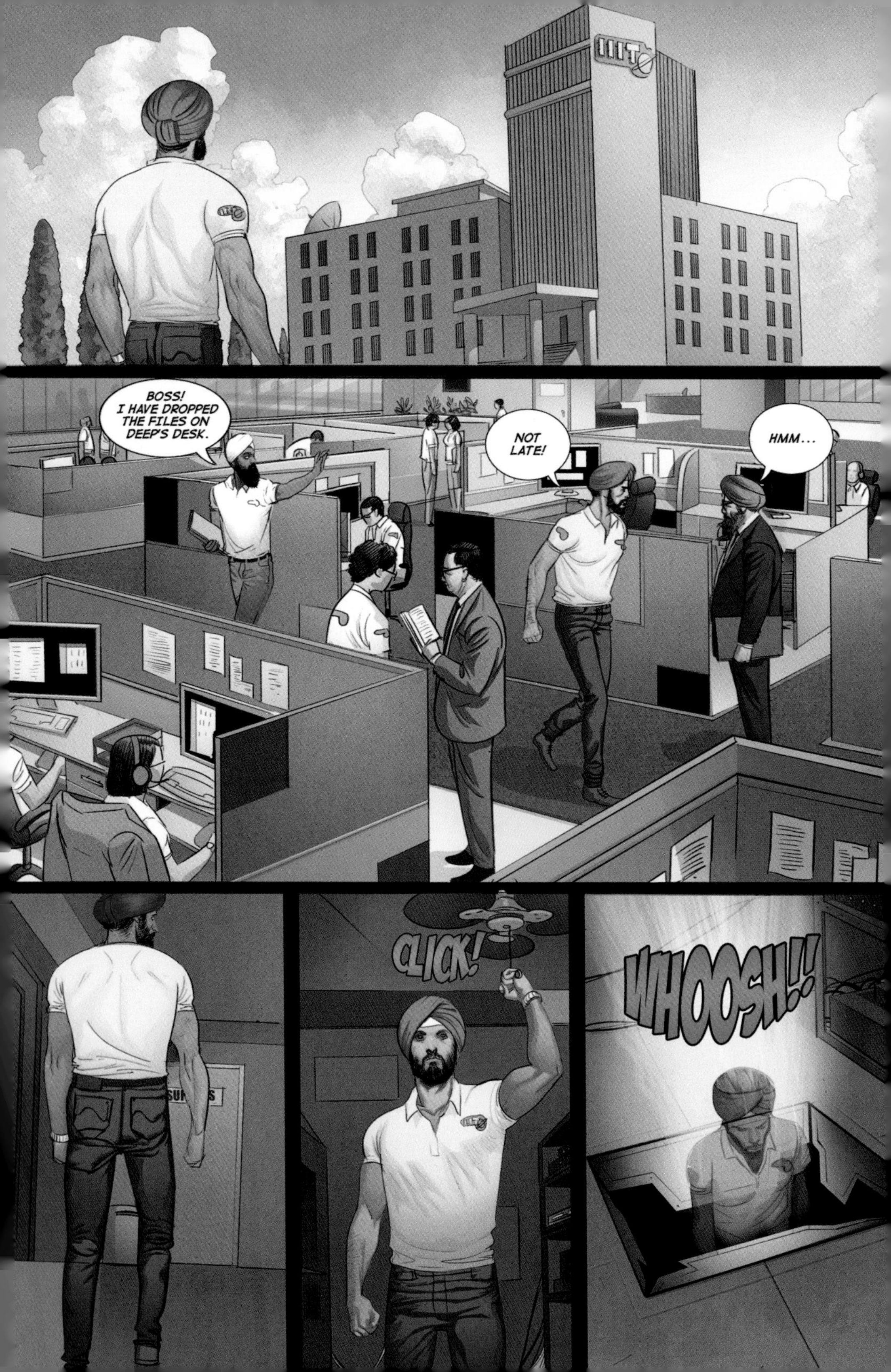
IIIT
BOSS! I HAVE DROPPED THE FILES ON DEEP'S DESK.
NOT LATE!
HMM...
CLICK!
WHOOSH!!

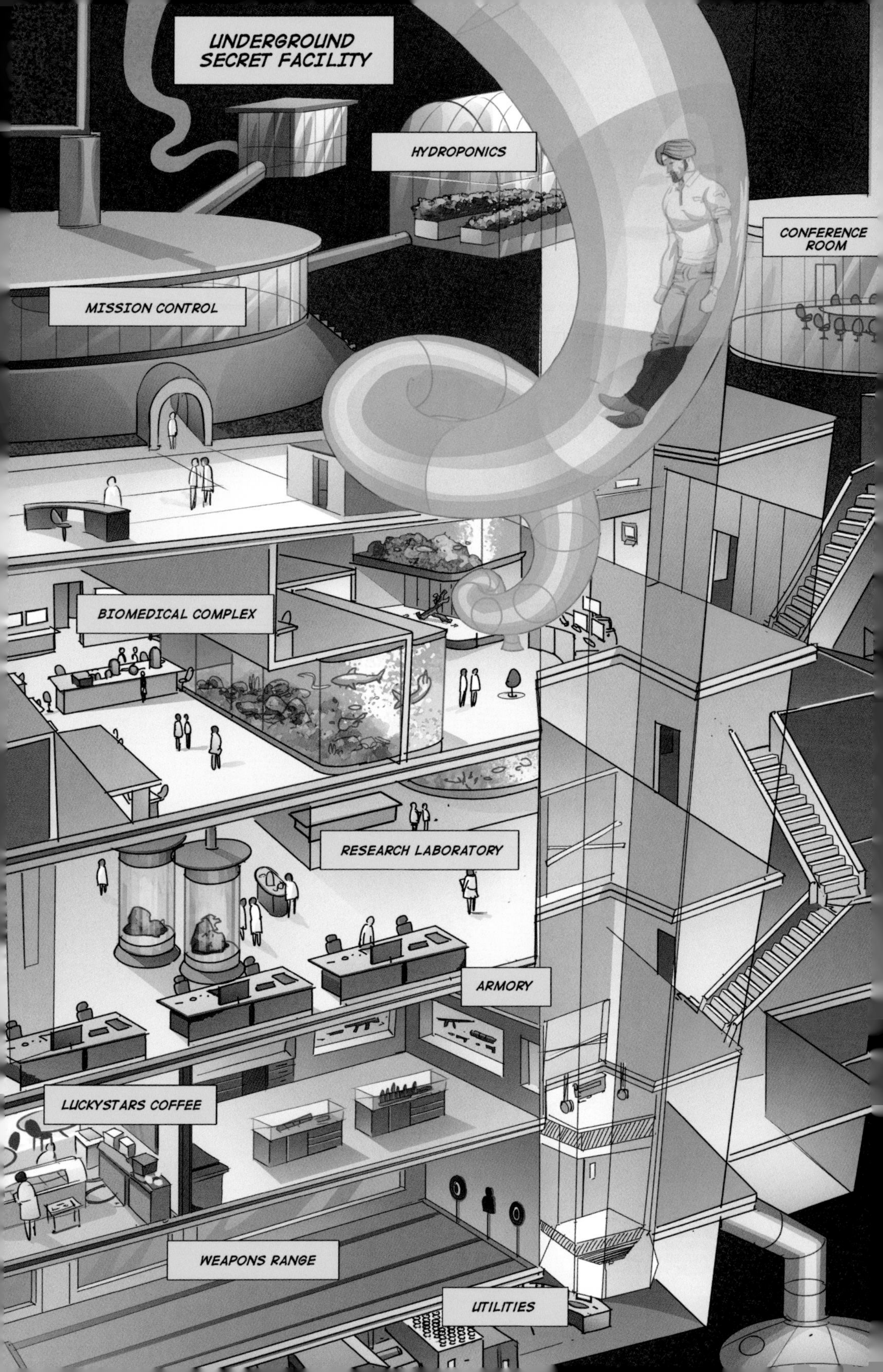
UNDERGROUND SECRET FACILITY
HYDROPONICS
CONFERENCE ROOM
MISSION CONTROL
BIOMEDICAL COMPLEX
RESEARCH LABORATORY
ARMORY
LUCKYSTARS COFFEE
WEAPONS RANGE
UTILITIES

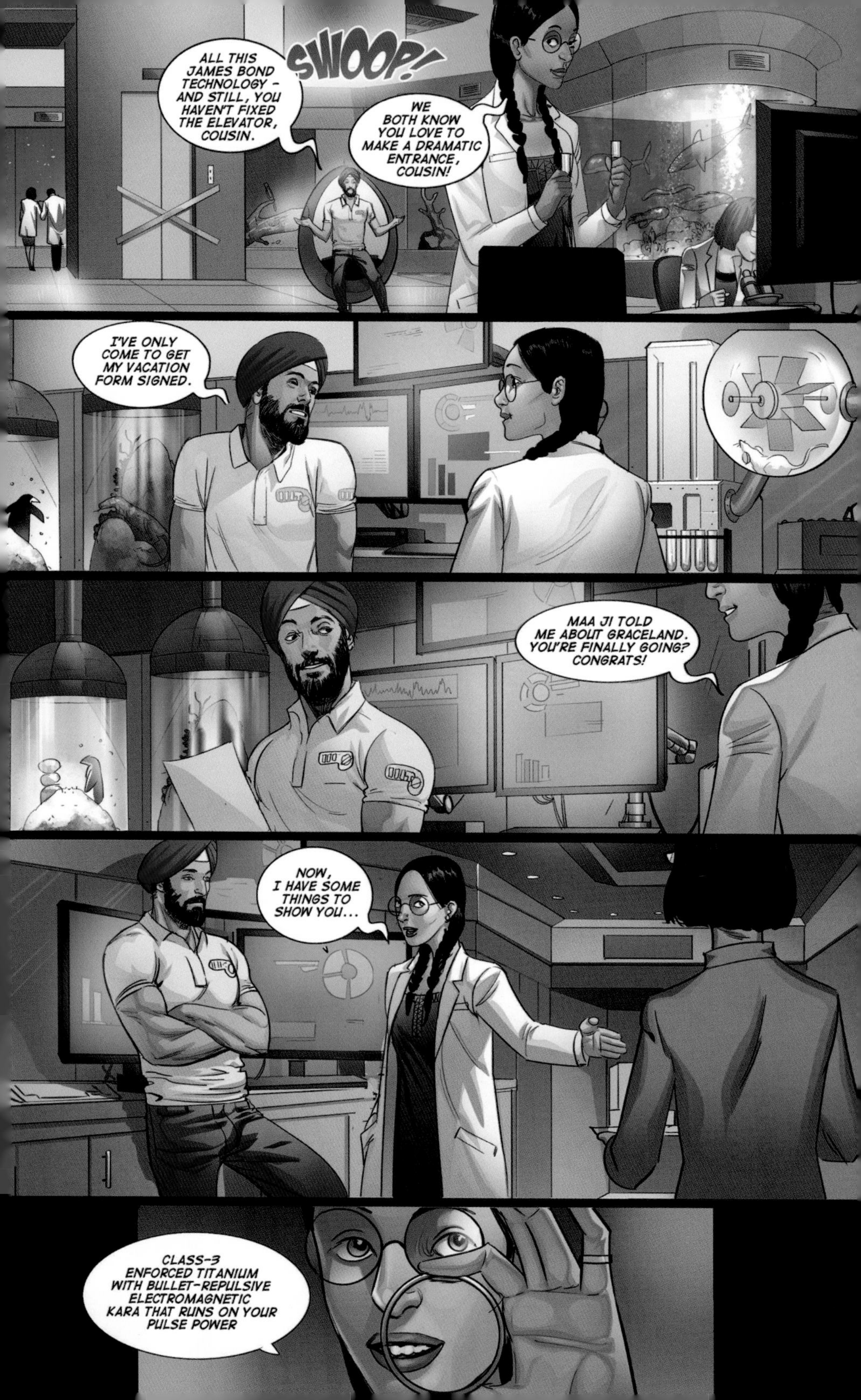
SWOOP!
ALL THIS JAMES BOND TECHNOLOGY - AND STILL, YOU HAVEN'T FIXED THE ELEVATOR, COUSIN.
WE BOTH KNOW YOU LOVE TO MAKE A DRAMATIC ENTRANCE, COUSIN!
I'VE ONLY COME TO GET MY VACATION FORM SIGNED.
MAA JI TOLD ME ABOUT GRACELAND. YOU'RE FINALLY GOING? CONGRATS!
NOW, I HAVE SOME THINGS TO SHOW YOU...
CLASS-3 ENFORCED TITANIUM WITH BULLET-REPULSIVE ELECTROMAGNETIC KARA THAT RUNS ON YOUR PULSE POWER

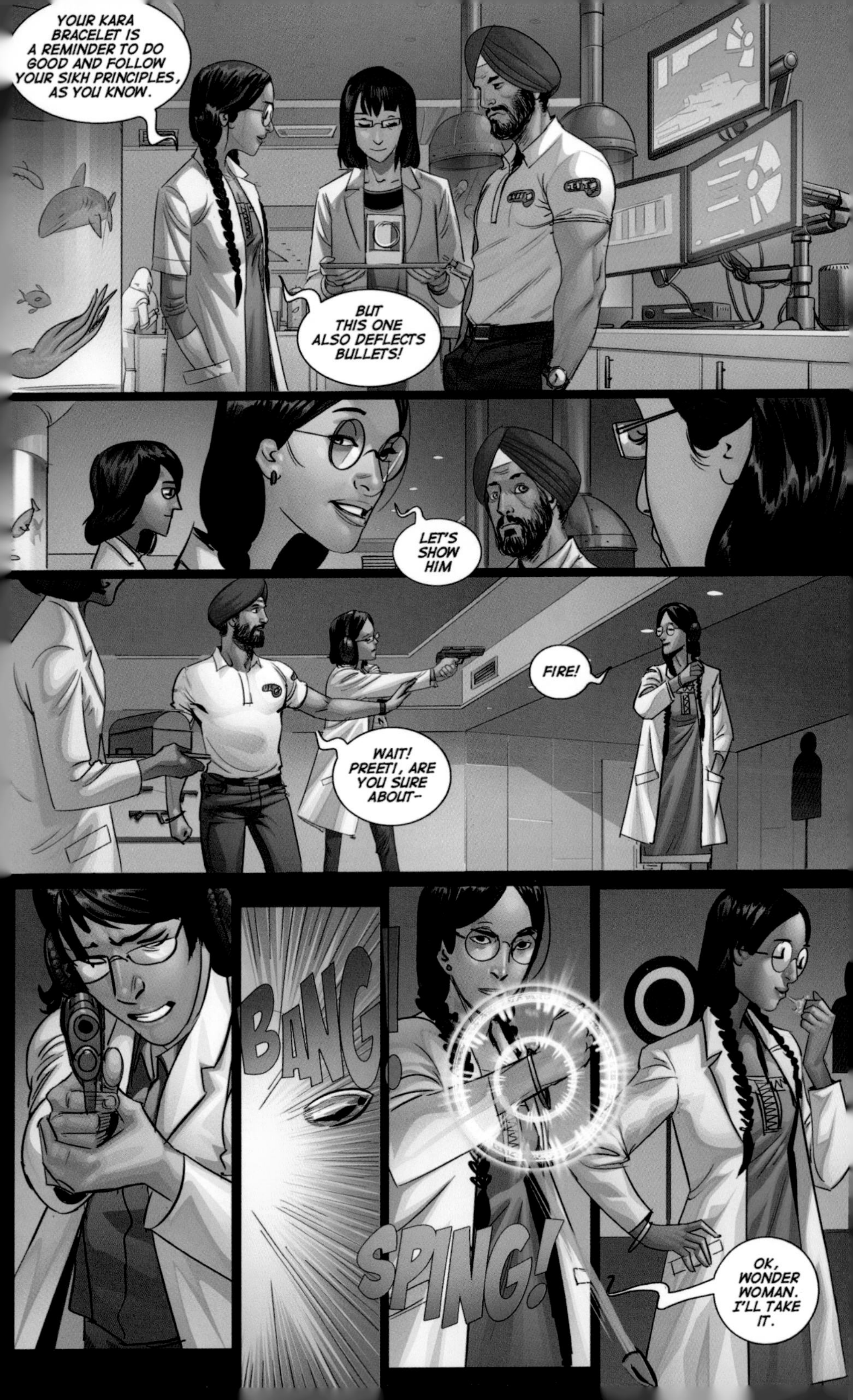
YOUR KARA BRACELET IS A REMINDER TO DO GOOD AND FOLLOW YOUR SIKH PRINCIPLES, AS YOU KNOW.
BUT THIS ONE ALSO DEFLECTS BULLETS!
LET'S SHOW HIM
FIRE!
WAIT! PREETI, ARE YOU SURE ABOUT-
BANG!
SPING!
OK, WONDER WOMAN. I'LL TAKE IT.

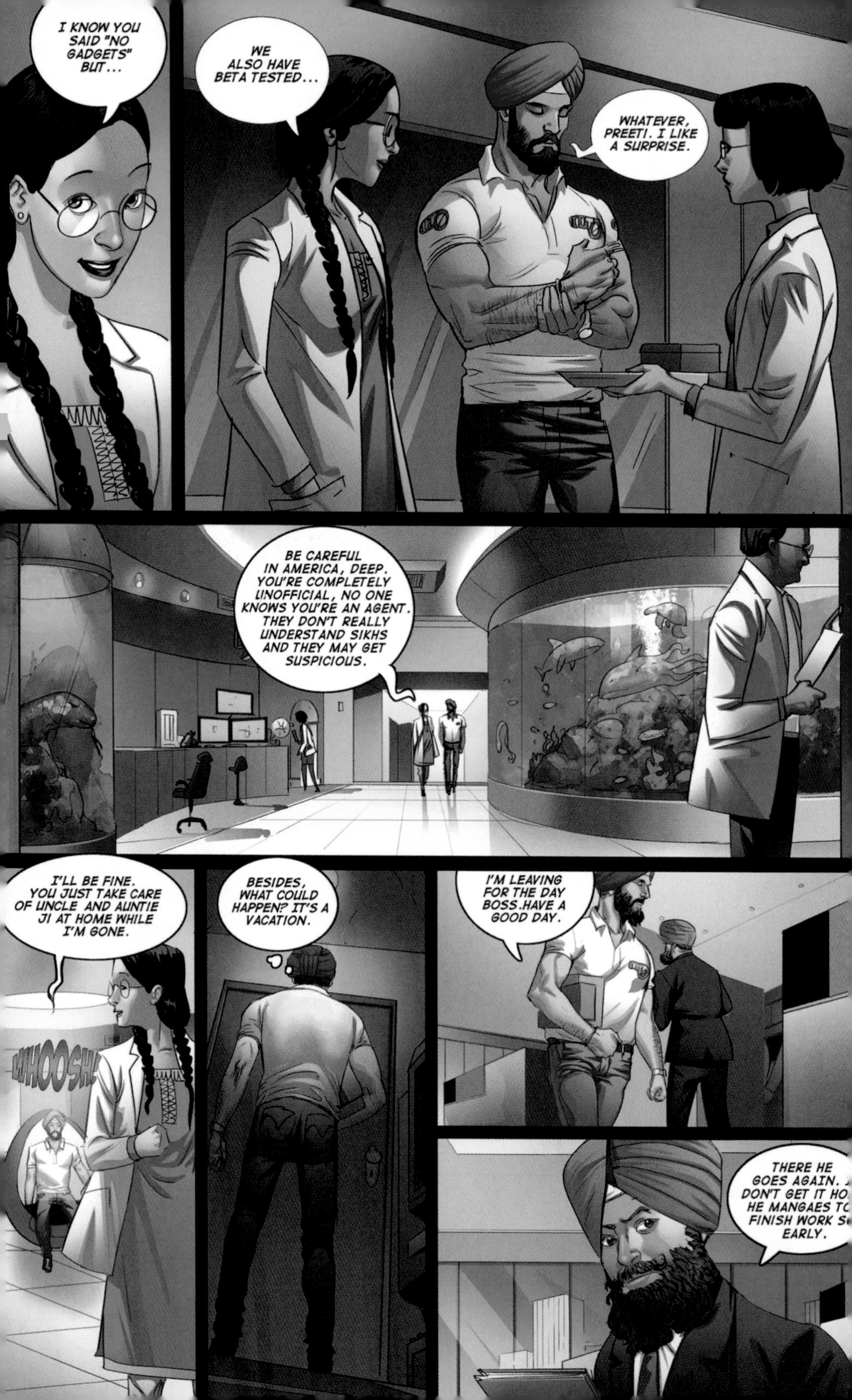
I KNOW YOU SAID "NO GADGETS" BUT...
WE ALSO HAVE BETA TESTED...
WHATEVER, PREETI. I LIKE A SURPRISE.
BE CAREFUL IN AMERICA, DEEP. YOU'RE COMPLETELY UNOFFICIAL, NO ONE KNOWS YOU'RE AN AGENT. THEY DON'T REALLY UNDERSTAND SIKHS AND THEY MAY GET SUSPICIOUS.
I'LL BE FINE. YOU JUST TAKE CARE OF UNCLE AND AUNTIE JI AT HOME WHILE I'M GONE.
WHOOSH!
BESIDES, WHAT COULD HAPPEN? IT'S A VACATION.
I'M LEAVING FOR THE DAY BOSS.HAVE A GOOD DAY.
THERE HE GOES AGAIN. DON'T GET IT HO HE MANGAES TO FINISH WORK S EARLY.

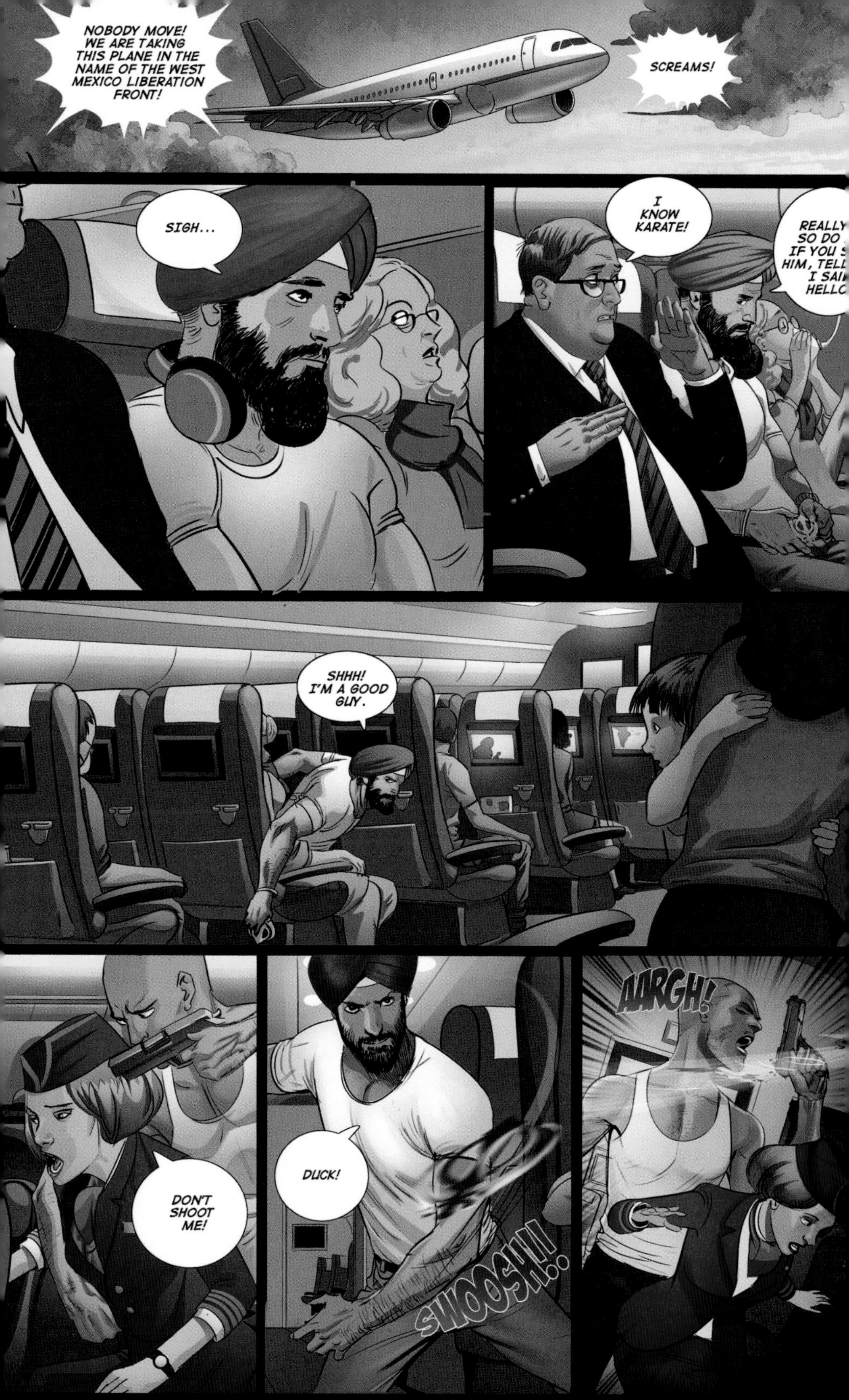
NOBODY MOVE! WE ARE TAKING THIS PLANE IN THE NAME OF THE WEST MEXICO LIBERATION FRONT!
SCREAMS!
SIGH...
I KNOW KARATE!
REALLY SO DO IF YOU S HIM, TELL I SAI HELLO
SHHH! I'M A GOOD GUY.
DON'T SHOOT ME!
DUCK!
SWOOSH!!
AARGH!

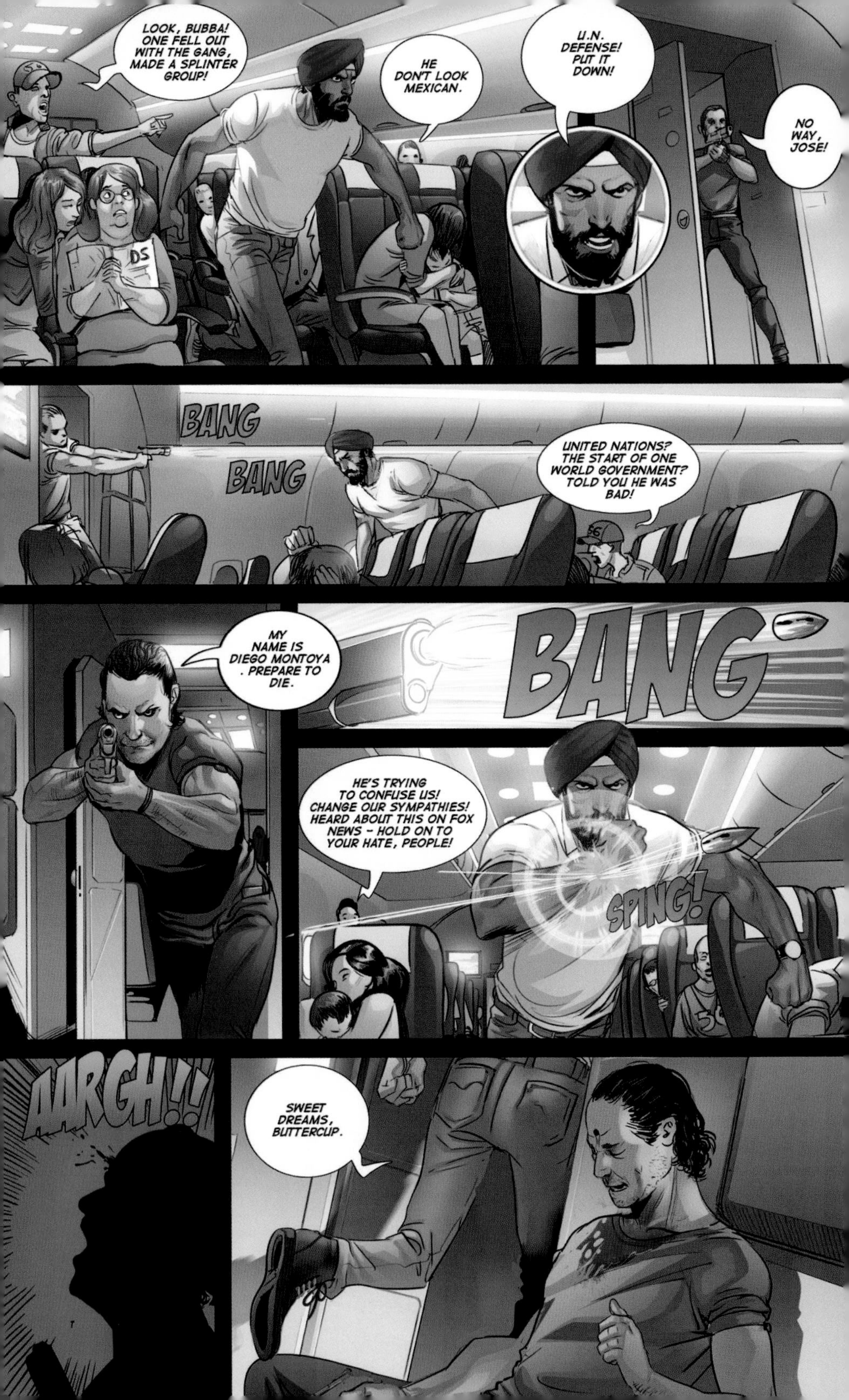
LOOK, BUBBA! ONE FELL OUT WITH THE GANG, MADE A SPLINTER GROUP!
HE DON'T LOOK MEXICAN.
U.N. DEFENSE! PUT IT DOWN!
NO WAY, JOSE!
BANG
BANG
UNITED NATIONS? THE START OF ONE WORLD GOVERNMENT? TOLD YOU HE WAS BAD!
MY NAME IS DIEGO MONTOYA . PREPARE TO DIE.
BANG
HE'S TRYING TO CONFUSE US! CHANGE OUR SYMPATHIES! HEARD ABOUT THIS ON FOX NEWS - HOLD ON TO YOUR HATE, PEOPLE!
SPING!
AARGH!!!
SWEET DREAMS, BUTTERCUP.

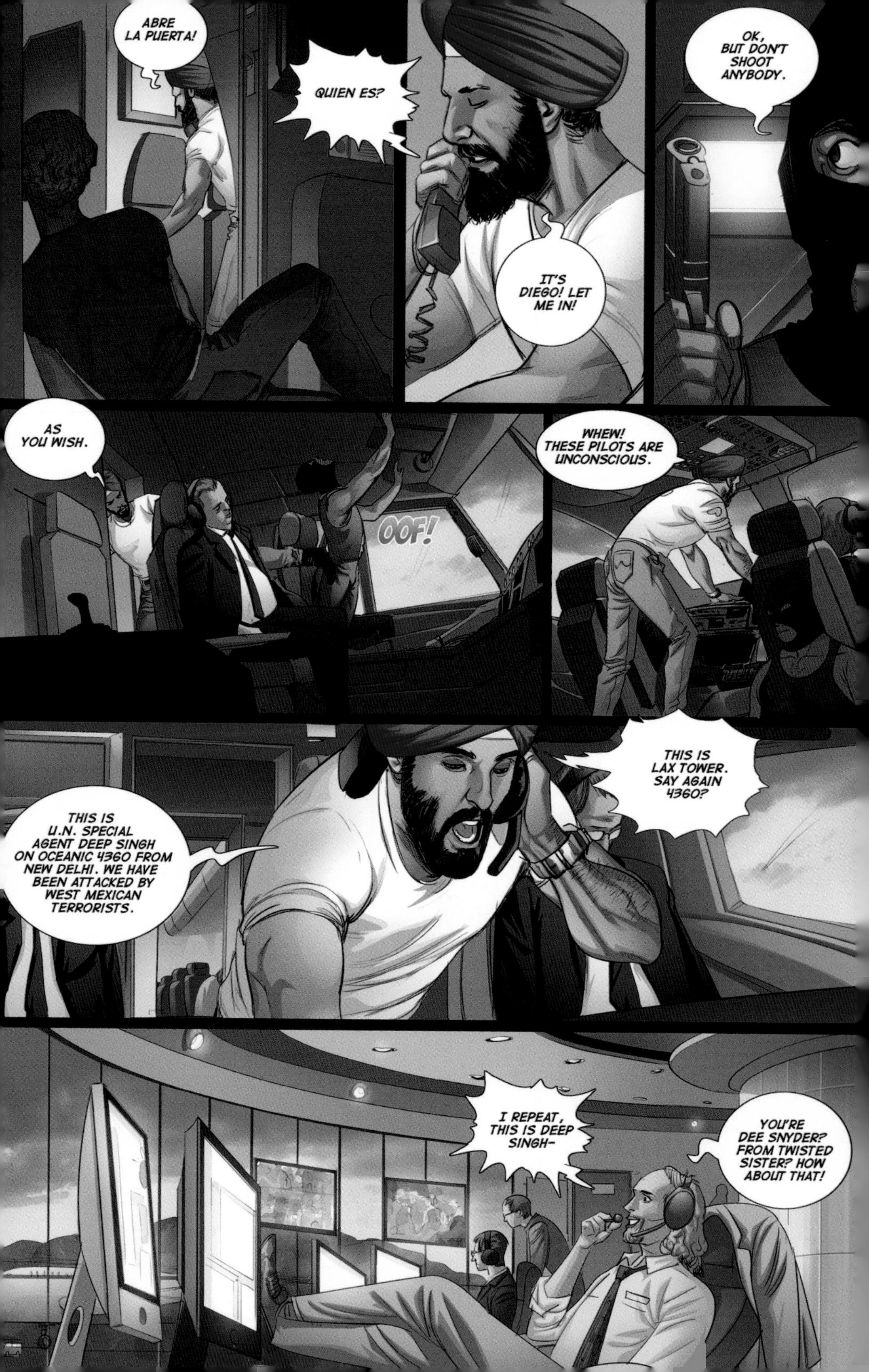
ABRE LA PUERTA!
QUIEN ES?
IT'S DIEGO! LET ME IN!
OK, BUT DON'T SHOOT ANYBODY.
AS YOU WISH.
OOF!
WHEW! THESE PILOTS ARE UNCONSCIOUS.
THIS IS U.N. SPECIAL AGENT DEEP SINGH ON OCEANIC 4360 FROM NEW DELHI. WE HAVE BEEN ATTACKED BY WEST MEXICAN TERRORISTS.
THIS IS LAX TOWER. SAY AGAIN 4360?
I REPEAT, THIS IS DEEP SINGH-
YOU'RE DEE SNYDER? FROM TWISTED SISTER? HOW ABOUT THAT!

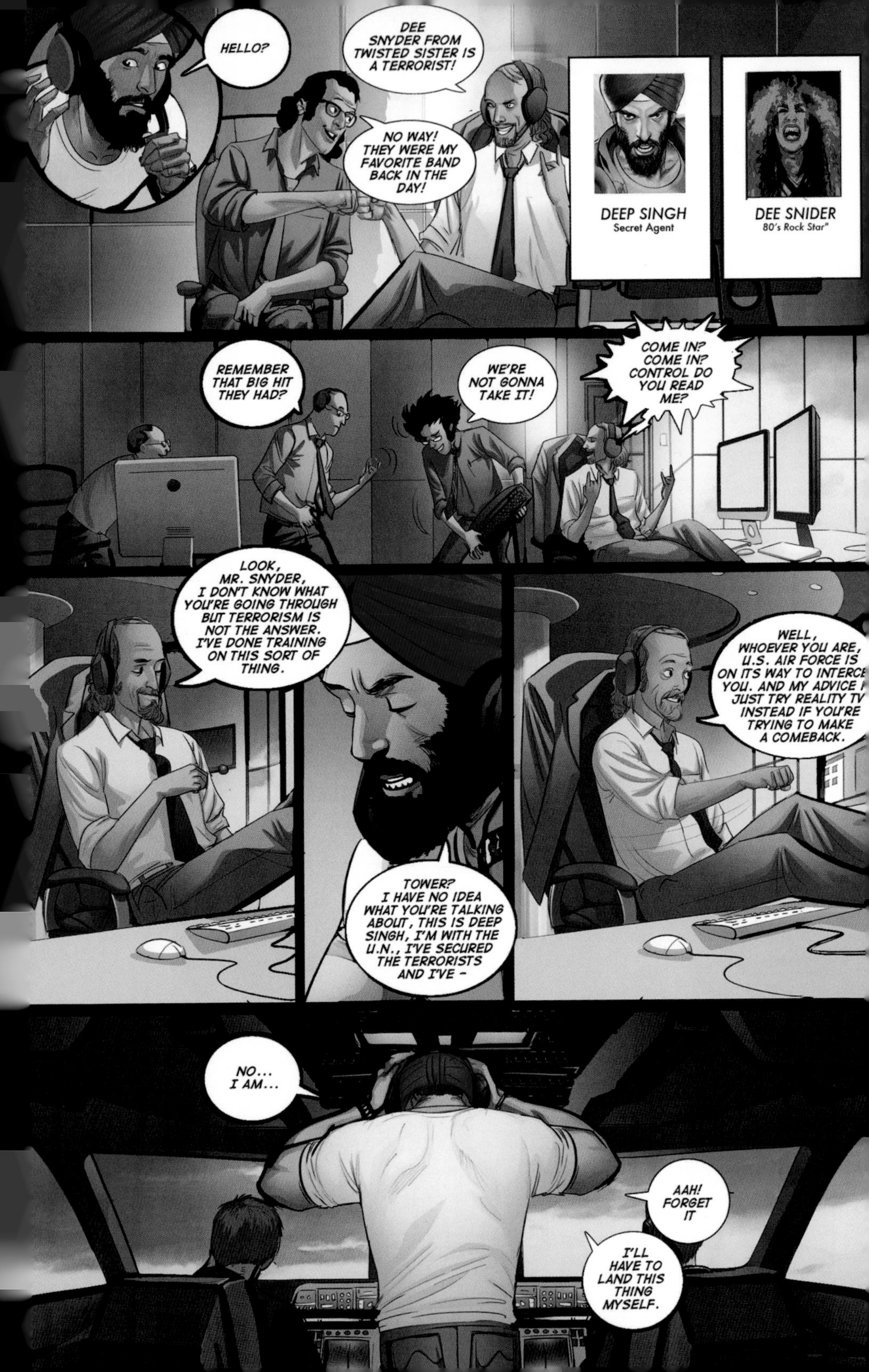
HELLO?
DEE SNYDER FROM TWISTED SISTER IS A TERRORIST!
NO WAY! THEY WERE MY FAVORITE BAND BACK IN THE DAY!
DEEP SINGH
Secret Agent
DEE SNIDER
80's Rock Star"
REMEMBER THAT BIG HIT THEY HAD?
WE'RE NOT GONNA TAKE IT!
COME IN? COME IN? CONTROL DO YOU READ ME?
LOOK, MR. SNYDER, I DON'T KNOW WHAT YOU'RE GOING THROUGH BUT TERRORISM IS NOT THE ANSWER. I'VE DONE TRAINING ON THIS SORT OF THING.
TOWER? I HAVE NO IDEA WHAT YOU'RE TALKING ABOUT, THIS IS DEEP SINGH, I'M WITH THE U.N., I'VE SECURED THE TERRORISTS AND I'VE -
WELL, WHOEVER YOU ARE, U.S. AIR FORCE IS ON ITS WAY TO INTERCE YOU. AND MY ADVICE I JUST TRY REALITY TV INSTEAD IF YOU'RE TRYING TO MAKE A COMEBACK.
NO... I AM...
AAH! FORGET IT
I'LL HAVE TO LAND THIS THING MYSELF.

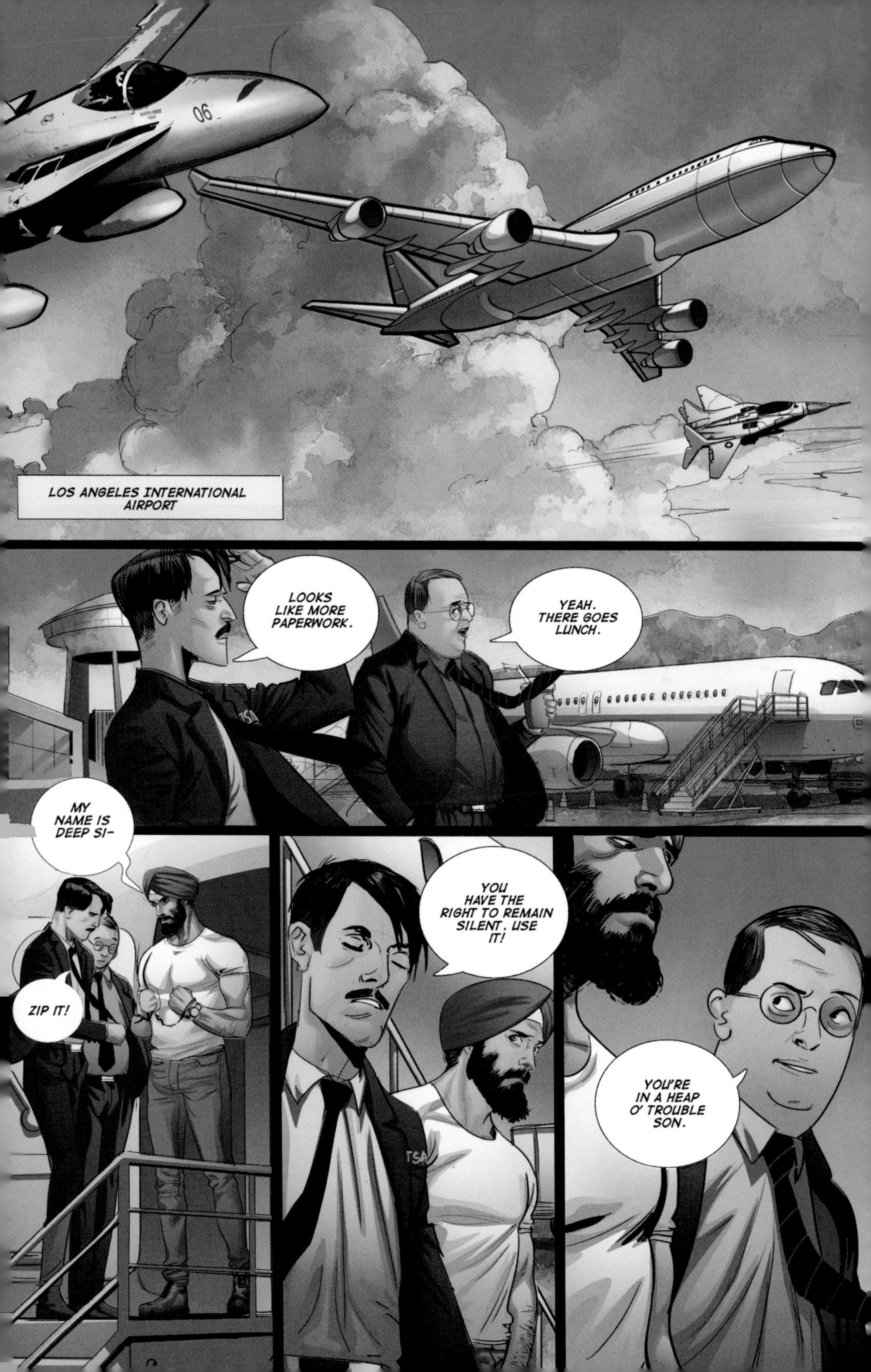
LOS ANGELES INTERNATIONAL AIRPORT
LOOKS LIKE MORE PAPERWORK.
YEAH. THERE GOES LUNCH.
MY NAME IS DEEP SI-
ZIP IT!
YOU HAVE THE RIGHT TO REMAIN SILENT. USE IT!
YOU'RE IN A HEAP O' TROUBLE SON.

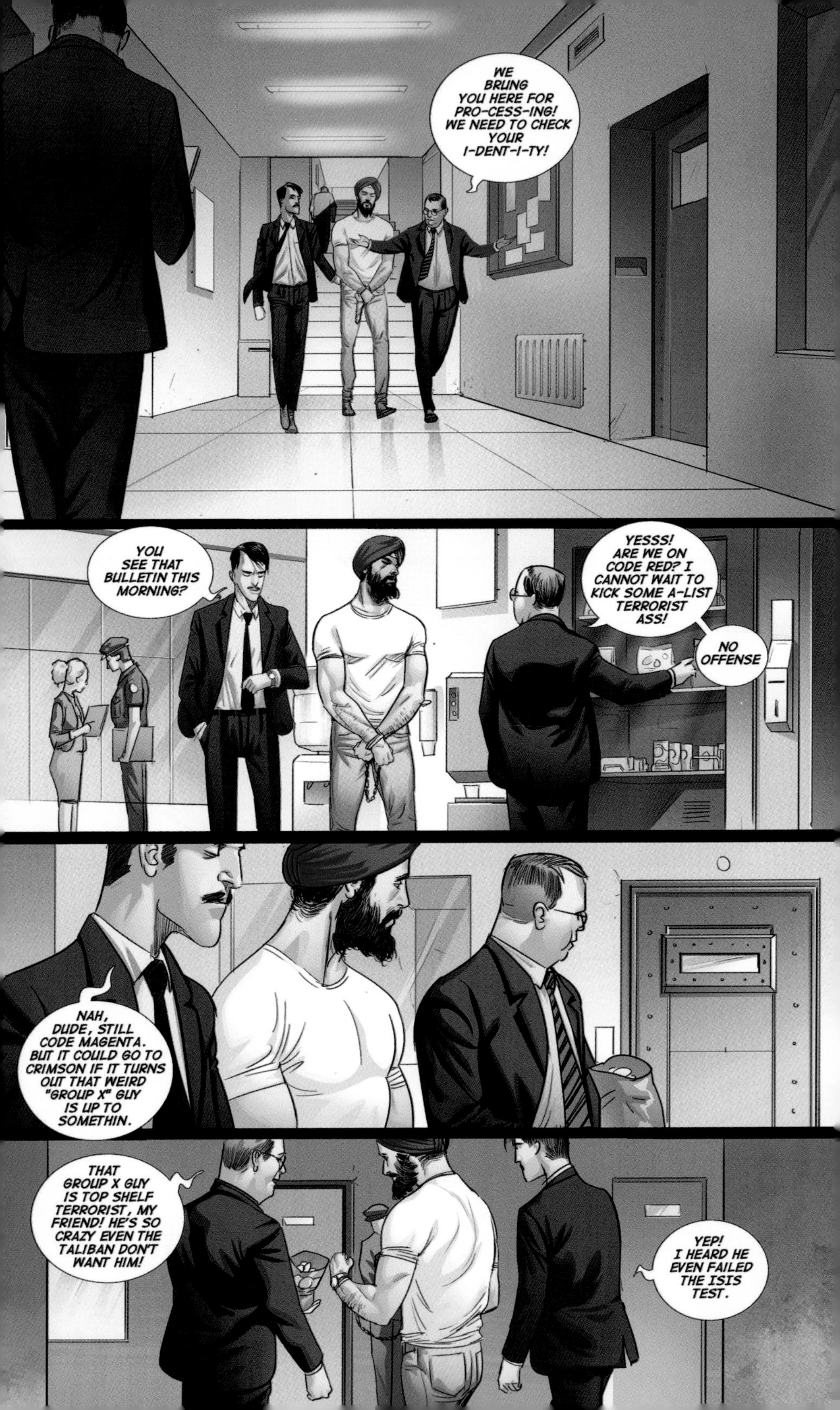
WE BRUNG YOU HERE FOR PRO-CESS-ING! WE NEED TO CHECK YOUR I-DENT-I-TY!
YOU SEE THAT BULLETIN THIS MORNING?
YESSS! ARE WE ON CODE RED? I CANNOT WAIT TO KICK SOME A-LIST TERRORIST ASS!
NO OFFENSE
NAH, DUDE, STILL CODE MAGENTA. BUT IT COULD GO TO CRIMSON IF IT TURNS OUT THAT WEIRD "GROUP X" GUY IS UP TO SOMETHIN.
THAT GROUP X GUY IS TOP SHELF TERRORIST, MY FRIEND! HE'S SO CRAZY EVEN THE TALIBAN DON'T WANT HIM!
YEP! I HEARD HE EVEN FAILED THE ISIS TEST.

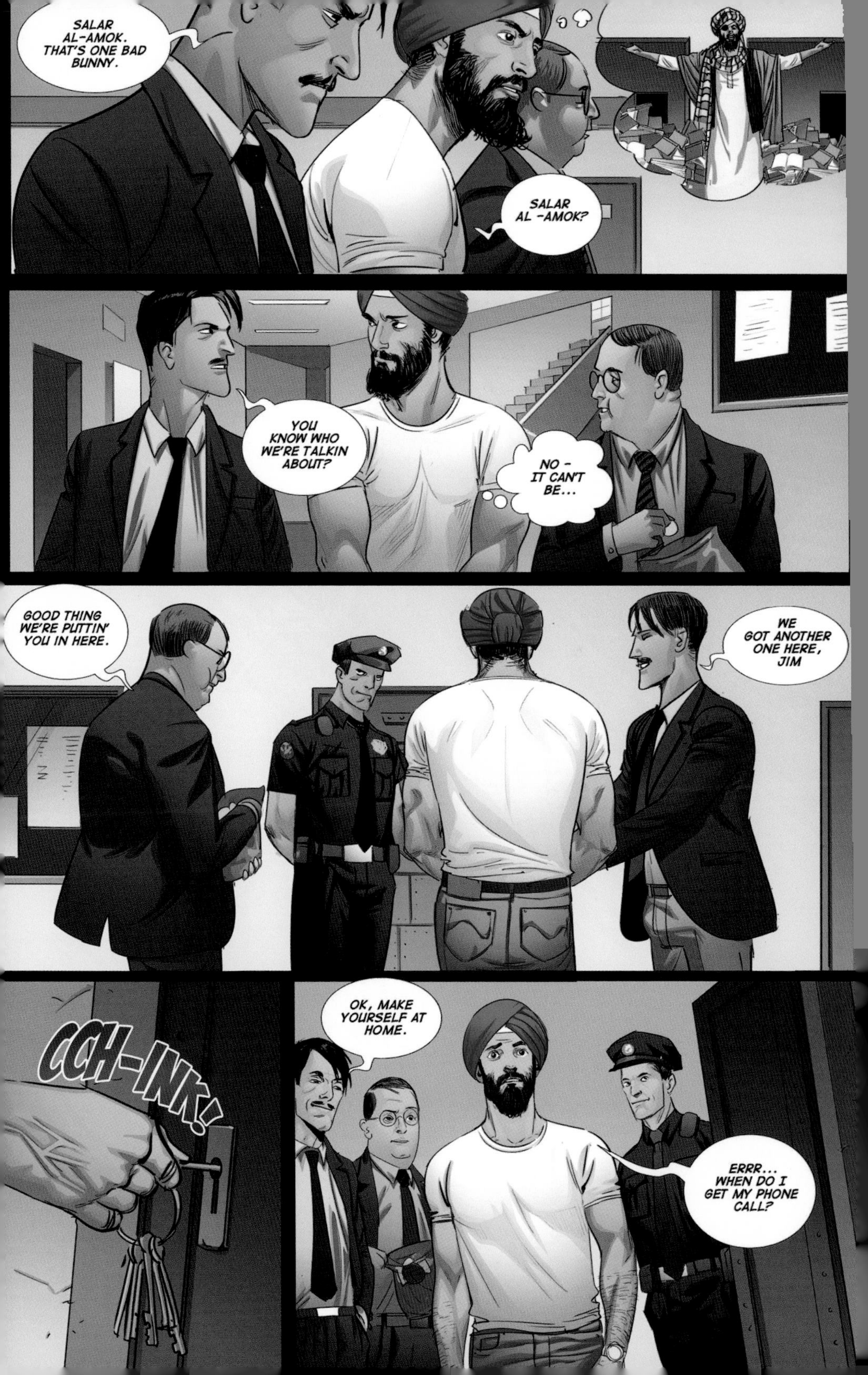
SALAR AL-AMOK. THAT'S ONE BAD BUNNY.
SALAR AL -AMOK?
YOU KNOW WHO WE'RE TALKIN ABOUT?
NO - IT CAN'T BE...
GOOD THING WE'RE PUTTIN' YOU IN HERE.
WE GOT ANOTHER ONE HERE, JIM
CCH-INK!
OK, MAKE YOURSELF AT HOME.
ERRR... WHEN DO I GET MY PHONE CALL?

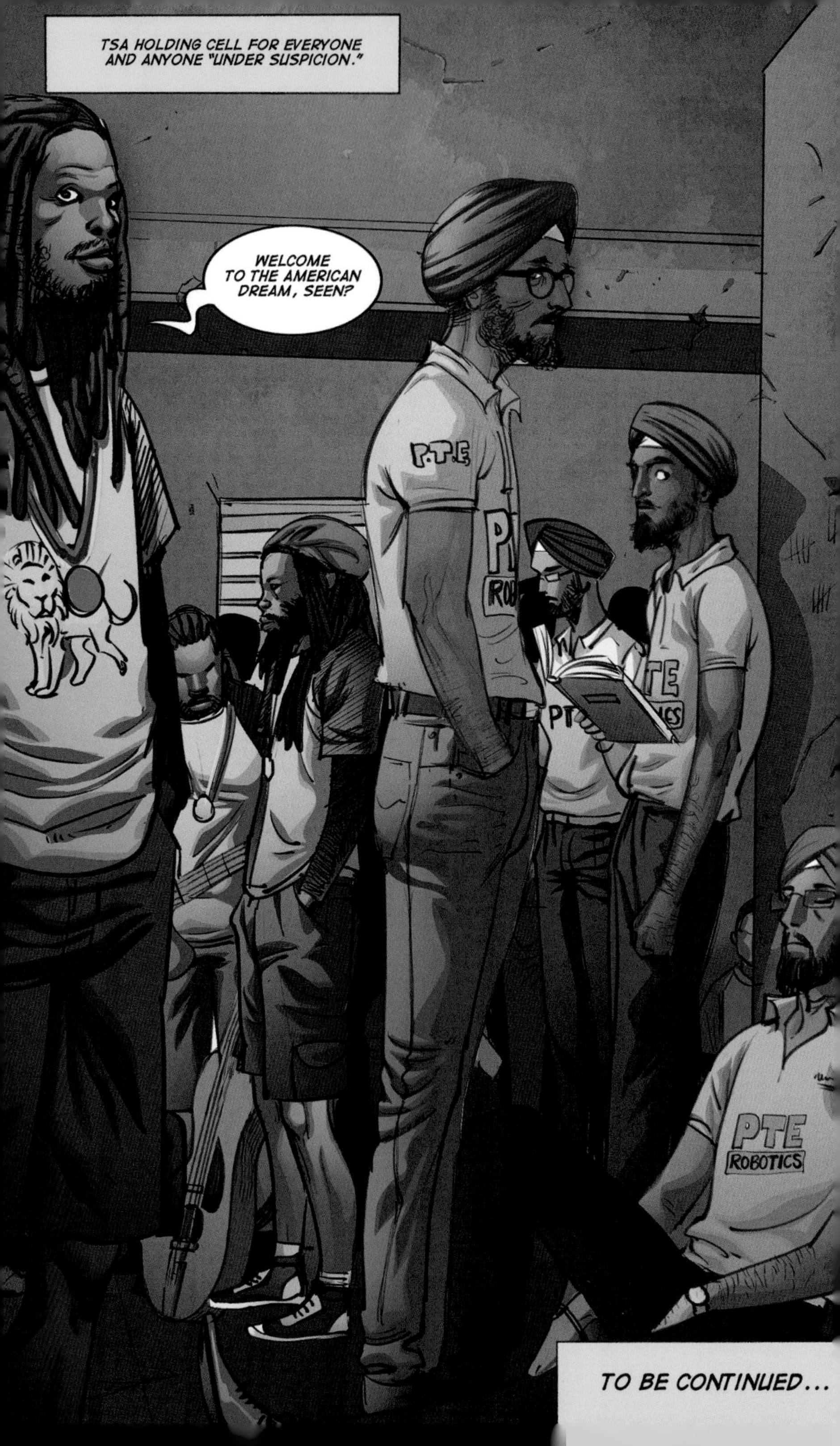
TSA HOLDING CELL FOR EVERYONE AND ANYONE "UNDER SUSPICION."
WELCOME TO THE AMERICAN DREAM, SEEN?
P.T.E
PTE ROBOTICS
PTE ROBOTICS
TO BE CONTINUED...

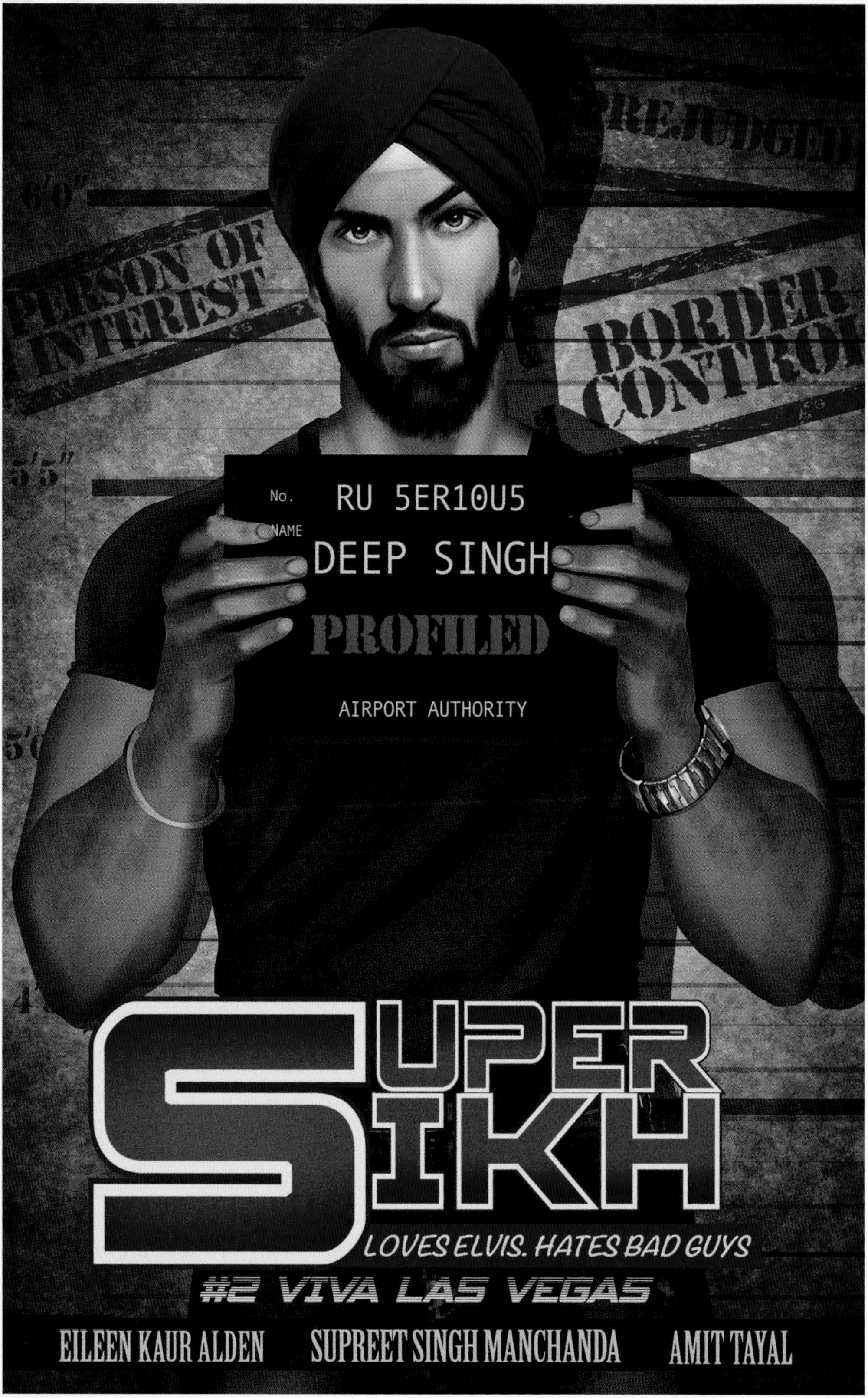
PREJUDGED
6'0"
PERSON OF INTEREST
BORDER CONTROL
5'5"
No. RU 5ER10U5
NAME DEEP SINGH
PROFILED
AIRPORT AUTHORITY
SUPER SIKH
LOVES ELVIS. HATES BAD GUYS
#2 VIVA LAS VEGAS
EILEEN KAUR ALDEN
SUPREET SINGH MANCHANDA
AMIT TAYAL

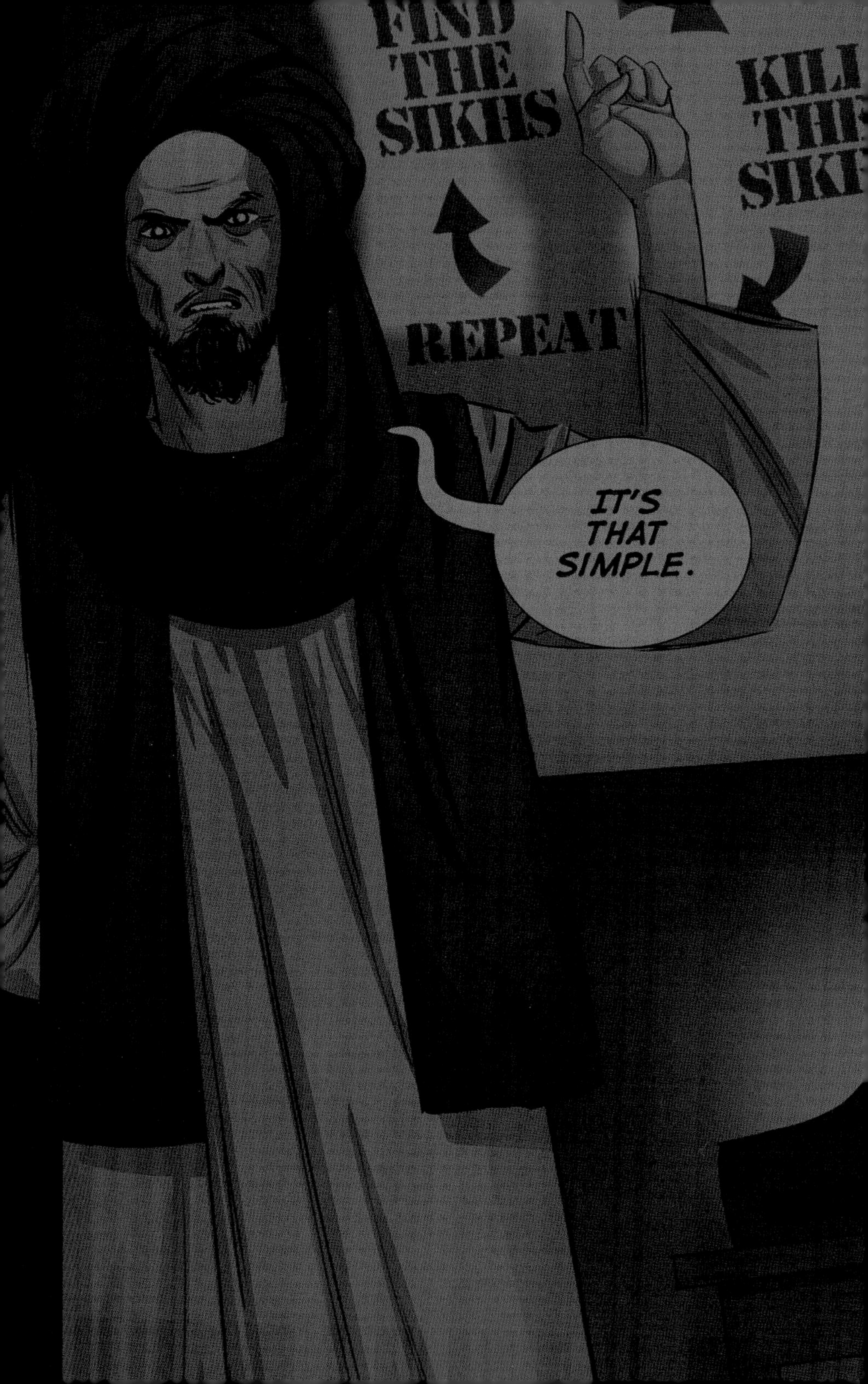
FIND THE SIKHS
REPEAT
IT'S THAT SIMPLE.

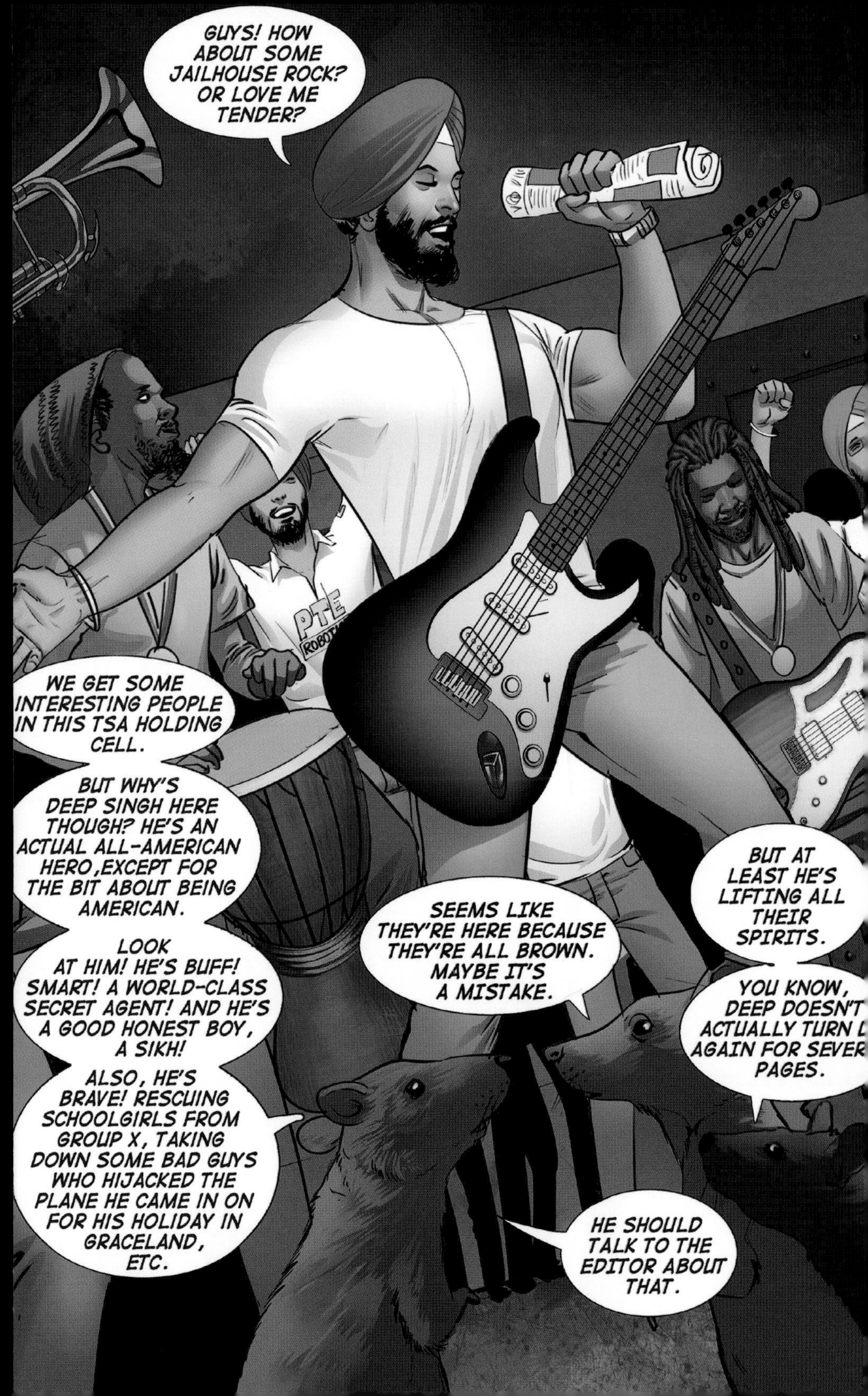
GUYS! HOW ABOUT SOME JAILHOUSE ROCK? OR LOVE ME TENDER?
WE GET SOME INTERESTING PEOPLE IN THIS TSA HOLDING CELL.
BUT WHY'S DEEP SINGH HERE THOUGH? HE'S AN ACTUAL ALL-AMERICAN HERO,EXCEPT FOR THE BIT ABOUT BEING AMERICAN.
LOOK AT HIM! HE'S BUFF! SMART! A WORLD-CLASS SECRET AGENT! AND HE'S A GOOD HONEST BOY, A SIKH!
ALSO, HE'S BRAVE! RESCUING SCHOOLGIRLS FROM GROUP X, TAKING DOWN SOME BAD GUYS WHO HIJACKED THE PLANE HE CAME IN ON FOR HIS HOLIDAY IN GRACELAND, ETC.
SEEMS LIKE THEY'RE HERE BECAUSE THEY'RE ALL BROWN. MAYBE IT'S A MISTAKE.
BUT AT LEAST HE'S LIFTING ALL THEIR SPIRITS.
YOU KNOW, DEEP DOESN'T ACTUALLY TURN
AGAIN FOR SEVER
PAGES.
HE SHOULD TALK TO THE EDITOR ABOUT THAT.

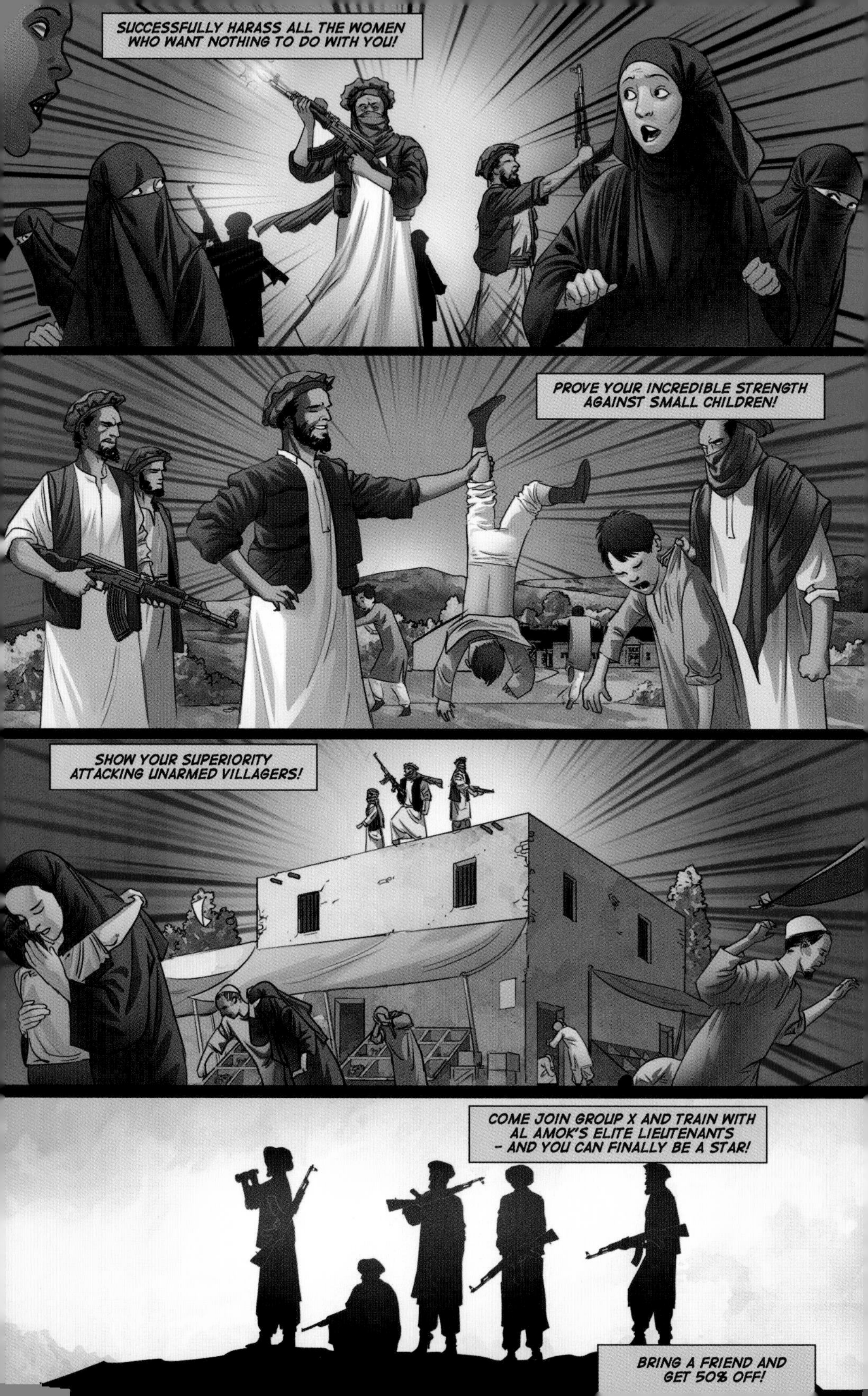
SUCCESSFULLY HARASS ALL THE WOMEN WHO WANT NOTHING TO DO WITH YOU!
PROVE YOUR INCREDIBLE STRENGTH AGAINST SMALL CHILDREN!
SHOW YOUR SUPERIORITY ATTACKING UNARMED VILLAGERS!
COME JOIN GROUP X AND TRAIN WITH AL AMOK'S ELITE LIEUTENANTS - AND YOU CAN FINALLY BE A STAR!
BRING A FRIEND AND GET 50% OFF!

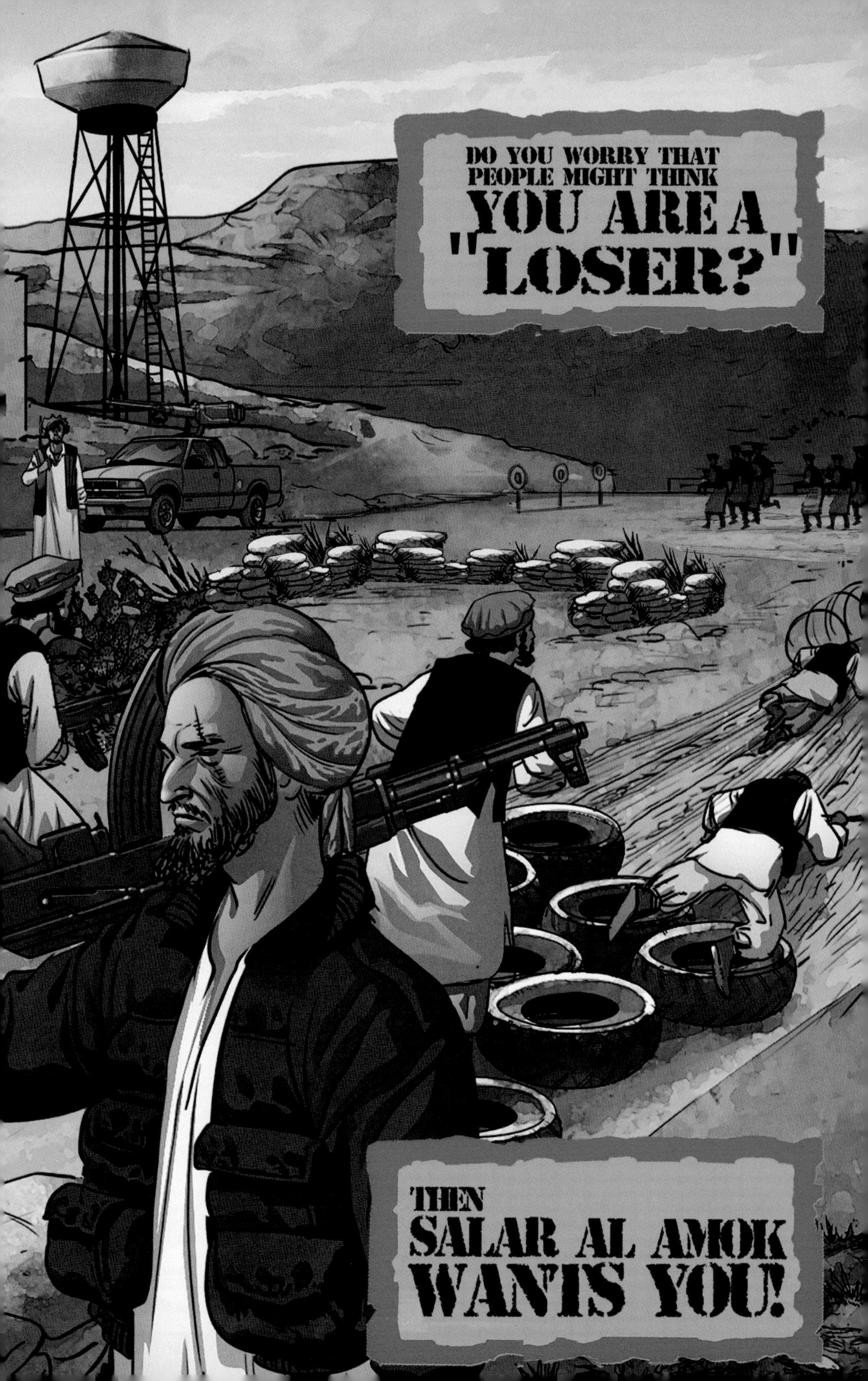
DO YOU WORRY THAT PEOPLE MIGHT THINK
YOU ARE A "LOSER?"
THEN
SALAR AL AMOK
WANTS YOU!

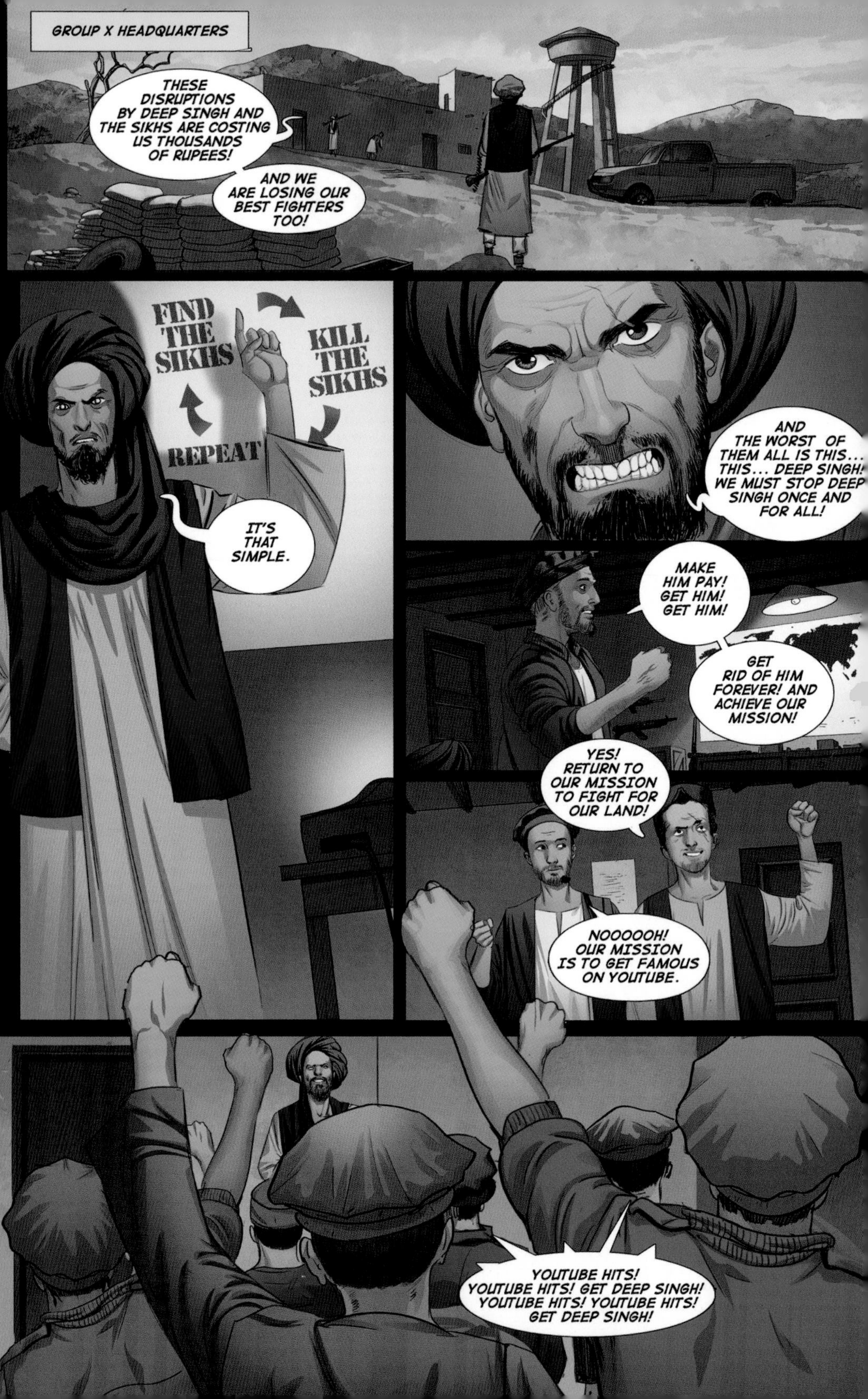
GROUP X HEADQUARTERS
THESE DISRUPTIONS BY DEEP SINGH AND THE SIKHS ARE COSTING US THOUSANDS OF RUPEES!
AND WE ARE LOSING OUR BEST FIGHTERS TOO!
FIND THE SIKHS
KILL THE SIKHS
REPEAT
IT'S THAT SIMPLE.
AND THE WORST OF THEM ALL IS THIS... THIS... DEEP SINGH! WE MUST STOP DEEP SINGH ONCE AND FOR ALL!
MAKE HIM PAY! GET HIM! GET HIM!
GET RID OF HIM FOREVER! AND ACHIEVE OUR MISSION!
YES! RETURN TO OUR MISSION TO FIGHT FOR OUR LAND!
NOOOOOH! OUR MISSION IS TO GET FAMOUS ON YOUTUBE.
YOUTUBE HITS! YOUTUBE HITS! GET DEEP SINGH! YOUTUBE HITS! YOUTUBE HITS! GET DEEP SINGH!

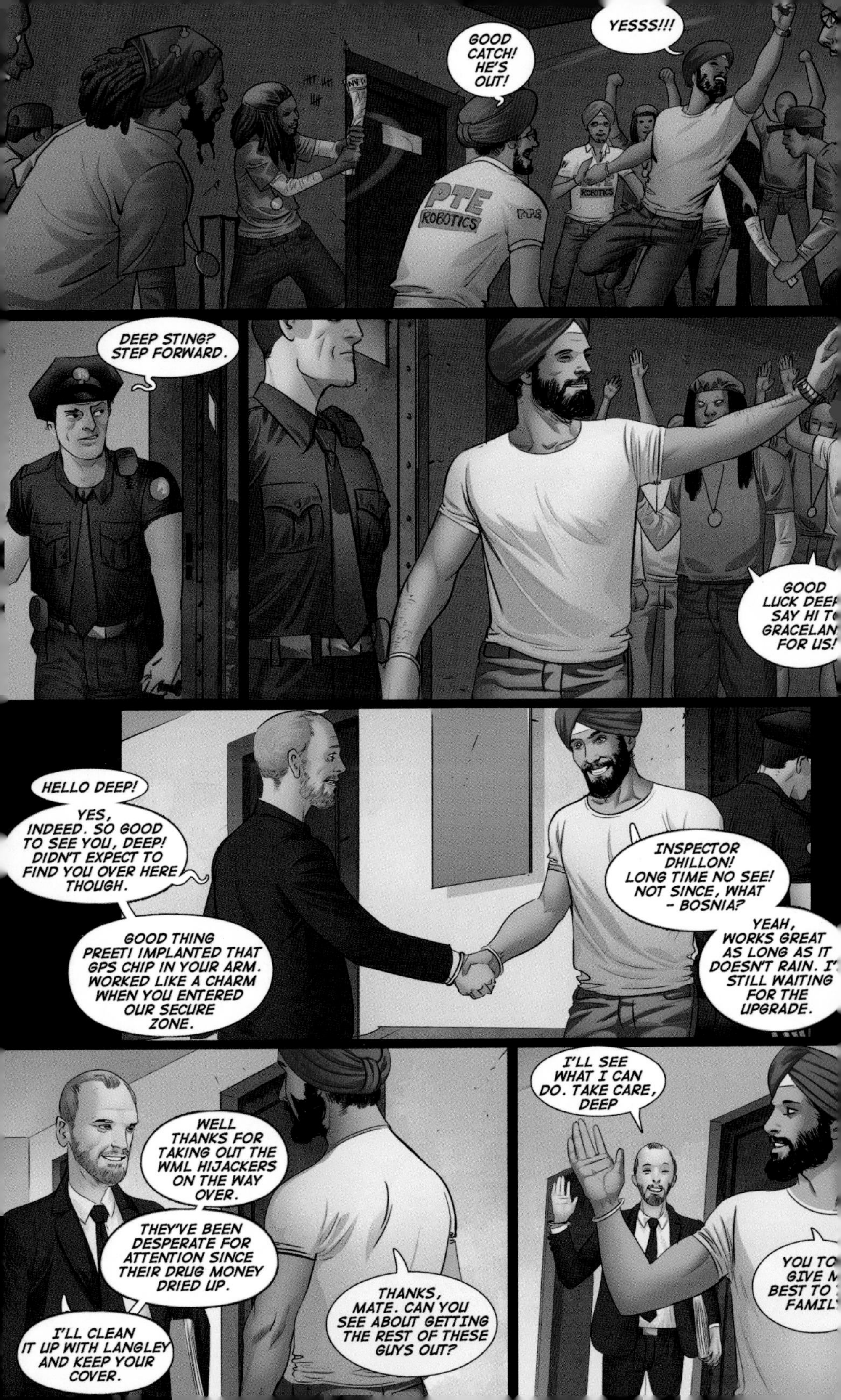
GOOD CATCH! HE'S OUT!
YESSS!!!
PTE ROBOTICS
DEEP STING? STEP FORWARD.
GOOD LUCK DEEP SAY HI T GRACELAN FOR US!
HELLO DEEP!
YES, INDEED. SO GOOD TO SEE YOU, DEEP! DIDN'T EXPECT TO FIND YOU OVER HERE THOUGH.
INSPECTOR DHILLON! LONG TIME NO SEE! NOT SINCE, WHAT - BOSNIA?
GOOD THING PREETI IMPLANTED THAT GPS CHIP IN YOUR ARM. WORKED LIKE A CHARM WHEN YOU ENTERED OUR SECURE ZONE.
YEAH, WORKS GREAT AS LONG AS IT DOESN'T RAIN. I' STILL WAITING FOR THE UPGRADE.
WELL THANKS FOR TAKING OUT THE WML HIJACKERS ON THE WAY OVER.
THEY'VE BEEN DESPERATE FOR ATTENTION SINCE THEIR DRUG MONEY DRIED UP.
I'LL CLEAN IT UP WITH LANGLEY AND KEEP YOUR COVER.
THANKS, MATE. CAN YOU SEE ABOUT GETTING THE REST OF THESE GUYS OUT?
I'LL SEE WHAT I CAN DO. TAKE CARE, DEEP
YOU TO GIVE M BEST TO FAMIL

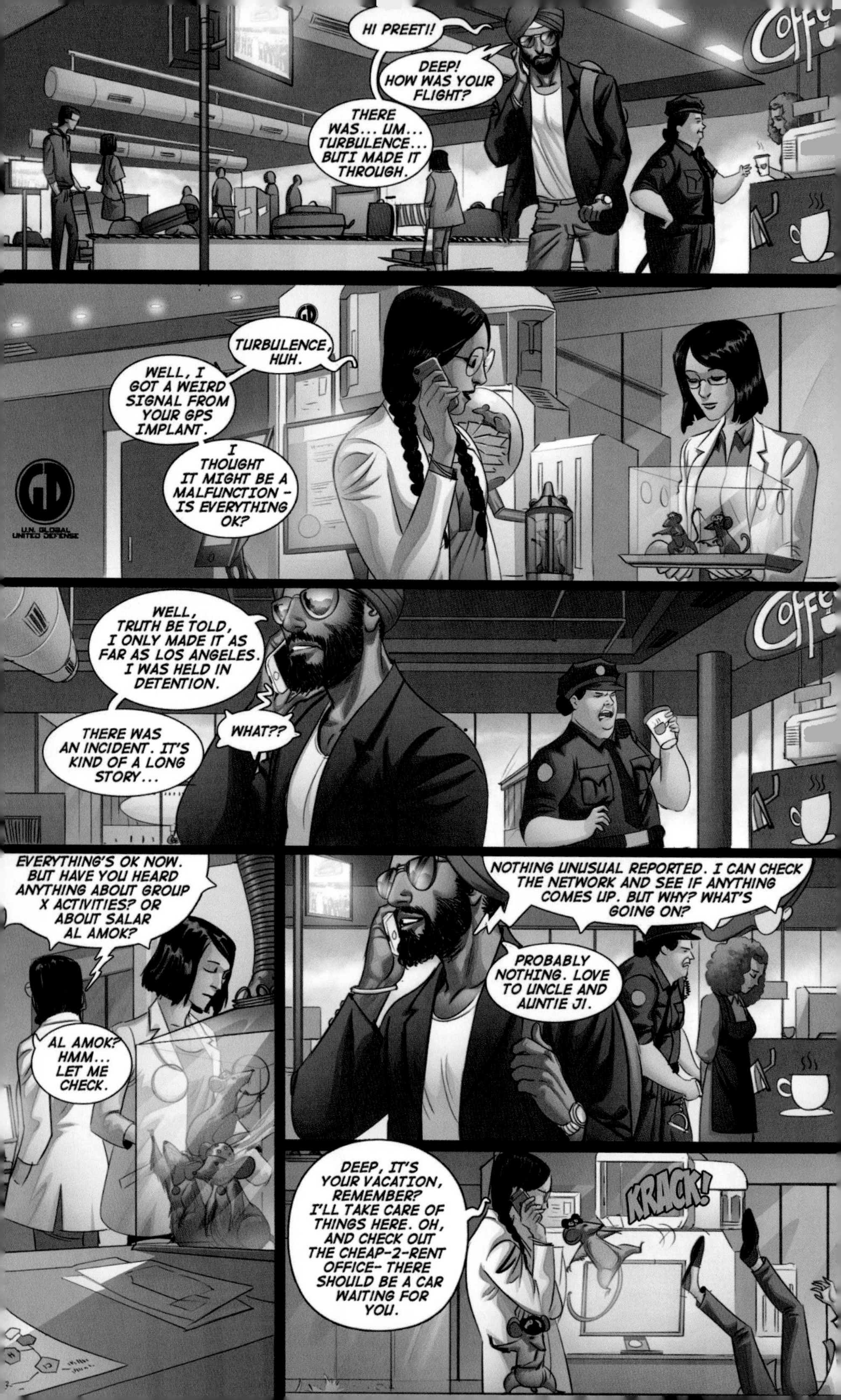
HI PREETI!
DEEP! HOW WAS YOUR FLIGHT?
THERE WAS... UM... TURBULENCE... BUT I MADE IT THROUGH.
TURBULENCE, HUH.
WELL, I GOT A WEIRD SIGNAL FROM YOUR GPS IMPLANT.
I THOUGHT IT MIGHT BE A MALFUNCTION - IS EVERYTHING OK?
U.N. GLOBAL UNITED DEFENSE
WELL, TRUTH BE TOLD, I ONLY MADE IT AS FAR AS LOS ANGELES. I WAS HELD IN DETENTION.
THERE WAS AN INCIDENT. IT'S KIND OF A LONG STORY...
WHAT??
EVERYTHING'S OK NOW. BUT HAVE YOU HEARD ANYTHING ABOUT GROUP X ACTIVITIES? OR ABOUT SALAR AL AMOK?
AL AMOK? HMM... LET ME CHECK.
NOTHING UNUSUAL REPORTED. I CAN CHECK THE NETWORK AND SEE IF ANYTHING COMES UP. BUT WHY? WHAT'S GOING ON?
PROBABLY NOTHING. LOVE TO UNCLE AND AUNTIE JI.
DEEP, IT'S YOUR VACATION, REMEMBER? I'LL TAKE CARE OF THINGS HERE. OH, AND CHECK OUT THE CHEAP-2-RENT OFFICE- THERE SHOULD BE A CAR WAITING FOR YOU.
KRACK!

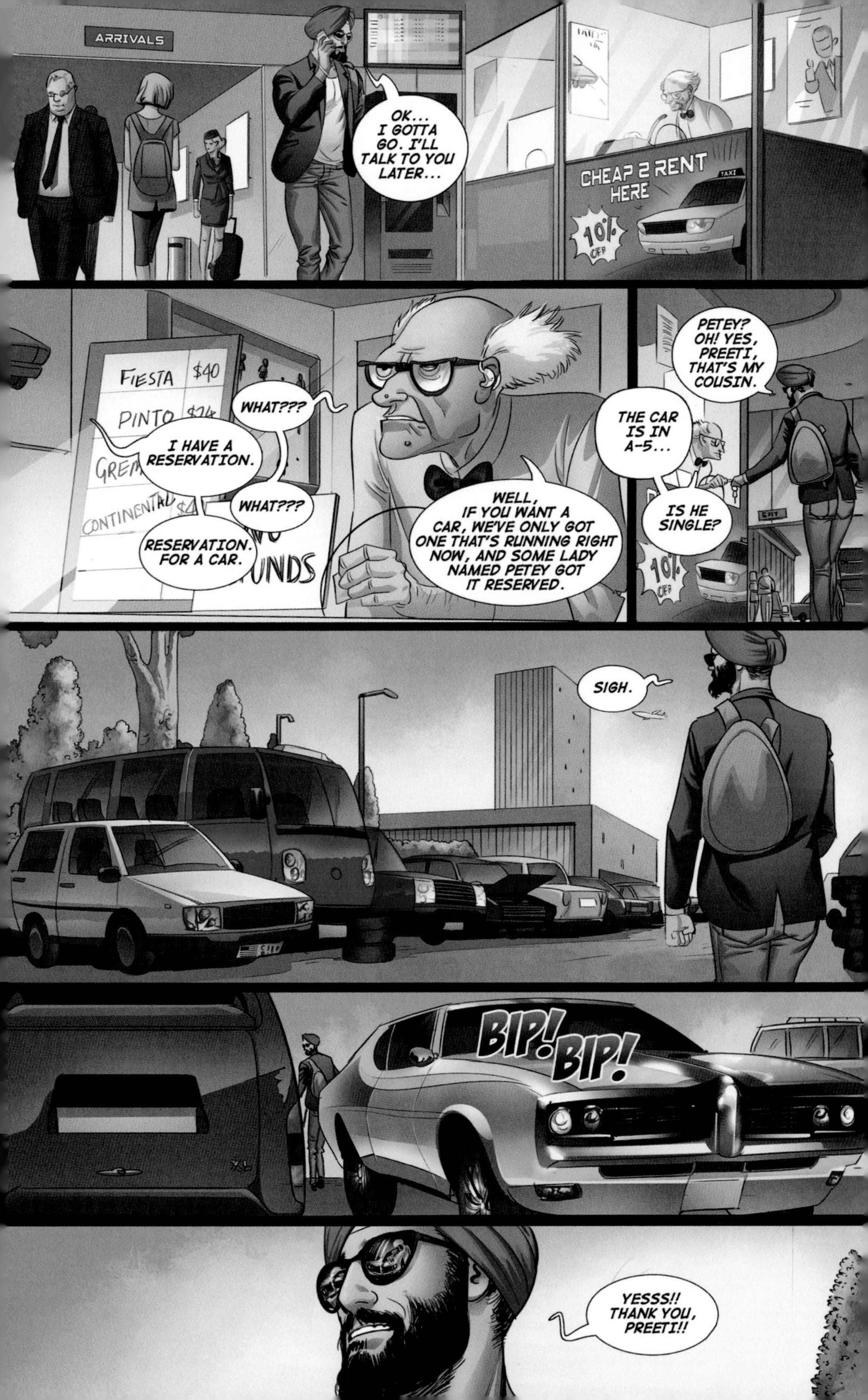
ARRIVALS
OK... I GOTTA GO. I'LL TALK TO YOU LATER...
CHEAP 2 RENT HERE
10% OFF
TAXI
FIESTA $40
PINTO
GREM
CONTINENTAL
I HAVE A RESERVATION.
WHAT???
WHAT???
RESERVATION. FOR A CAR.
WELL, IF YOU WANT A CAR, WE'VE ONLY GOT ONE THAT'S RUNNING RIGHT NOW, AND SOME LADY NAMED PETEY GOT IT RESERVED.
PETEY? OH! YES, PREETI, THAT'S MY COUSIN.
THE CAR IS IN A-5...
IS HE SINGLE?
10% OFF
SIGH.
BIP! BIP!
YESSS!! THANK YOU, PREETI!!

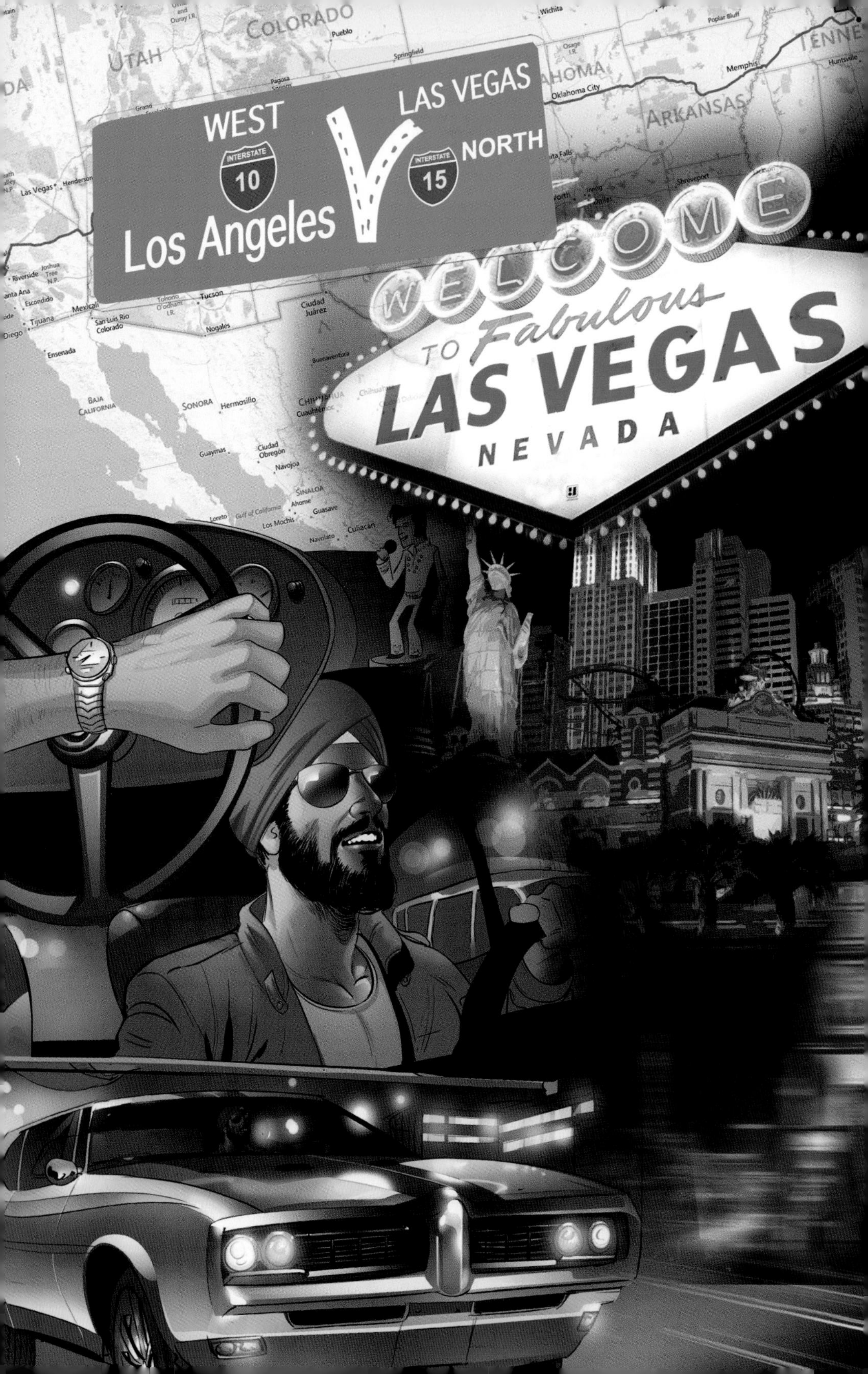

WEST
INTERSTATE 10
Los Angeles
LAS VEGAS
INTERSTATE 15
NORTH
WELCOME
TO Fabulous
LAS VEGAS
NEVADA

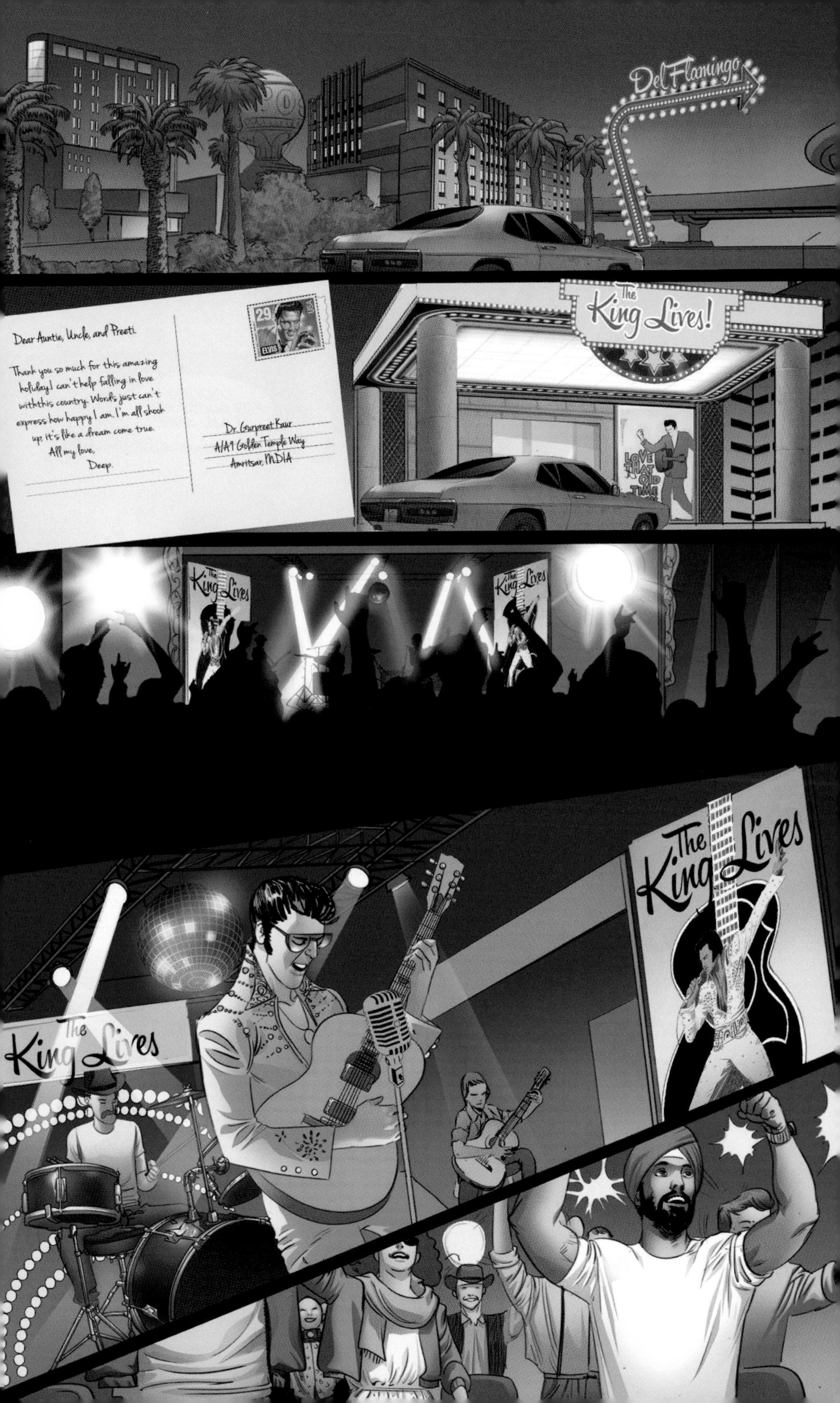

Del Flamingo
Dear Auntie, Uncle, and Preeti.
Thank you so much for this amazing holiday! I can't help falling in love with this country. Words just can't express how happy I am. I'm all shook up, it's like a dream come true.
All my love,
Deep.
Dr. Gurpreet Kaur
A/A9 Golden Temple Way
Amritsar, INDIA
29 ELVIS USA
The King Lives!
LOVE THAT OLD TIME
The King Lives
The King Lives
The King Lives
The King Lives

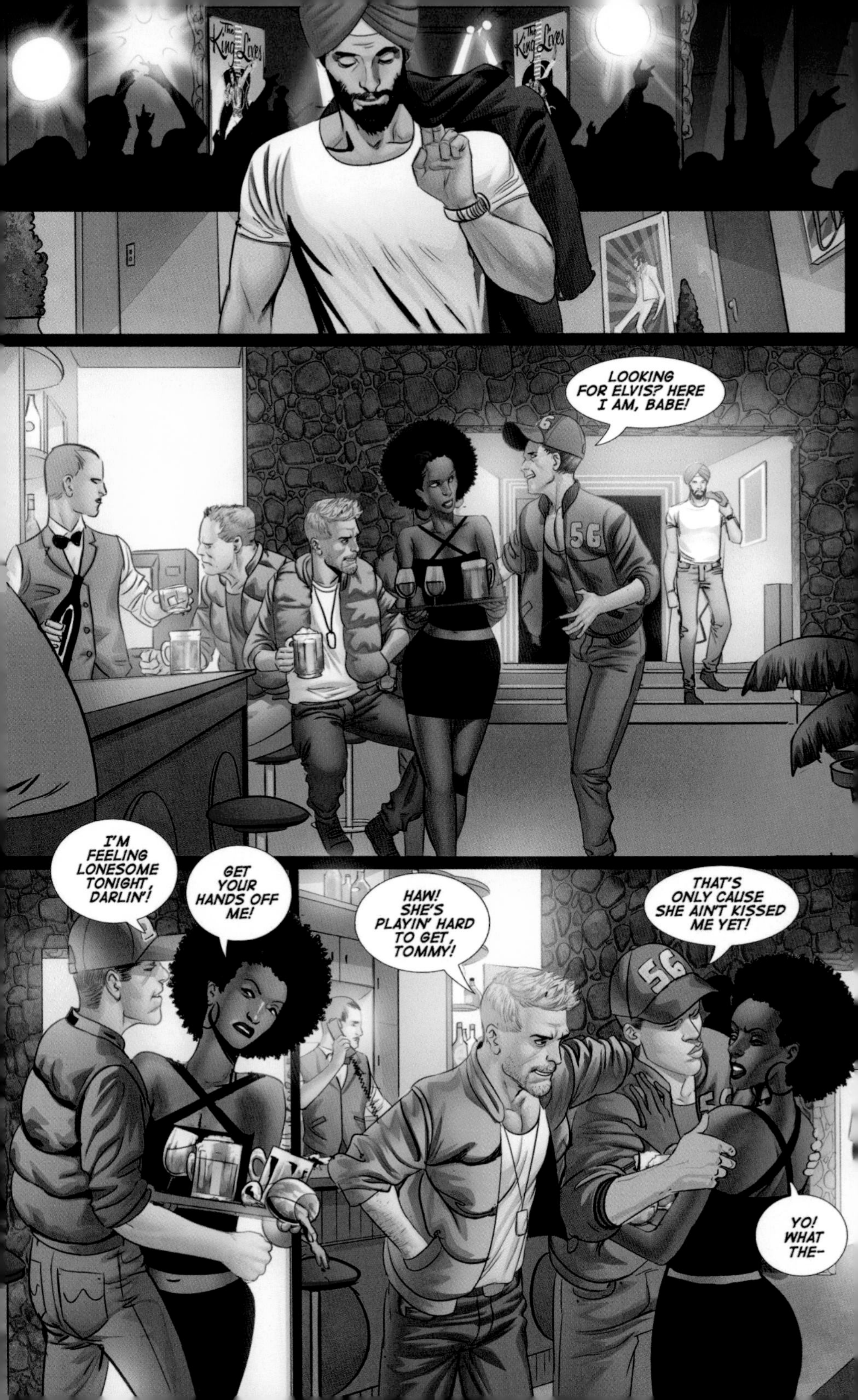
The King Lives
The King Lives
LOOKING FOR ELVIS? HERE I AM, BABE!
I'M FEELING LONESOME TONIGHT, DARLIN'!
GET YOUR HANDS OFF ME!
HAW! SHE'S PLAYIN' HARD TO GET, TOMMY!
THAT'S ONLY CAUSE SHE AIN'T KISSED ME YET!
YO! WHAT THE-

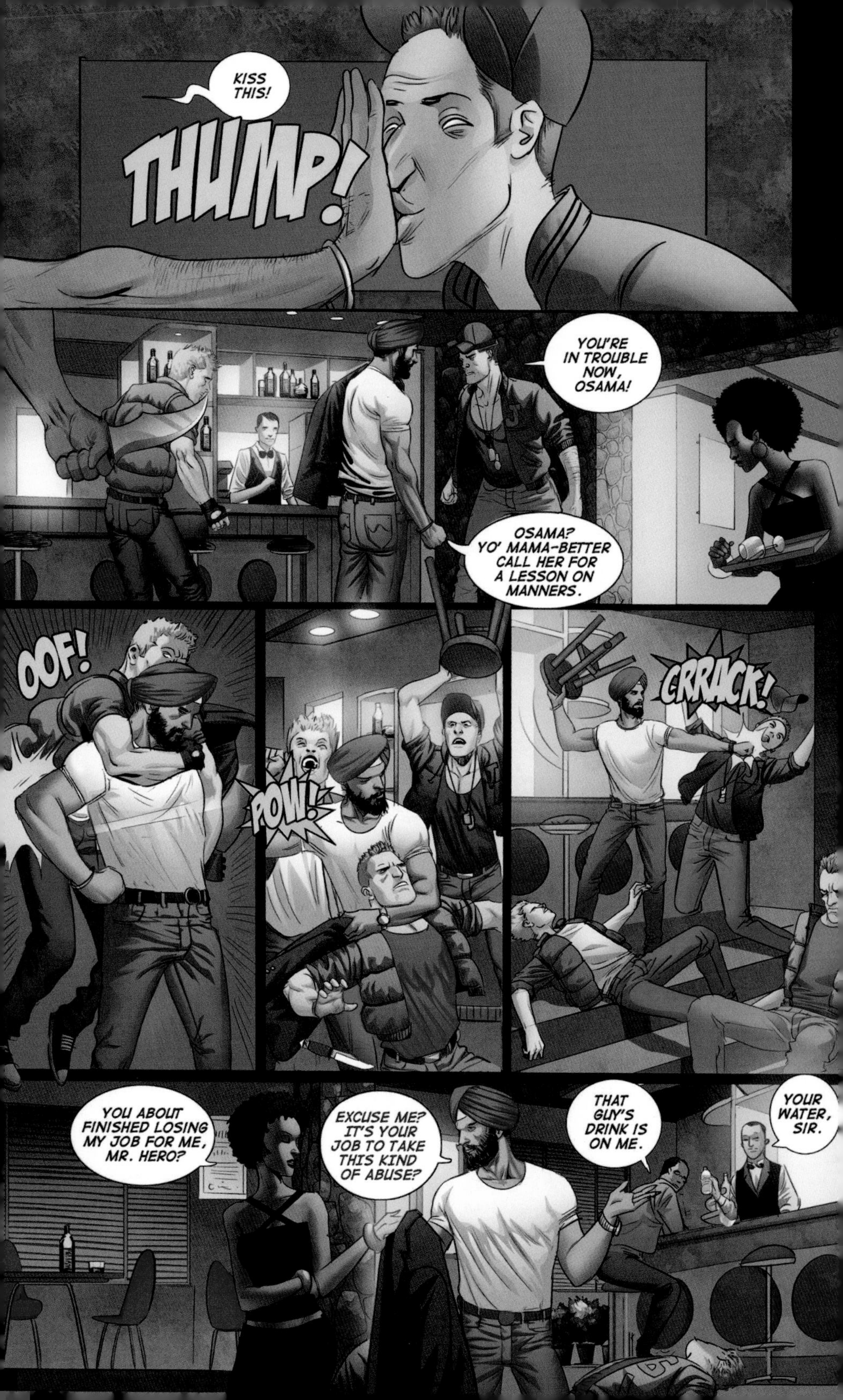

KISS THIS!
THUMP!
YOU'RE IN TROUBLE NOW, OSAMA!
OSAMA? YO' MAMA-BETTER CALL HER FOR A LESSON ON MANNERS.
OOF!
POW!
CRRACK!
YOU ABOUT FINISHED LOSING MY JOB FOR ME, MR. HERO?
EXCUSE ME? IT'S YOUR JOB TO TAKE THIS KIND OF ABUSE?
THAT GUY'S DRINK IS ON ME.
YOUR WATER, SIR.

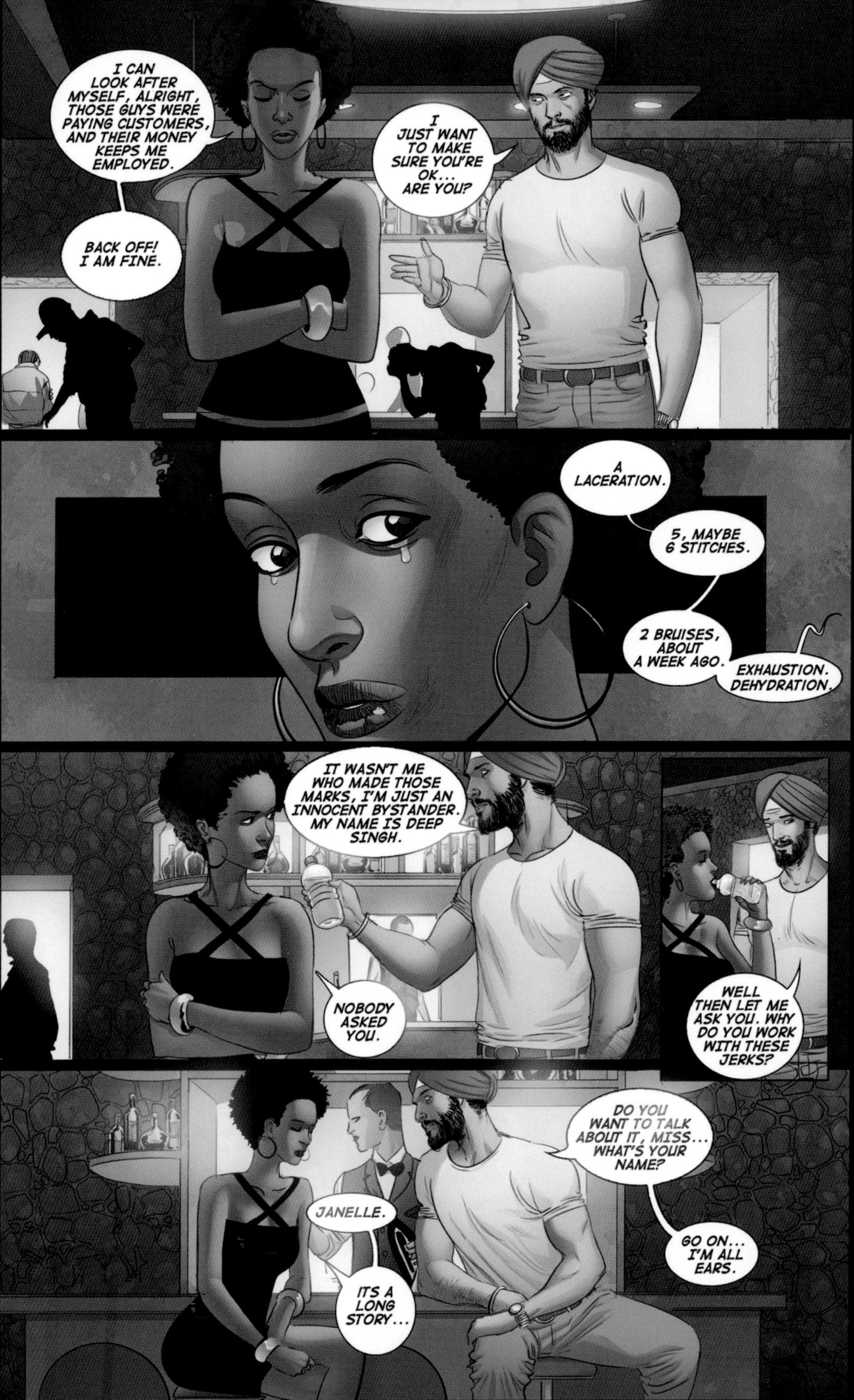
I CAN LOOK AFTER MYSELF, ALRIGHT, THOSE GUYS WERE PAYING CUSTOMERS, AND THEIR MONEY KEEPS ME EMPLOYED.
I JUST WANT TO MAKE SURE YOU'RE OK... ARE YOU?
BACK OFF! I AM FINE.
A LACERATION.
5, MAYBE 6 STITCHES.
2 BRUISES, ABOUT A WEEK AGO.
EXHAUSTION. DEHYDRATION.
IT WASN'T ME WHO MADE THOSE MARKS, I'M JUST AN INNOCENT BYSTANDER. MY NAME IS DEEP SINGH.
NOBODY ASKED YOU.
WELL THEN LET ME ASK YOU. WHY DO YOU WORK WITH THESE JERKS?
DO YOU WANT TO TALK ABOUT IT, MISS... WHAT'S YOUR NAME?
JANELLE.
ITS A LONG STORY...
GO ON... I'M ALL EARS.

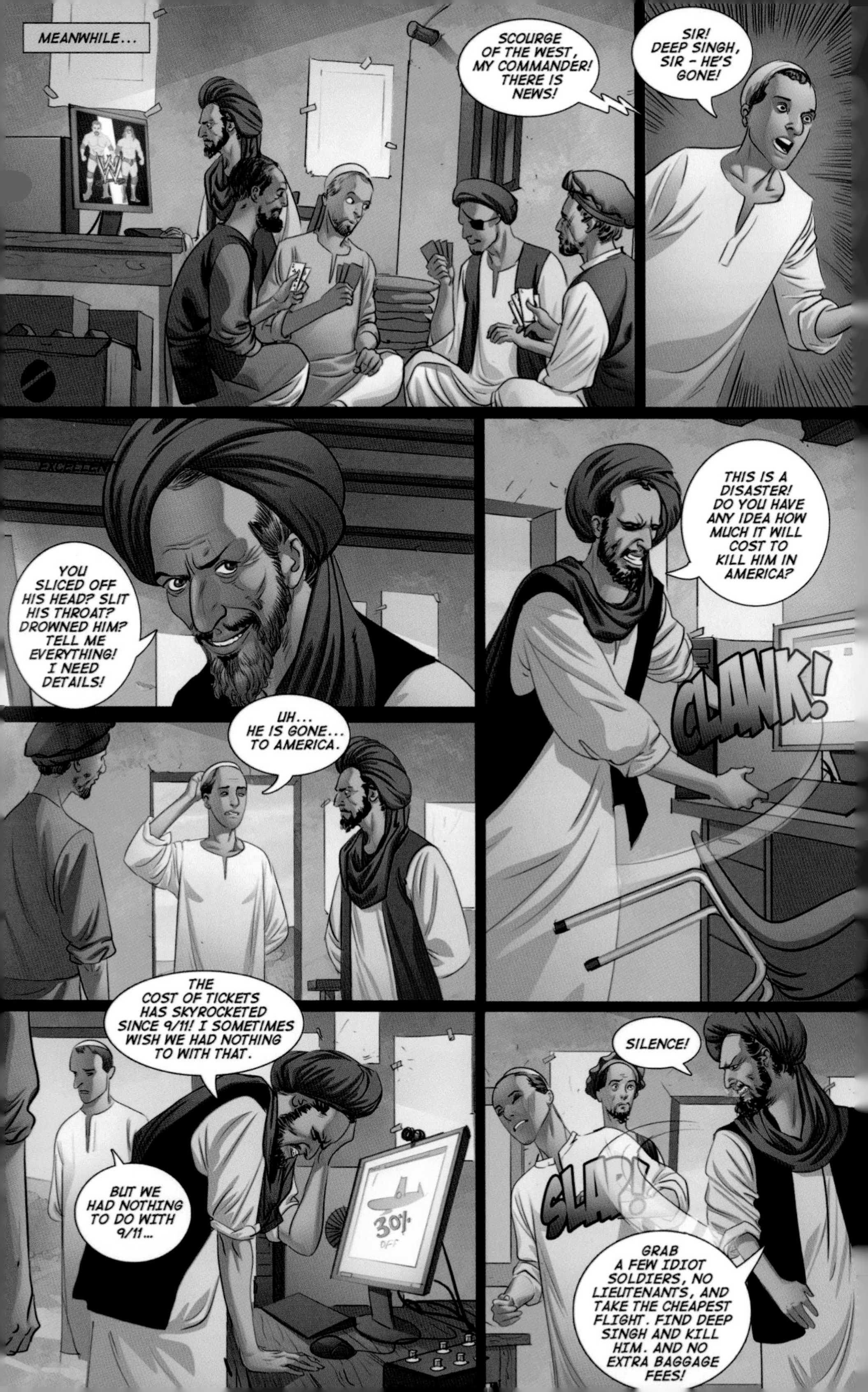
MEANWHILE...
SCOURGE OF THE WEST, MY COMMANDER! THERE IS NEWS!
SIR! DEEP SINGH, SIR - HE'S GONE!
YOU SLICED OFF HIS HEAD? SLIT HIS THROAT? DROWNED HIM? TELL ME EVERYTHING! I NEED DETAILS!
UH... HE IS GONE... TO AMERICA.
THIS IS A DISASTER! DO YOU HAVE ANY IDEA HOW MUCH IT WILL COST TO KILL HIM IN AMERICA?
CLANK!
THE COST OF TICKETS HAS SKYROCKETED SINCE 9/11! I SOMETIMES WISH WE HAD NOTHING TO WITH THAT.
BUT WE HAD NOTHING TO DO WITH 9/11...
30% OFF
SILENCE!
SLAP!
GRAB A FEW IDIOT SOLDIERS, NO LIEUTENANTS, AND TAKE THE CHEAPEST FLIGHT. FIND DEEP SINGH AND KILL HIM. AND NO EXTRA BAGGAGE FEES!

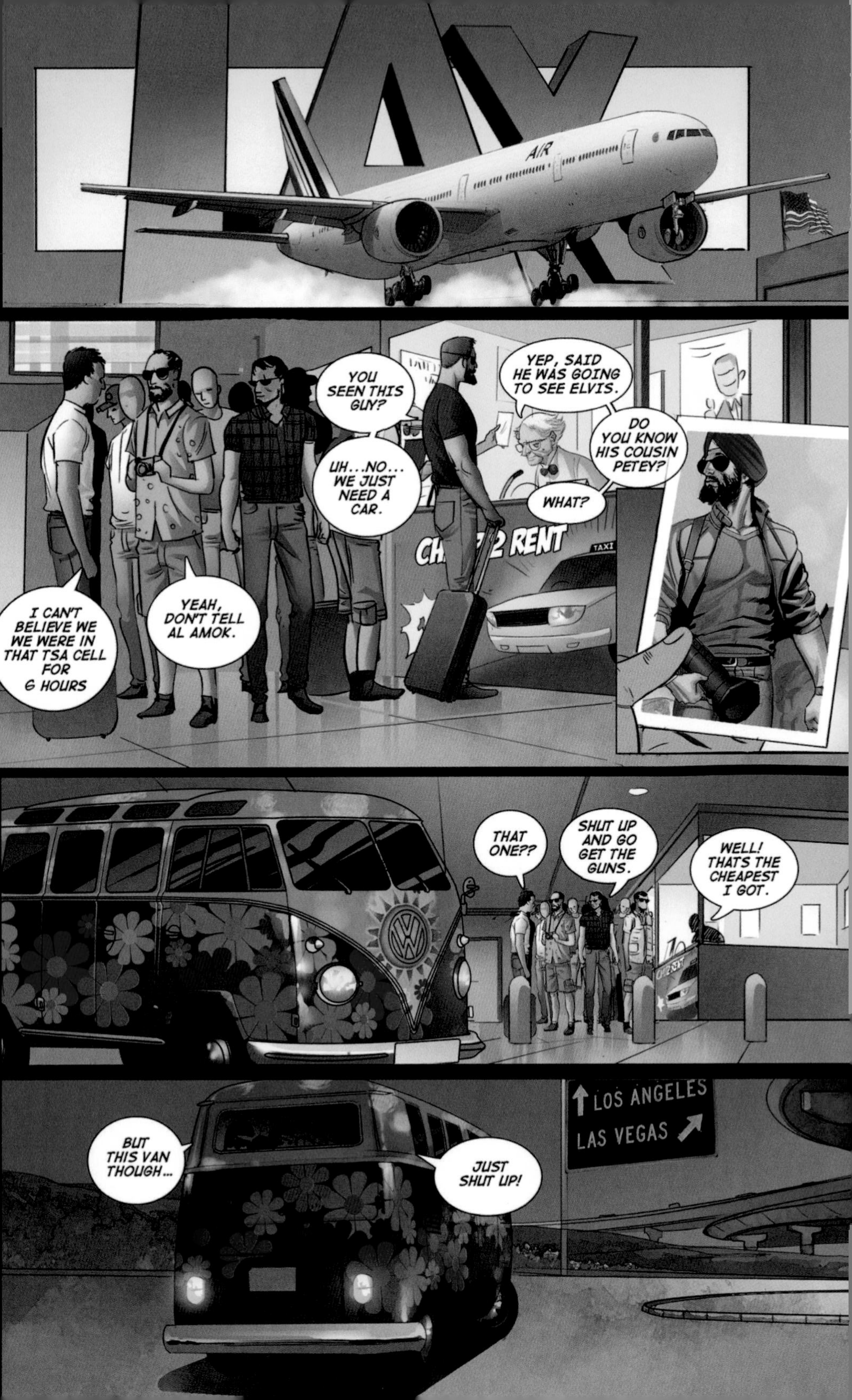

AIR
YOU SEEN THIS GUY?
YEP, SAID HE WAS GOING TO SEE ELVIS.
UH...NO... WE JUST NEED A CAR.
DO YOU KNOW HIS COUSIN PETEY?
WHAT?
I CAN'T BELIEVE WE WE WERE IN THAT TSA CELL FOR 6 HOURS
YEAH, DON'T TELL AL AMOK.
THAT ONE??
SHUT UP AND GO GET THE GUNS.
WELL! THATS THE CHEAPEST I GOT.
LOS ANGELES
LAS VEGAS
BUT THIS VAN THOUGH...
JUST SHUT UP!

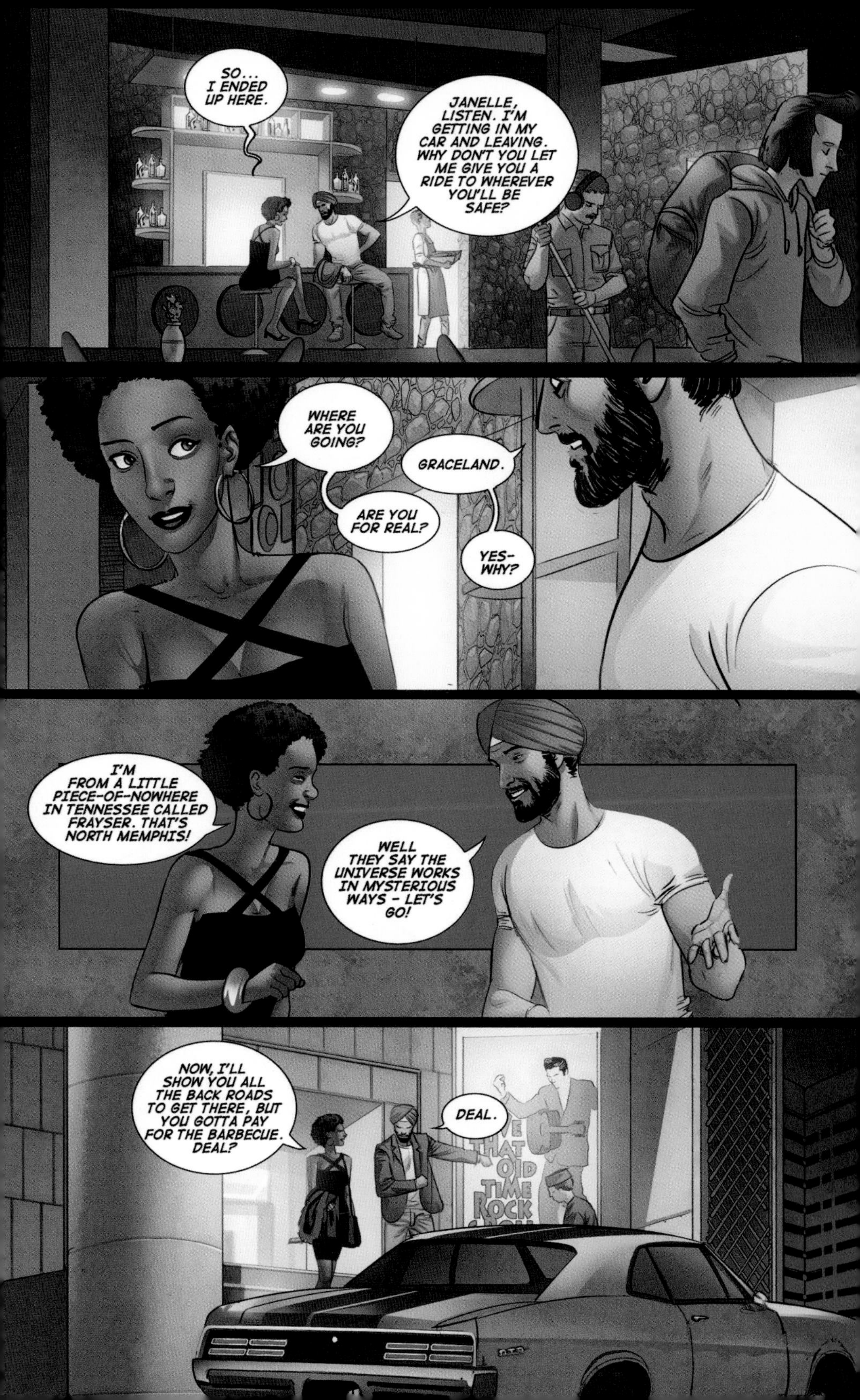
SO... I ENDED UP HERE.
JANELLE, LISTEN. I'M GETTING IN MY CAR AND LEAVING. WHY DON'T YOU LET ME GIVE YOU A RIDE TO WHEREVER YOU'LL BE SAFE?
WHERE ARE YOU GOING?
GRACELAND.
ARE YOU FOR REAL?
YES- WHY?
I'M FROM A LITTLE PIECE-OF-NOWHERE IN TENNESSEE CALLED FRAYSER. THAT'S NORTH MEMPHIS!
WELL THEY SAY THE UNIVERSE WORKS IN MYSTERIOUS WAYS - LET'S GO!
NOW, I'LL SHOW YOU ALL THE BACK ROADS TO GET THERE, BUT YOU GOTTA PAY FOR THE BARBECUE. DEAL?
DEAL.
THAT OLD TIME ROCK

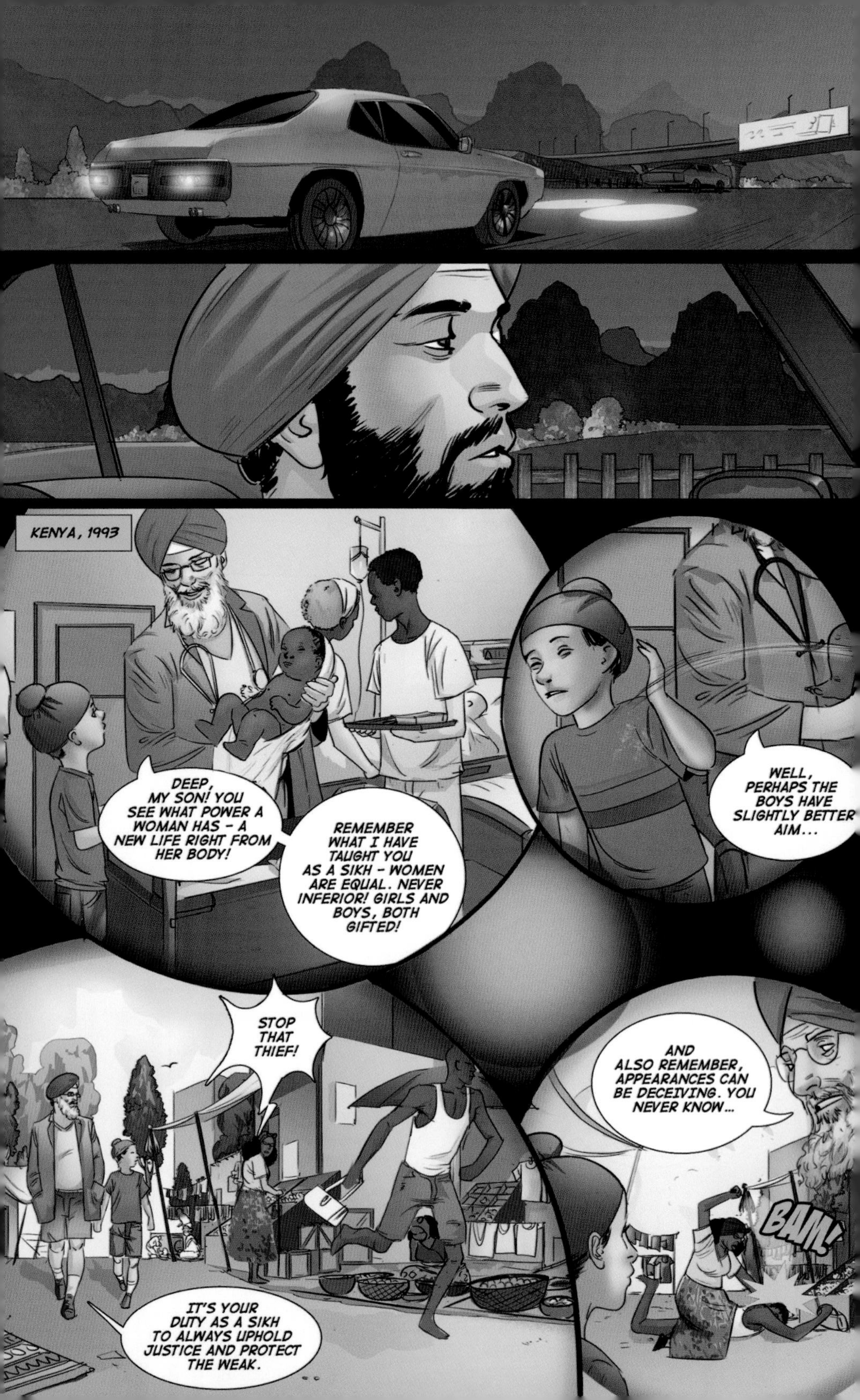
KENYA, 1993
DEEP, MY SON! YOU SEE WHAT POWER A WOMAN HAS - A NEW LIFE RIGHT FROM HER BODY!
REMEMBER WHAT I HAVE TAUGHT YOU AS A SIKH - WOMEN ARE EQUAL. NEVER INFERIOR! GIRLS AND BOYS, BOTH GIFTED!
WELL, PERHAPS THE BOYS HAVE SLIGHTLY BETTER AIM...
STOP THAT THIEF!
IT'S YOUR DUTY AS A SIKH TO ALWAYS UPHOLD JUSTICE AND PROTECT THE WEAK.
AND ALSO REMEMBER, APPEARANCES CAN BE DECEIVING. YOU NEVER KNOW...
BAM!

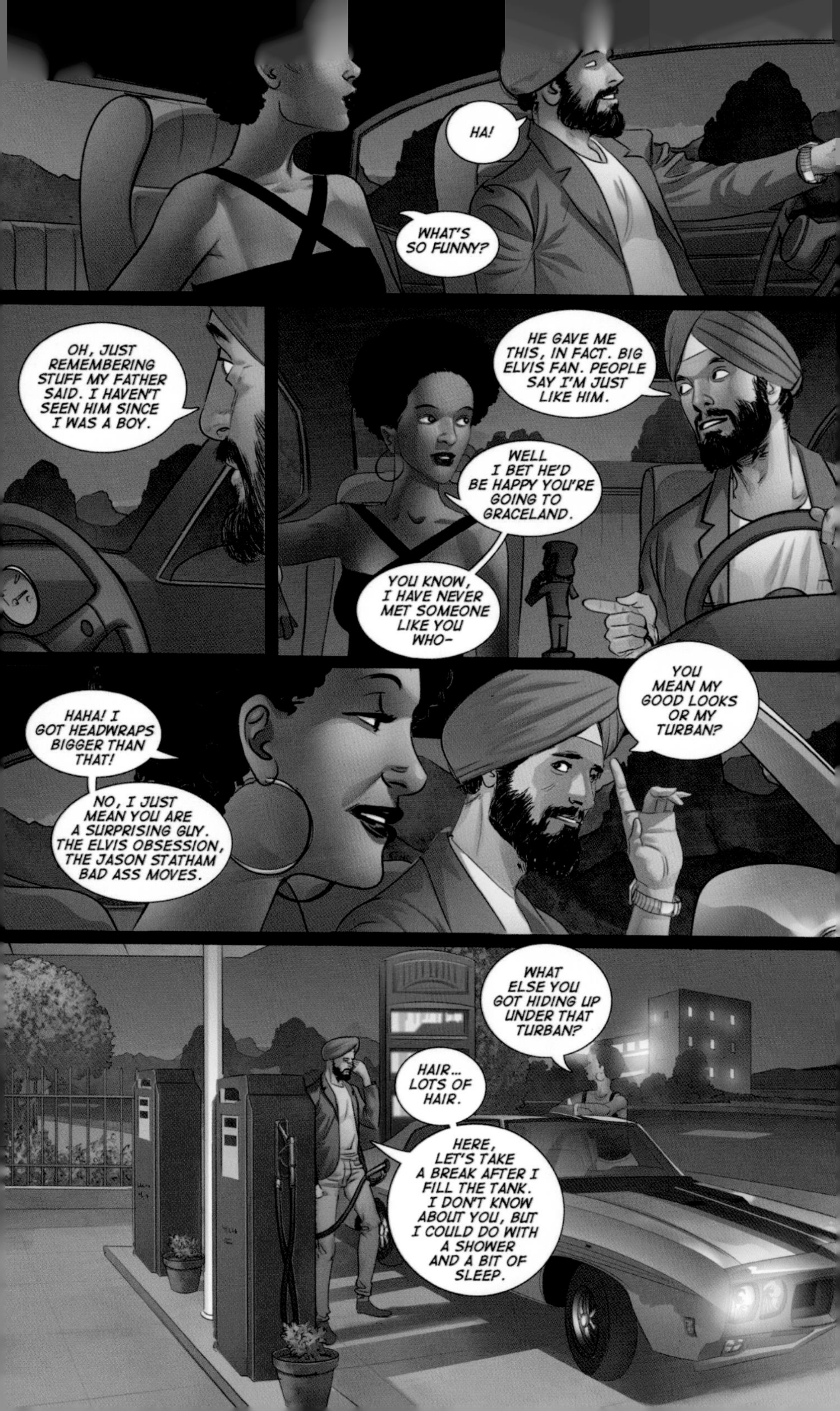
HA!
WHAT'S SO FUNNY?
OH, JUST REMEMBERING STUFF MY FATHER SAID. I HAVEN'T SEEN HIM SINCE I WAS A BOY.
HE GAVE ME THIS, IN FACT. BIG ELVIS FAN. PEOPLE SAY I'M JUST LIKE HIM.
WELL I BET HE'D BE HAPPY YOU'RE GOING TO GRACELAND.
YOU KNOW, I HAVE NEVER MET SOMEONE LIKE YOU WHO-
YOU MEAN MY GOOD LOOKS OR MY TURBAN?
HAHA! I GOT HEADWRAPS BIGGER THAN THAT!
NO, I JUST MEAN YOU ARE A SURPRISING GUY. THE ELVIS OBSESSION, THE JASON STATHAM BAD ASS MOVES.
WHAT ELSE YOU GOT HIDING UP UNDER THAT TURBAN?
HAIR... LOTS OF HAIR.
HERE, LET'S TAKE A BREAK AFTER I FILL THE TANK. I DON'T KNOW ABOUT YOU, BUT I COULD DO WITH A SHOWER AND A BIT OF SLEEP.

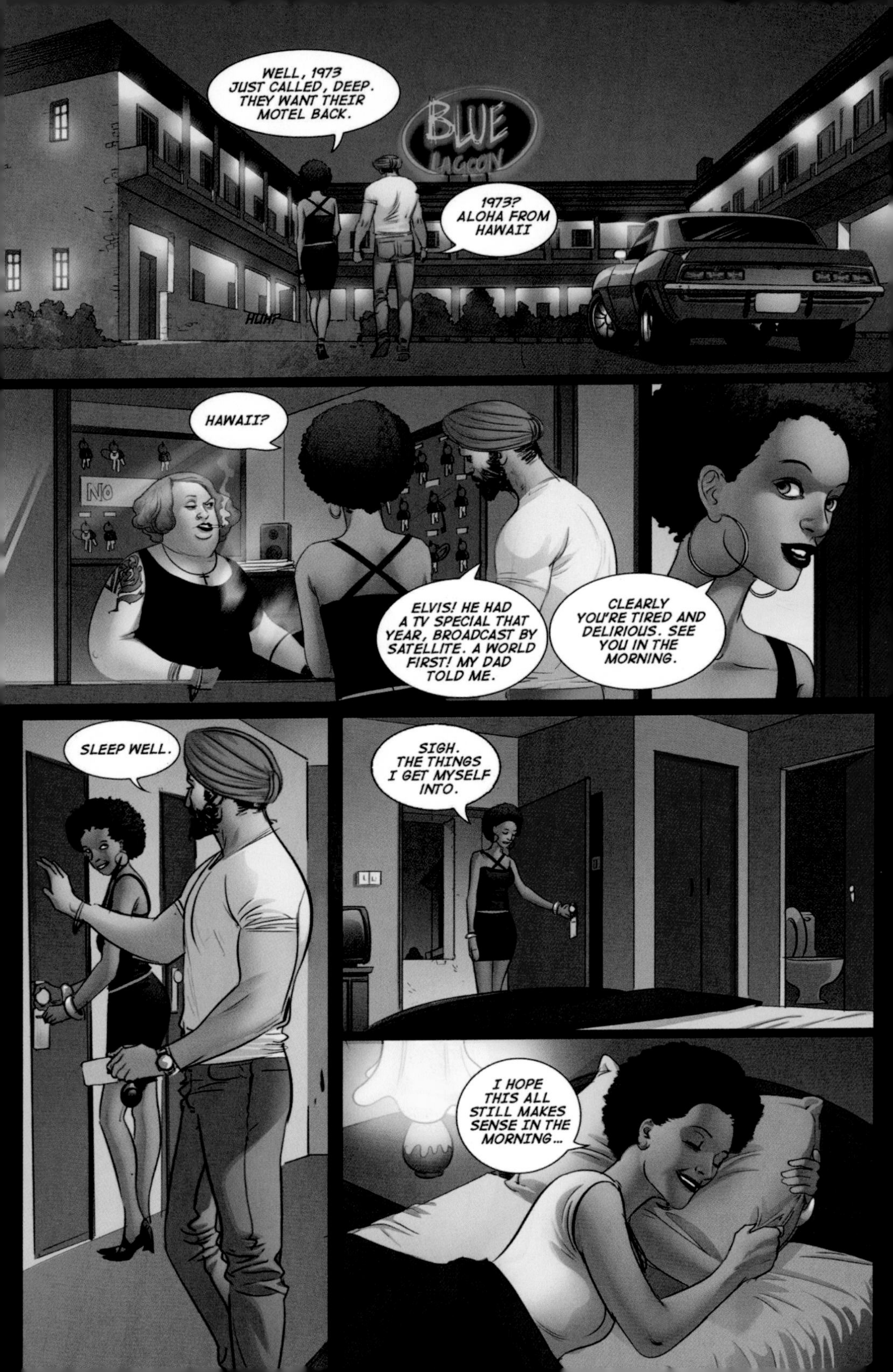

WELL, 1973 JUST CALLED, DEEP. THEY WANT THEIR MOTEL BACK.
BLUE LAGOON
1973? ALOHA FROM HAWAII
HUH?
HAWAII?
NO
ELVIS! HE HAD A TV SPECIAL THAT YEAR, BROADCAST BY SATELLITE. A WORLD FIRST! MY DAD TOLD ME.
CLEARLY YOU'RE TIRED AND DELIRIOUS. SEE YOU IN THE MORNING.
SLEEP WELL.
SIGH. THE THINGS I GET MYSELF INTO.
I HOPE THIS ALL STILL MAKES SENSE IN THE MORNING...

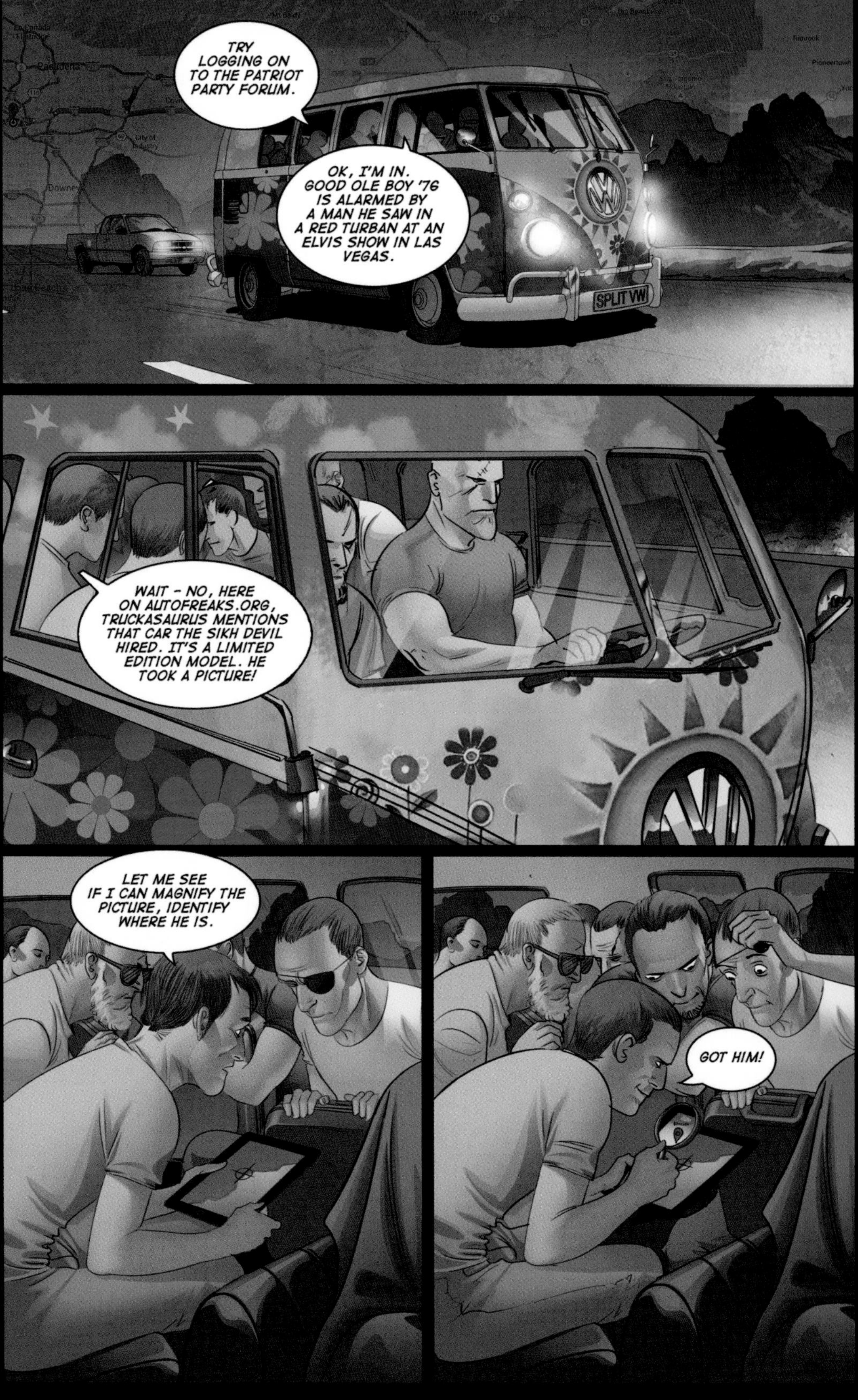
TRY LOGGING ON TO THE PATRIOT PARTY FORUM.
OK, I'M IN. GOOD OLE BOY '76 IS ALARMED BY A MAN HE SAW IN A RED TURBAN AT AN ELVIS SHOW IN LAS VEGAS.
SPLIT VW
WAIT - NO, HERE ON AUTOFREAKS.ORG, TRUCKASAURUS MENTIONS THAT CAR THE SIKH DEVIL HIRED. IT'S A LIMITED EDITION MODEL. HE TOOK A PICTURE!
LET ME SEE IF I CAN MAGNIFY THE PICTURE, IDENTIFY WHERE HE IS.
GOT HIM!

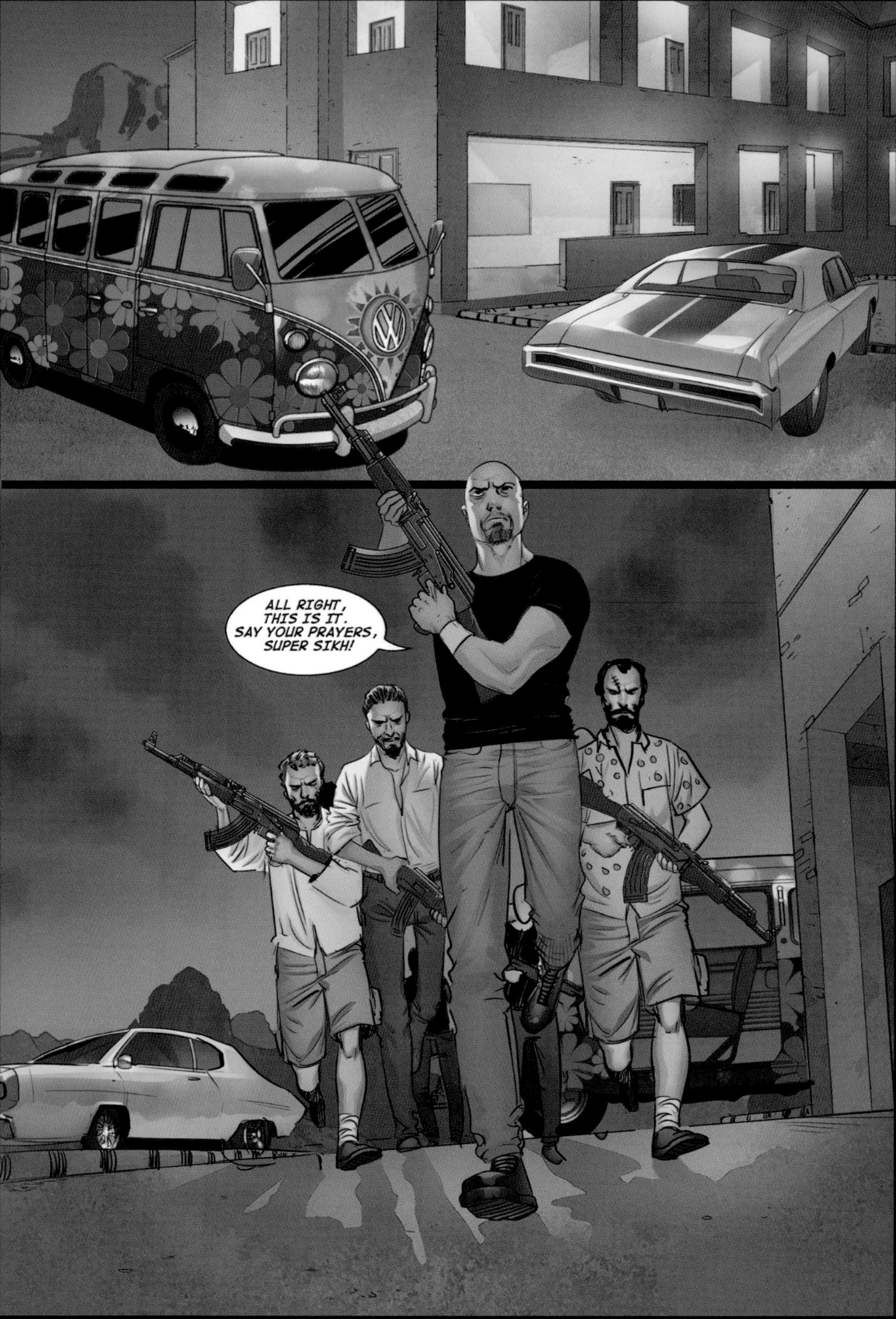
ALL RIGHT, THIS IS IT. SAY YOUR PRAYERS, SUPER SIKH!

TO BE CONTINUED...

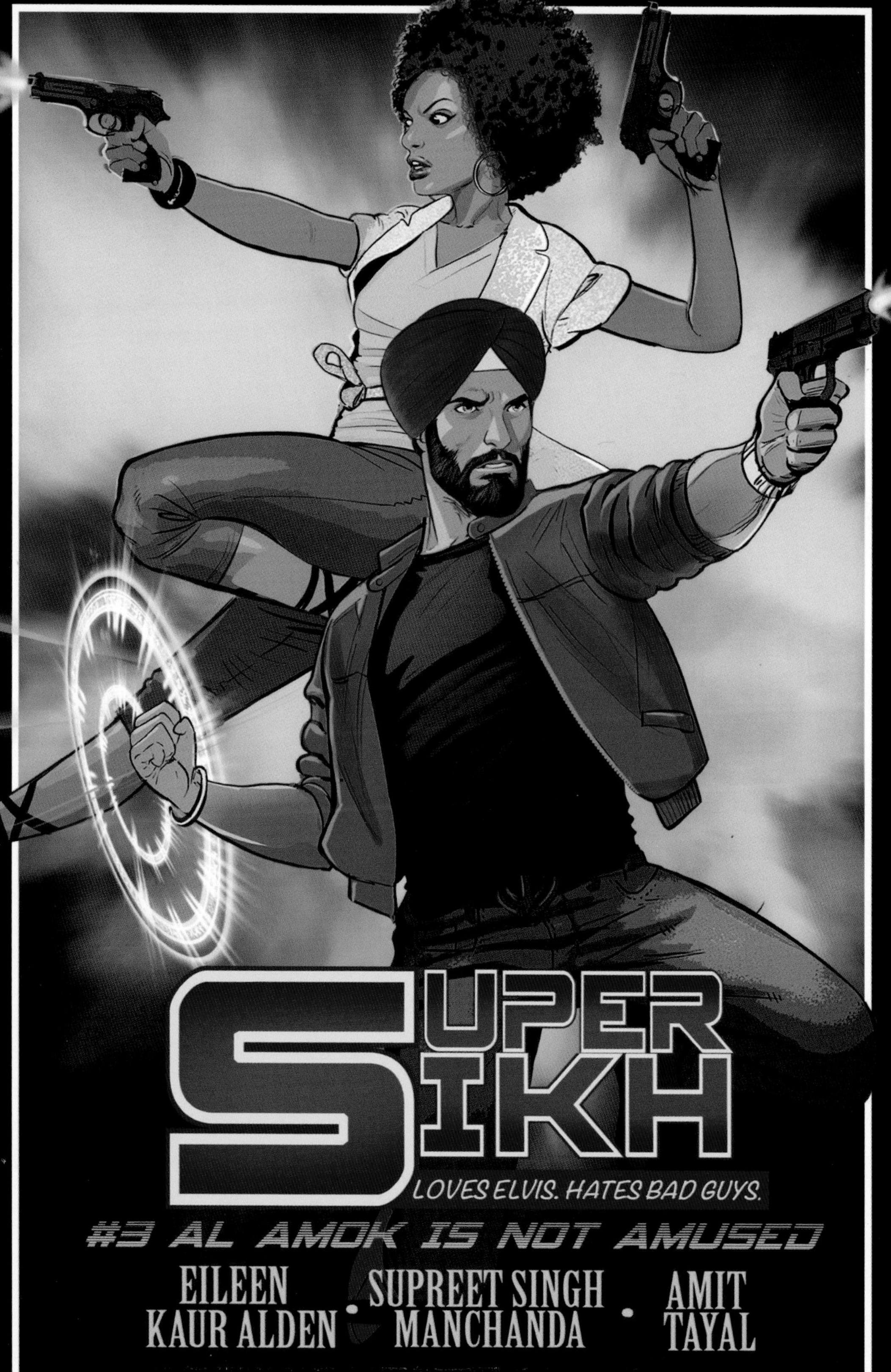
SUPER SIKH
LOVES ELVIS. HATES BAD GUYS.
#3 AL AMOK IS NOT AMUSED
EILEEN KAUR ALDEN
SUPREET SINGH MANCHANDA
AMIT TAYAL

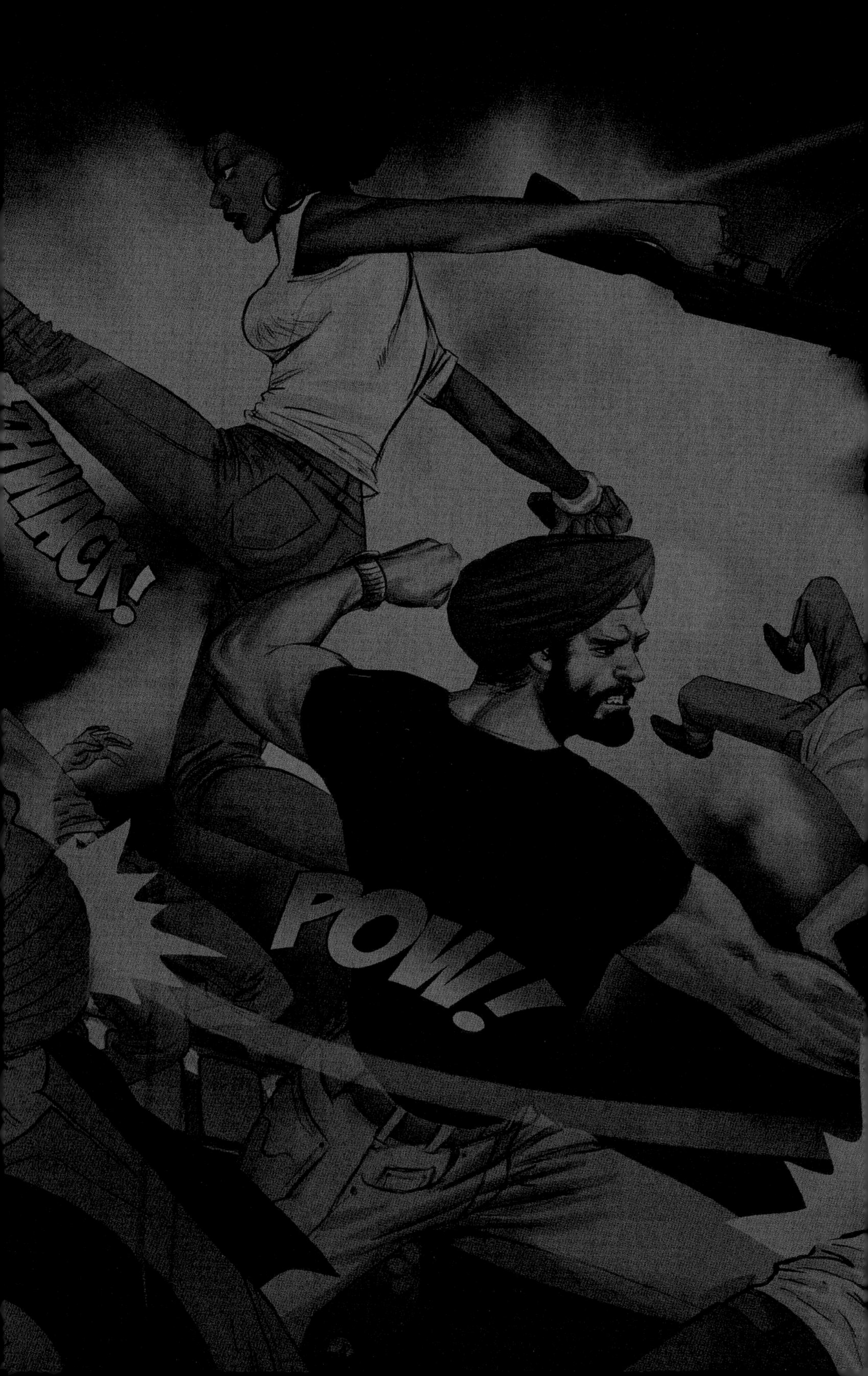
HWACK!
POW!

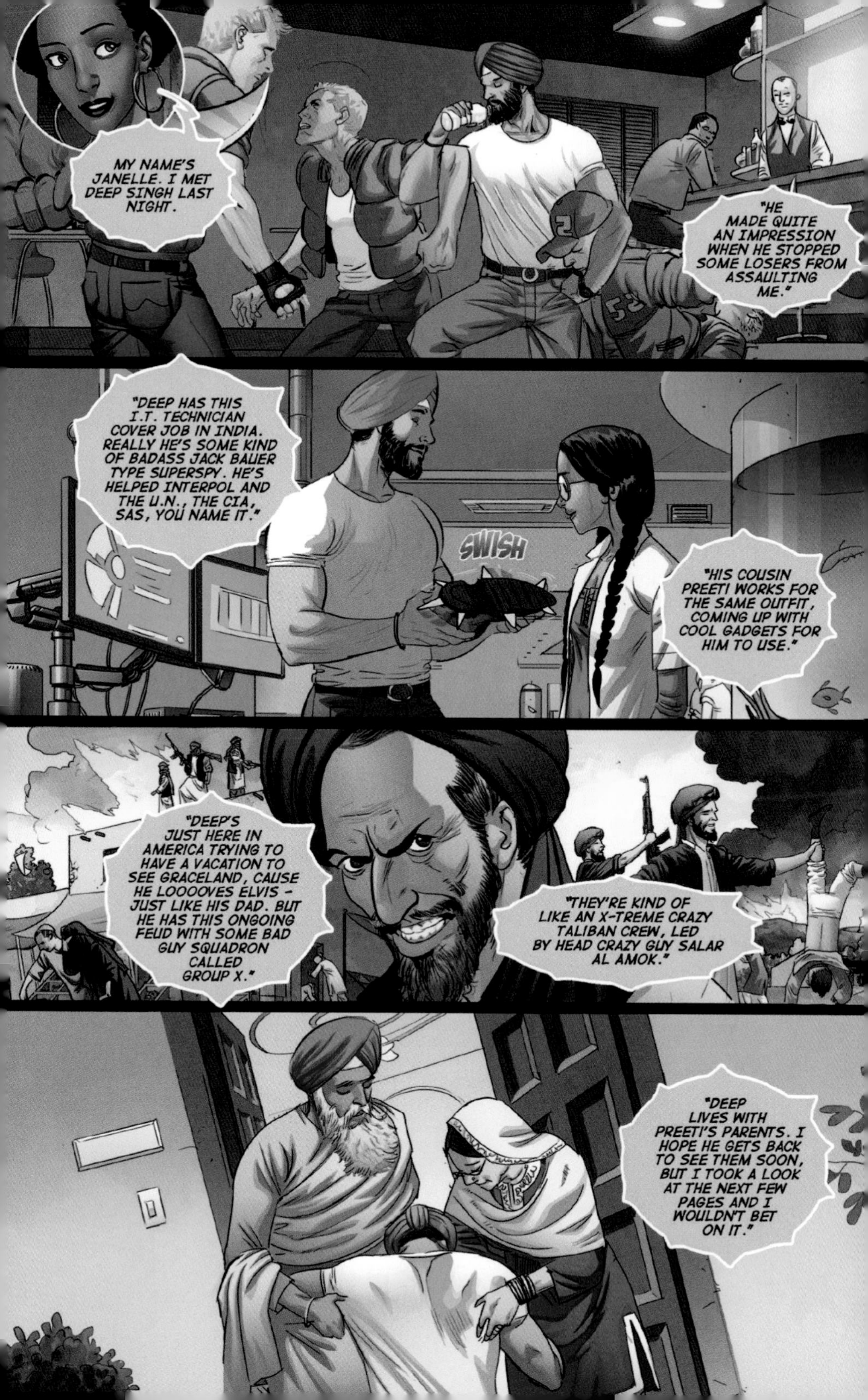
MY NAME'S JANELLE. I MET DEEP SINGH LAST NIGHT.
"HE MADE QUITE AN IMPRESSION WHEN HE STOPPED SOME LOSERS FROM ASSAULTING ME."
"DEEP HAS THIS I.T. TECHNICIAN COVER JOB IN INDIA. REALLY HE'S SOME KIND OF BADASS JACK BAUER TYPE SUPERSPY. HE'S HELPED INTERPOL AND THE U.N., THE CIA, SAS, YOU NAME IT."
SWISH
"HIS COUSIN PREETI WORKS FOR THE SAME OUTFIT, COMING UP WITH COOL GADGETS FOR HIM TO USE."
"DEEP'S JUST HERE IN AMERICA TRYING TO HAVE A VACATION TO SEE GRACELAND, CAUSE HE LOOOOVES ELVIS - JUST LIKE HIS DAD. BUT HE HAS THIS ONGOING FEUD WITH SOME BAD GUY SQUADRON CALLED GROUP X."
"THEY'RE KIND OF LIKE AN X-TREME CRAZY TALIBAN CREW, LED BY HEAD CRAZY GUY SALAR AL AMOK."
"DEEP LIVES WITH PREETI'S PARENTS. I HOPE HE GETS BACK TO SEE THEM SOON, BUT I TOOK A LOOK AT THE NEXT FEW PAGES AND I WOULDN'T BET ON IT."

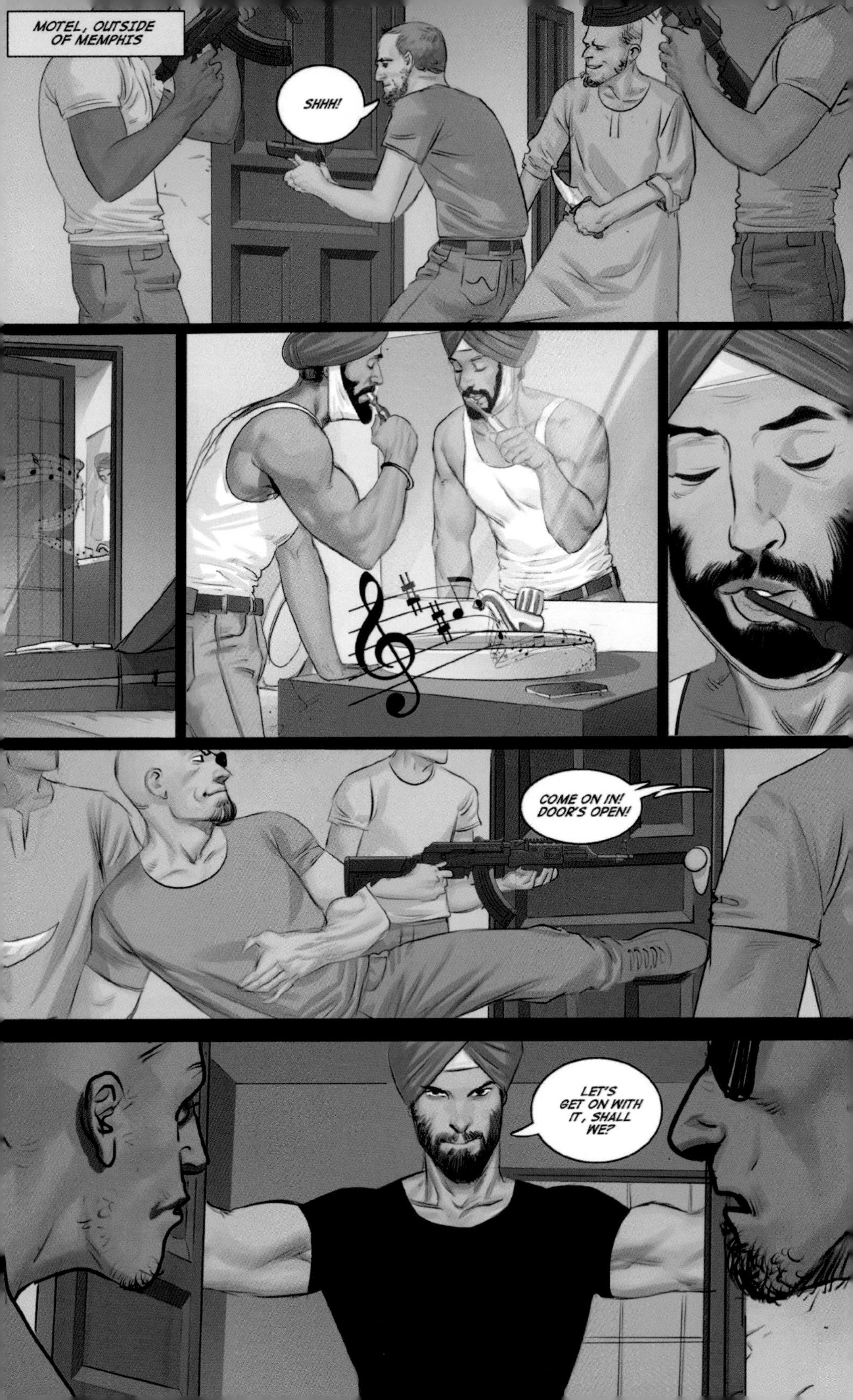
MOTEL, OUTSIDE OF MEMPHIS
SHHH!
COME ON IN! DOOR'S OPEN!
LET'S GET ON WITH IT, SHALL WE?

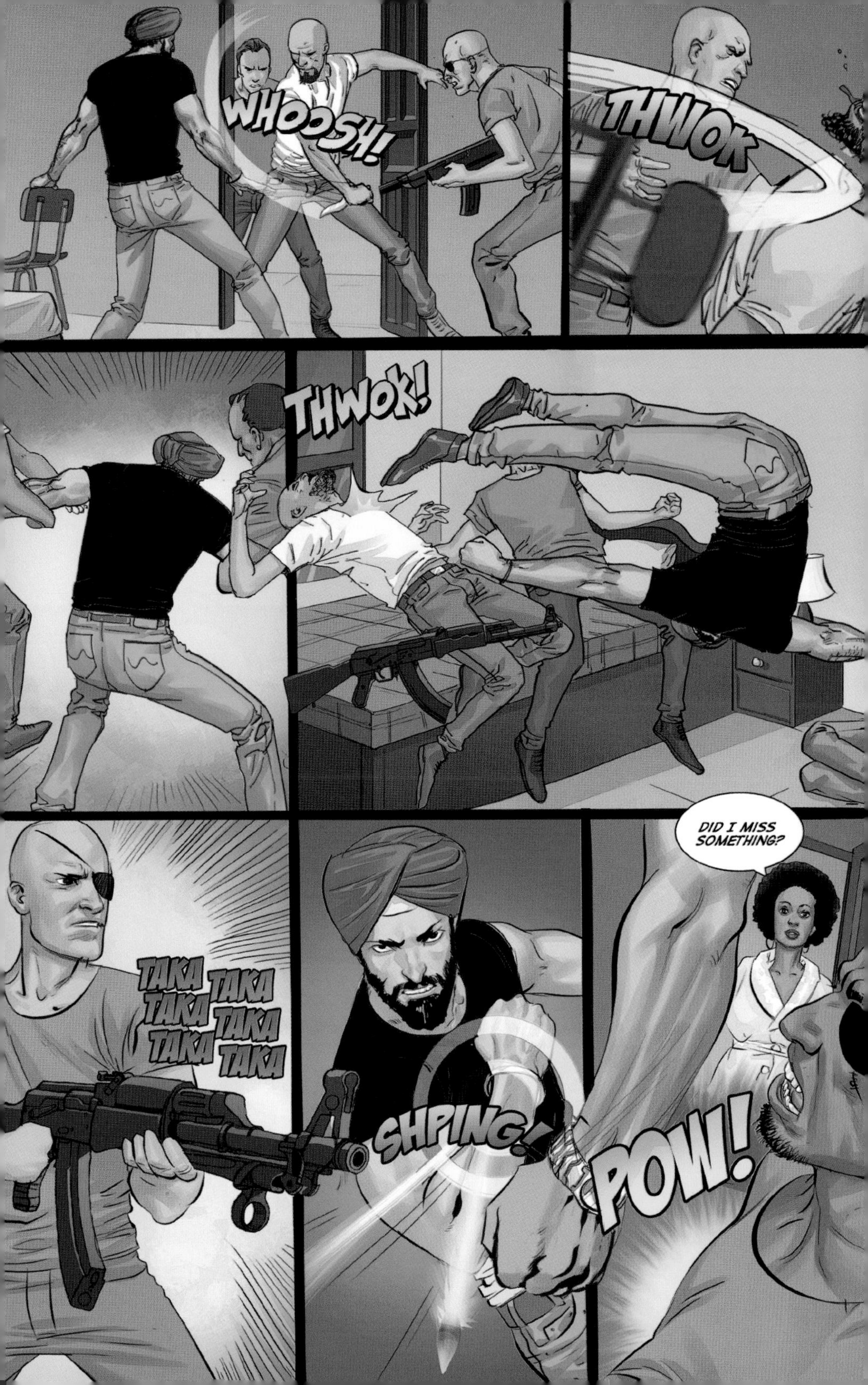
WHOOSH!
THWOK
THWOK!
TAKA TAKA TAKA
TAKA TAKA TAKA
SHPING!
DID I MISS SOMETHING?
POW!

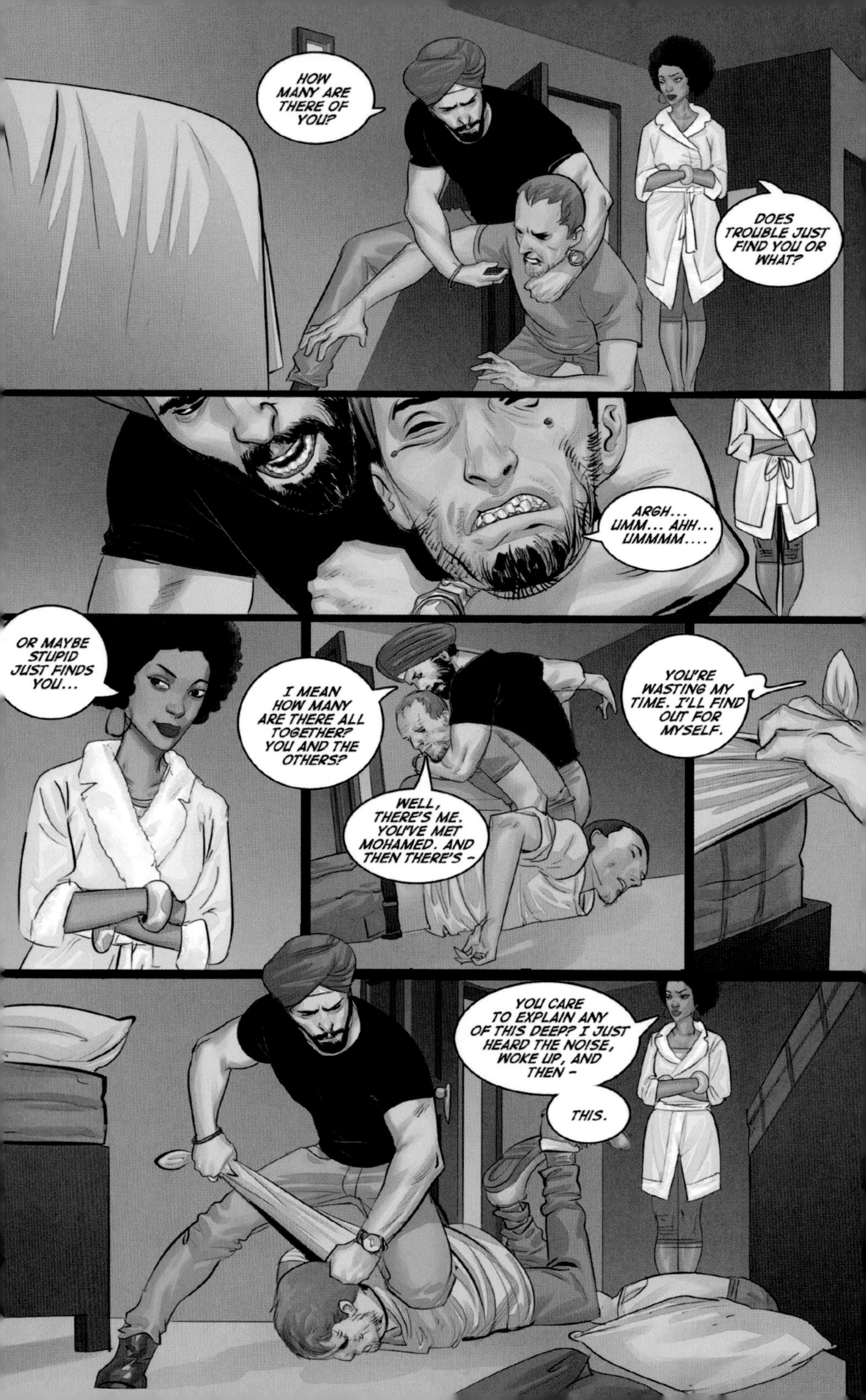
HOW MANY ARE THERE OF YOU?
DOES TROUBLE JUST FIND YOU OR WHAT?
ARGH... UMM... AHH... UMMMM....
OR MAYBE STUPID JUST FINDS YOU...
I MEAN HOW MANY ARE THERE ALL TOGETHER? YOU AND THE OTHERS?
WELL, THERE'S ME. YOU'VE MET MOHAMED. AND THEN THERE'S -
YOU'RE WASTING MY TIME. I'LL FIND OUT FOR MYSELF.
YOU CARE TO EXPLAIN ANY OF THIS DEEP? I JUST HEARD THE NOISE, WOKE UP, AND THEN -
THIS.

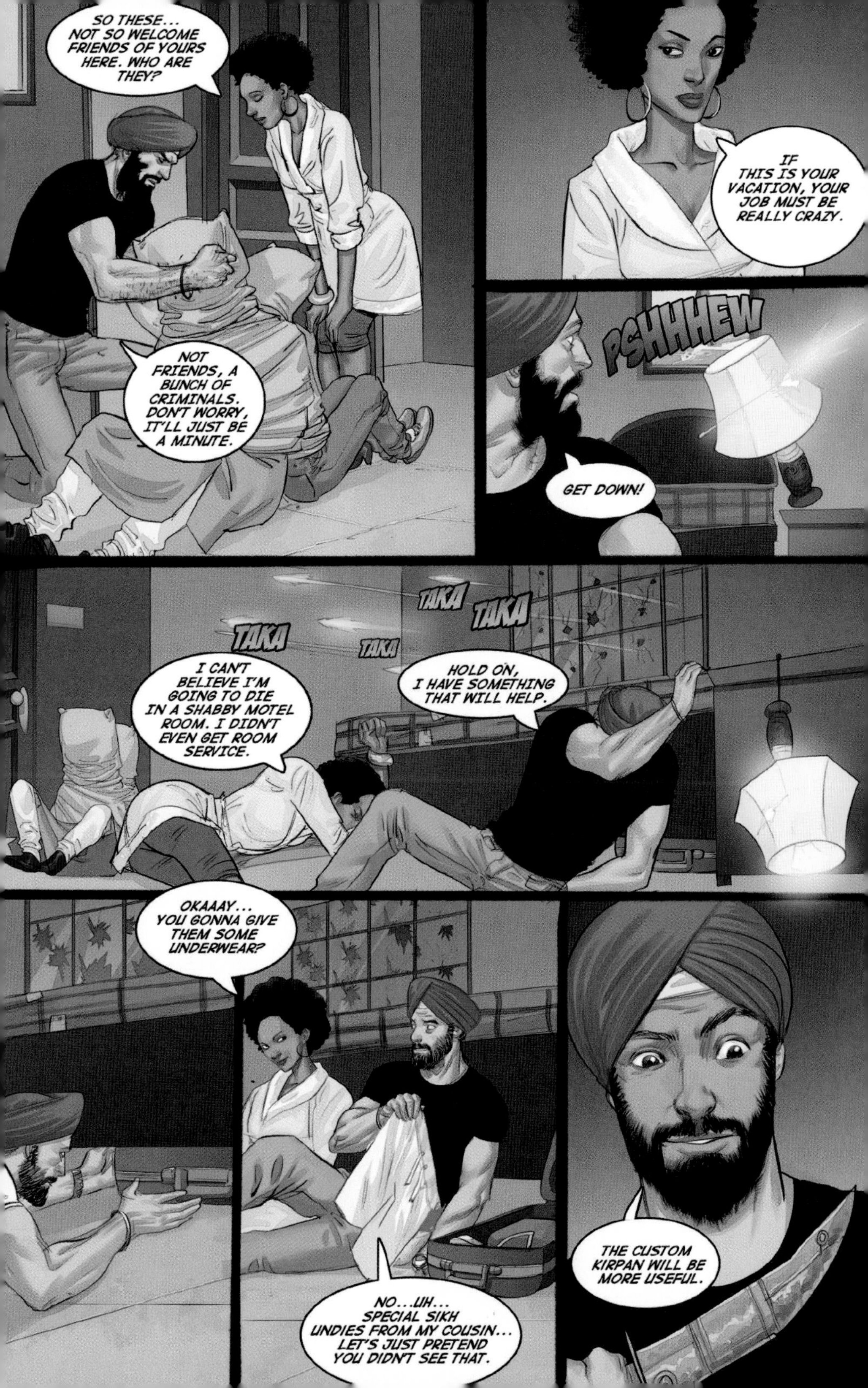
SO THESE... NOT SO WELCOME FRIENDS OF YOURS HERE. WHO ARE THEY?
NOT FRIENDS, A BUNCH OF CRIMINALS. DON'T WORRY, IT'LL JUST BE A MINUTE.
IF THIS IS YOUR VACATION, YOUR JOB MUST BE REALLY CRAZY.
PSHHHEW
GET DOWN!
TAKA
TAKA
TAKA
TAKA
I CAN'T BELIEVE I'M GOING TO DIE IN A SHABBY MOTEL ROOM. I DIDN'T EVEN GET ROOM SERVICE.
HOLD ON, I HAVE SOMETHING THAT WILL HELP.
OKAAAY... YOU GONNA GIVE THEM SOME UNDERWEAR?
NO...UH... SPECIAL SIKH UNDIES FROM MY COUSIN... LET'S JUST PRETEND YOU DIDN'T SEE THAT.
THE CUSTOM KIRPAN WILL BE MORE USEFUL.

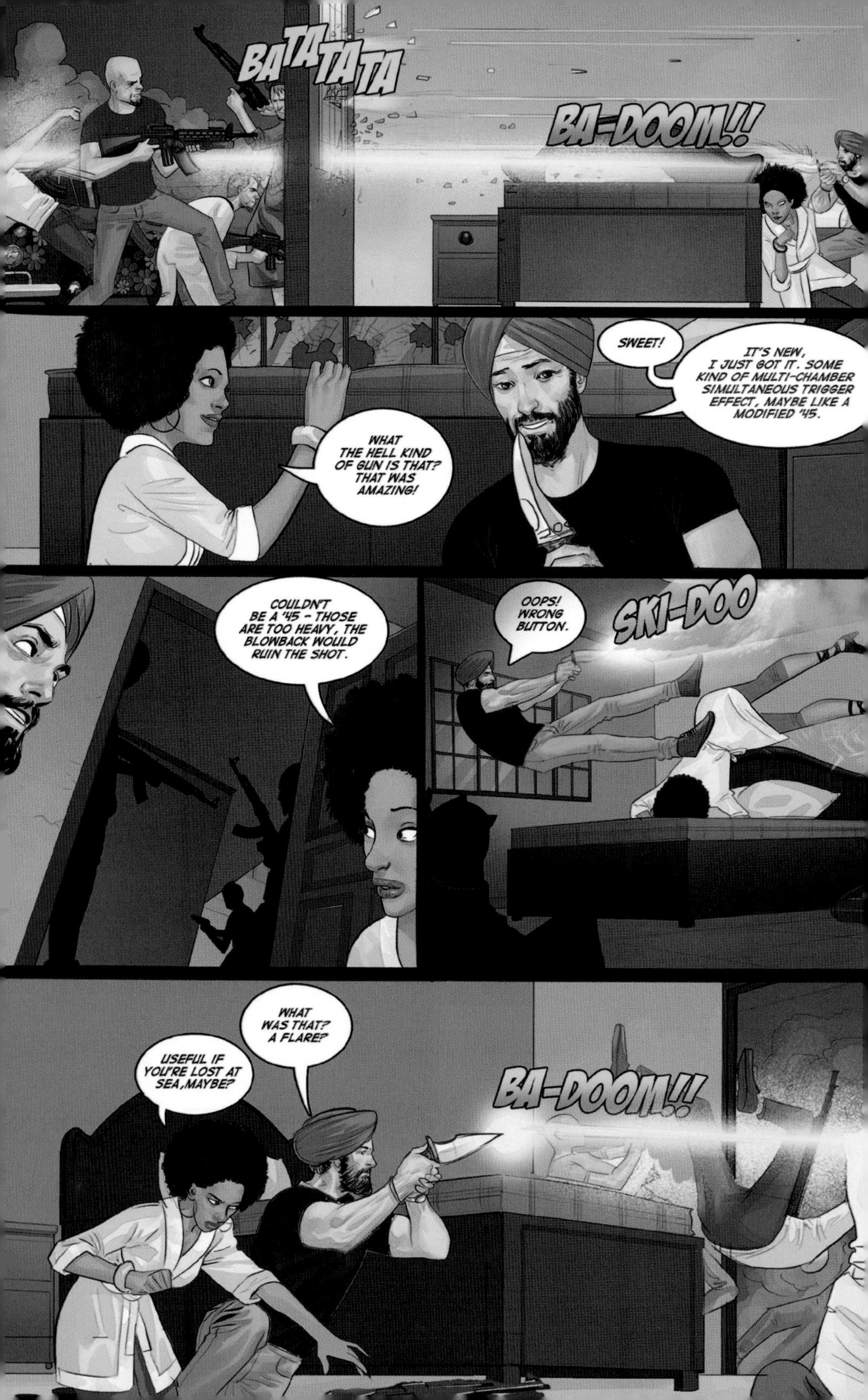
BATATATA
BA-DOOM!!
SWEET!
IT'S NEW, I JUST GOT IT. SOME KIND OF MULTI-CHAMBER SIMULTANEOUS TRIGGER EFFECT, MAYBE LIKE A MODIFIED '45.
WHAT THE HELL KIND OF GUN IS THAT? THAT WAS AMAZING!
COULDN'T BE A '45 - THOSE ARE TOO HEAVY, THE BLOWBACK WOULD RUIN THE SHOT.
OOPS! WRONG BUTTON.
SKI-DOO
WHAT WAS THAT? A FLARE?
USEFUL IF YOU'RE LOST AT SEA, MAYBE?
BA-DOOM!!

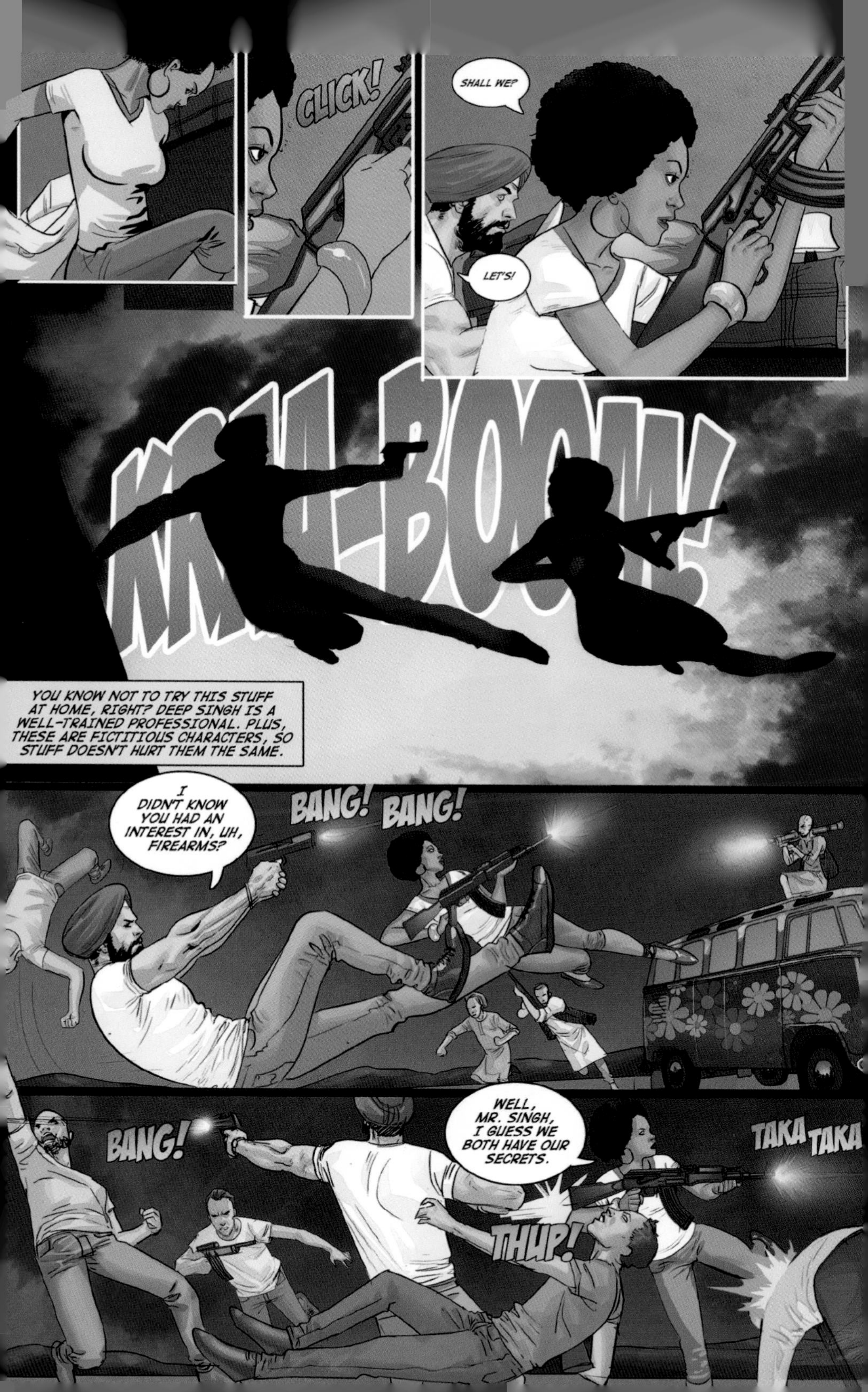
CLICK!
SHALL WE?
LET'S!
YOU KNOW NOT TO TRY THIS STUFF AT HOME, RIGHT? DEEP SINGH IS A WELL-TRAINED PROFESSIONAL. PLUS, THESE ARE FICTITIOUS CHARACTERS, SO STUFF DOESN'T HURT THEM THE SAME.
I DIDN'T KNOW YOU HAD AN INTEREST IN, UH, FIREARMS?
BANG! BANG!
BANG!
WELL, MR. SINGH, I GUESS WE BOTH HAVE OUR SECRETS.
TAKA TAKA
THUP!

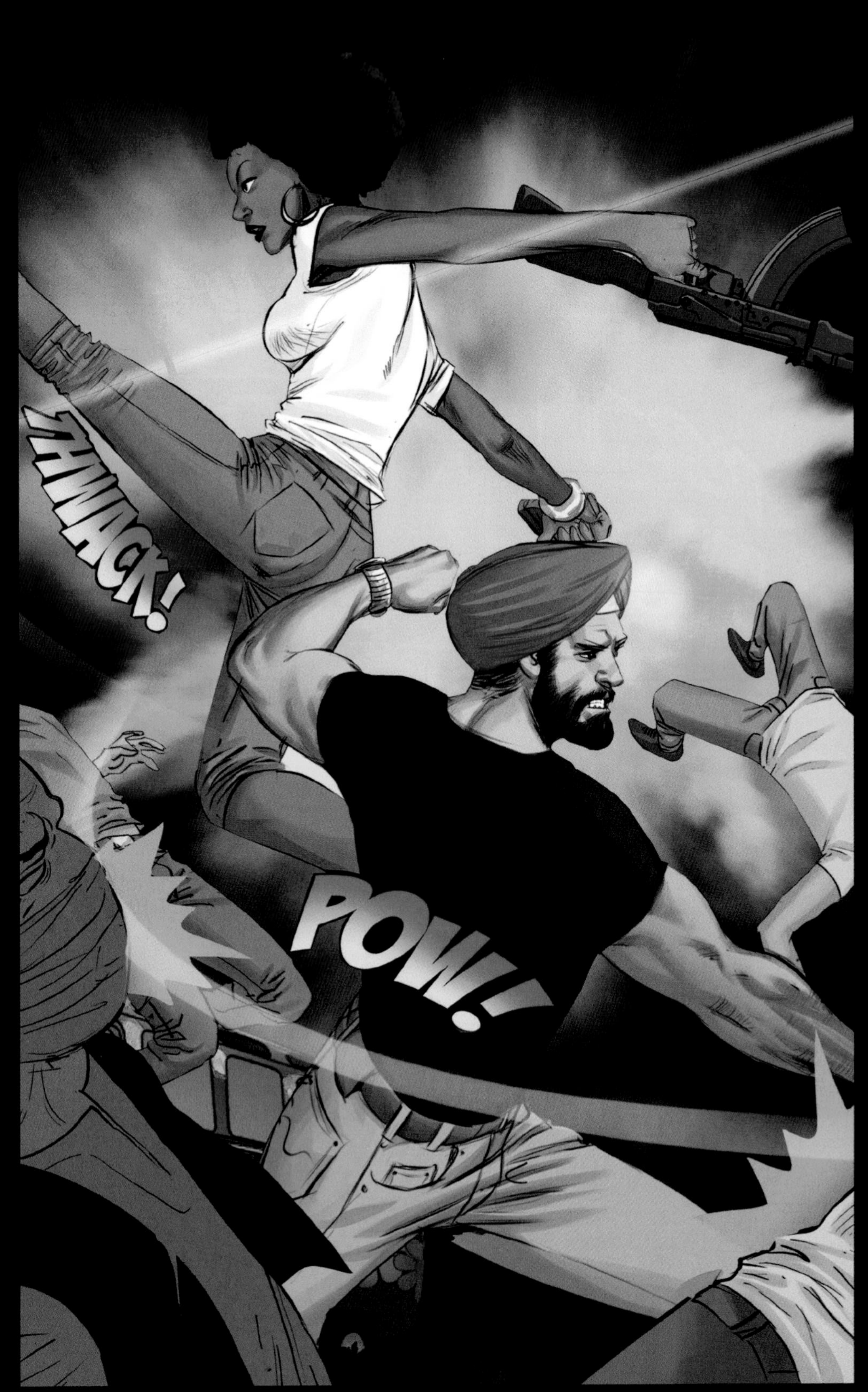
THWACK!
POW!

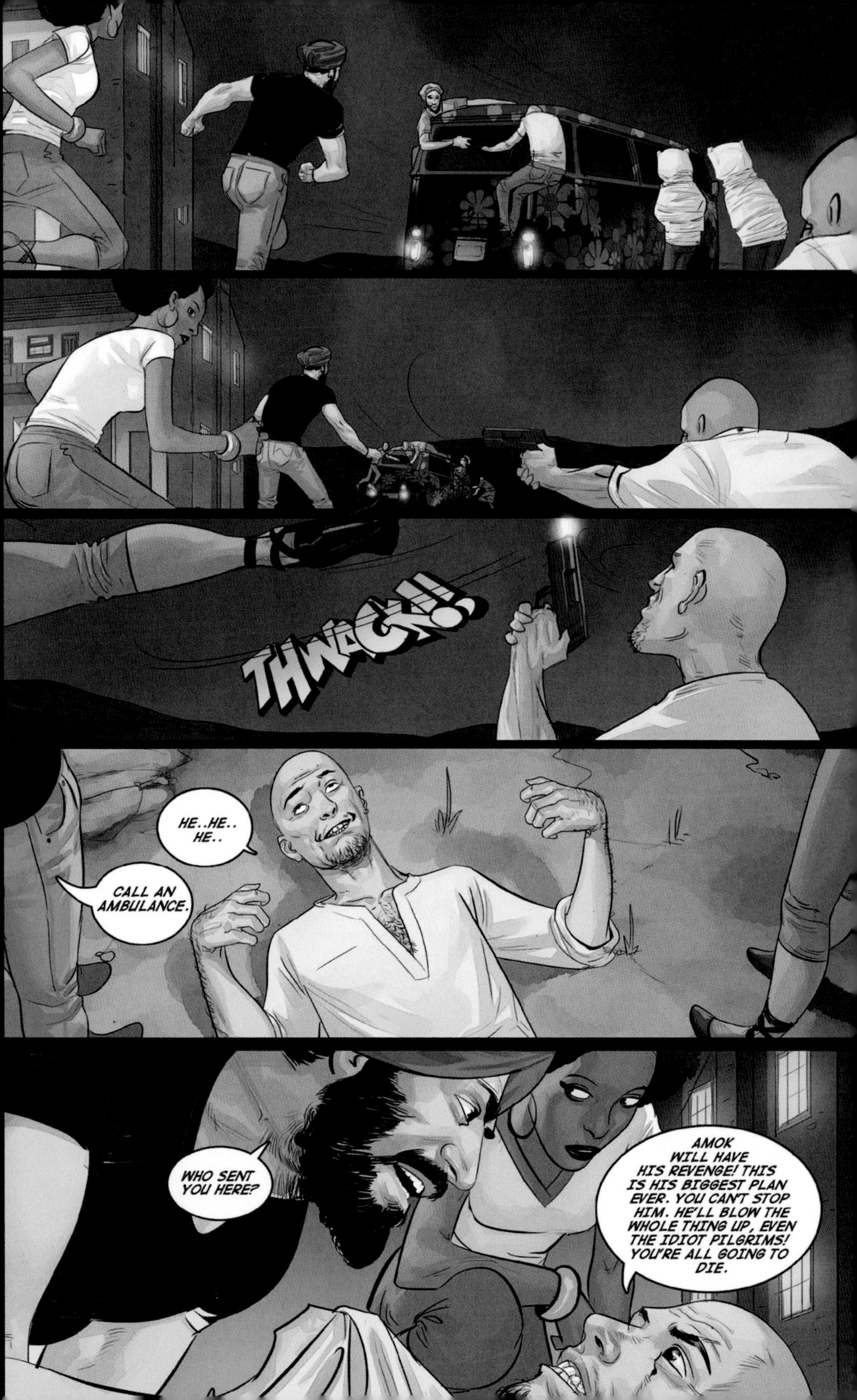
THWACK!!
HE..HE..
HE..
CALL AN AMBULANCE.
WHO SENT YOU HERE?
AMOK WILL HAVE HIS REVENGE! THIS IS HIS BIGGEST PLAN EVER. YOU CAN'T STOP HIM. HE'LL BLOW THE WHOLE THING UP, EVEN THE IDIOT PILGRIMS! YOU'RE ALL GOING TO DIE.

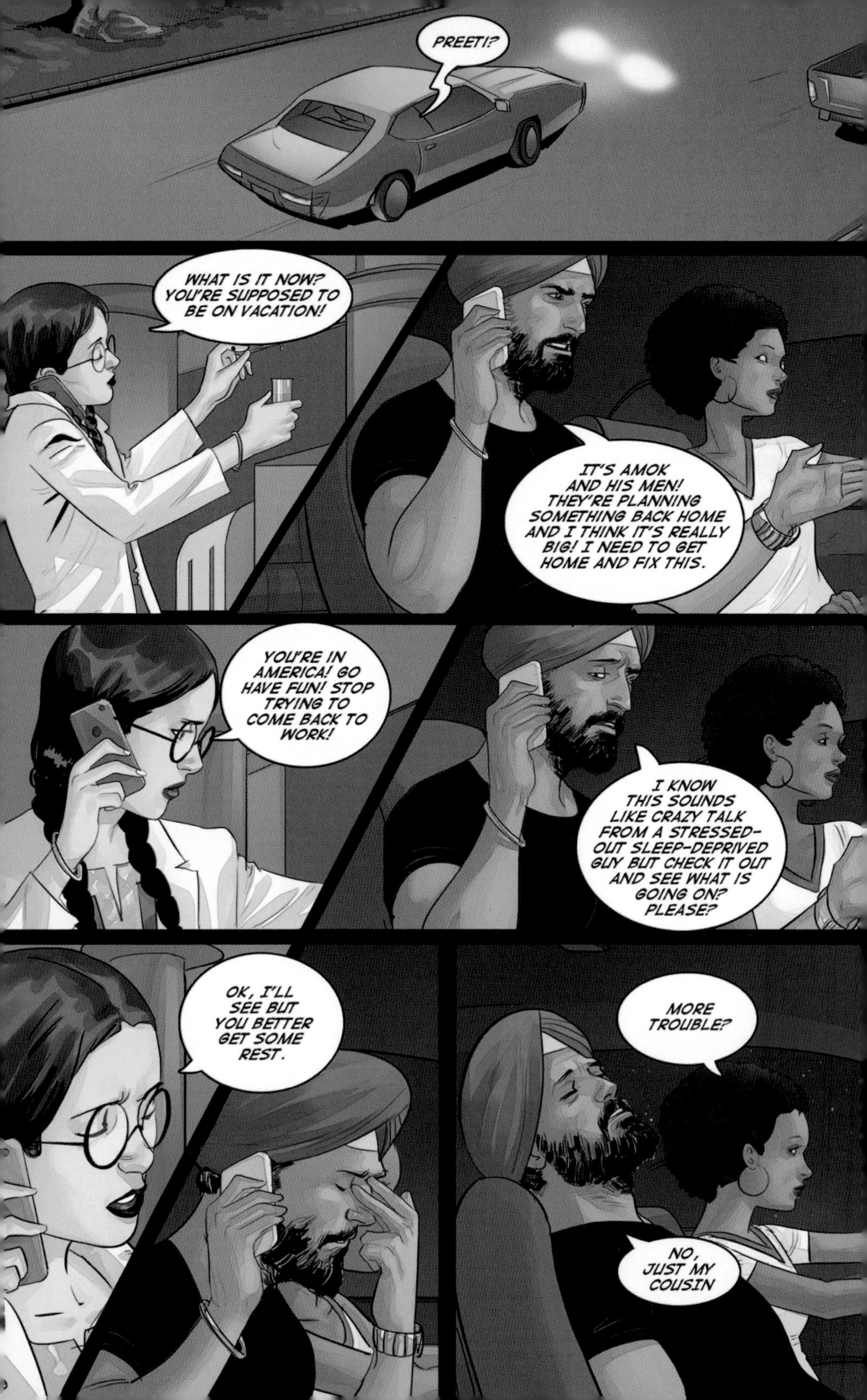
PREETI!?
WHAT IS IT NOW? YOU'RE SUPPOSED TO BE ON VACATION!
IT'S AMOK AND HIS MEN! THEY'RE PLANNING SOMETHING BACK HOME AND I THINK IT'S REALLY BIG! I NEED TO GET HOME AND FIX THIS.
YOU'RE IN AMERICA! GO HAVE FUN! STOP TRYING TO COME BACK TO WORK!
I KNOW THIS SOUNDS LIKE CRAZY TALK FROM A STRESSED-OUT SLEEP-DEPRIVED GUY BUT CHECK IT OUT AND SEE WHAT IS GOING ON? PLEASE?
OK, I'LL SEE BUT YOU BETTER GET SOME REST.
MORE TROUBLE?
NO, JUST MY COUSIN

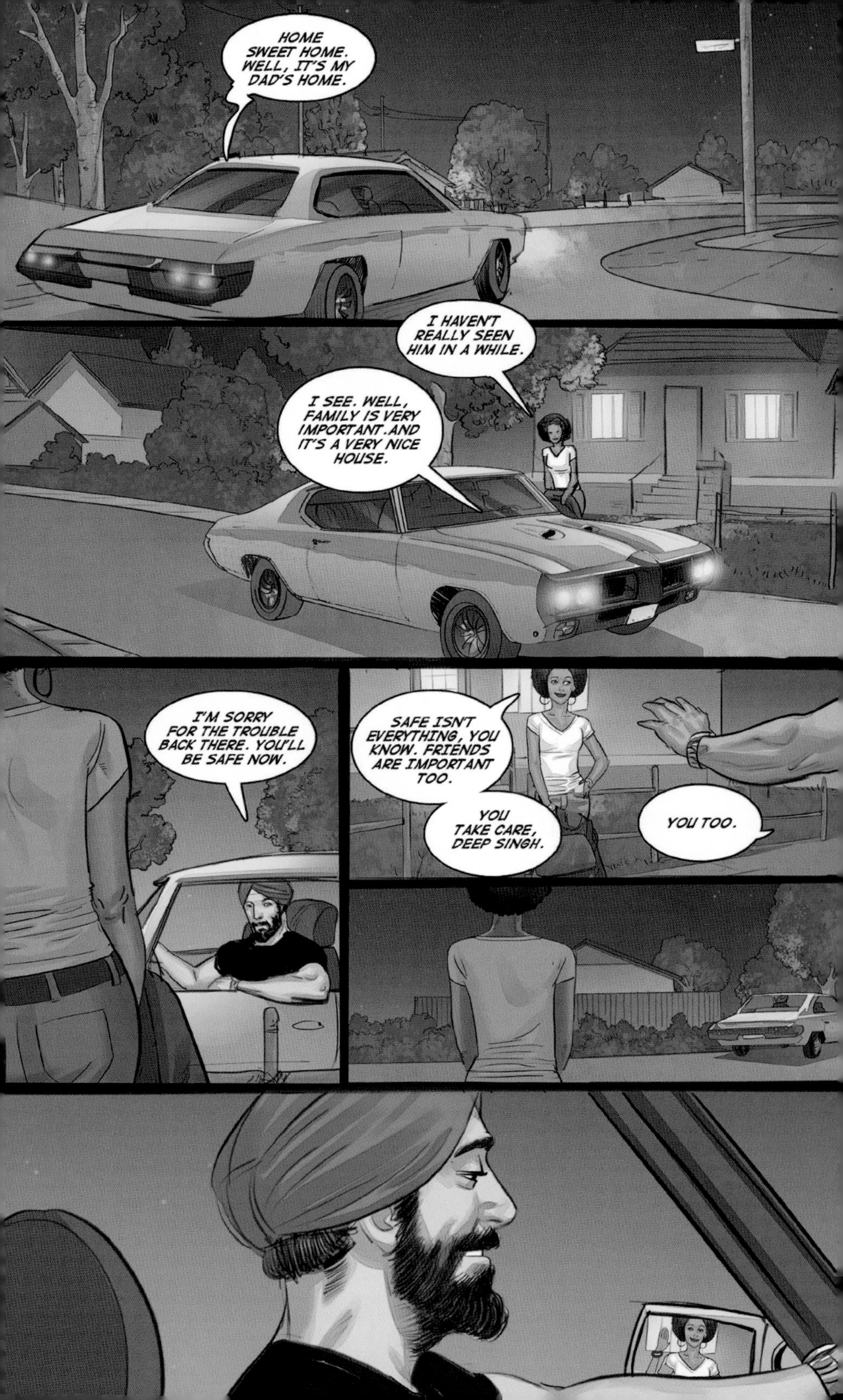
HOME SWEET HOME. WELL, IT'S MY DAD'S HOME.
I HAVEN'T REALLY SEEN HIM IN A WHILE.
I SEE. WELL, FAMILY IS VERY IMPORTANT.AND IT'S A VERY NICE HOUSE.
I'M SORRY FOR THE TROUBLE BACK THERE. YOU'LL BE SAFE NOW.
SAFE ISN'T EVERYTHING, YOU KNOW. FRIENDS ARE IMPORTANT TOO.
YOU TAKE CARE, DEEP SINGH.
YOU TOO.

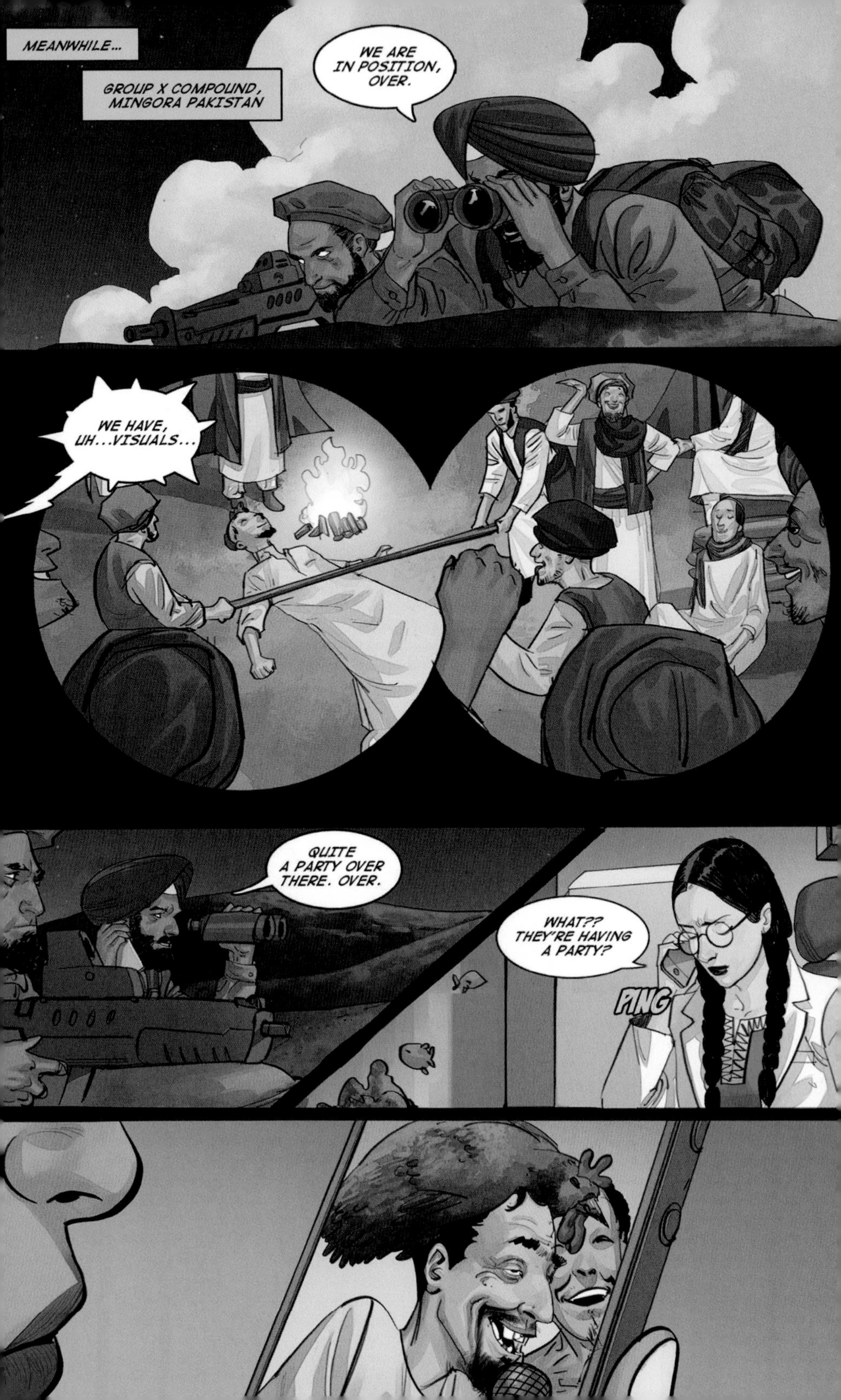
MEANWHILE...
GROUP X COMPOUND, MINGORA PAKISTAN
WE ARE IN POSITION, OVER.
WE HAVE, UH...VISUALS...
QUITE A PARTY OVER THERE. OVER.
WHAT?? THEY'RE HAVING A PARTY?
PING

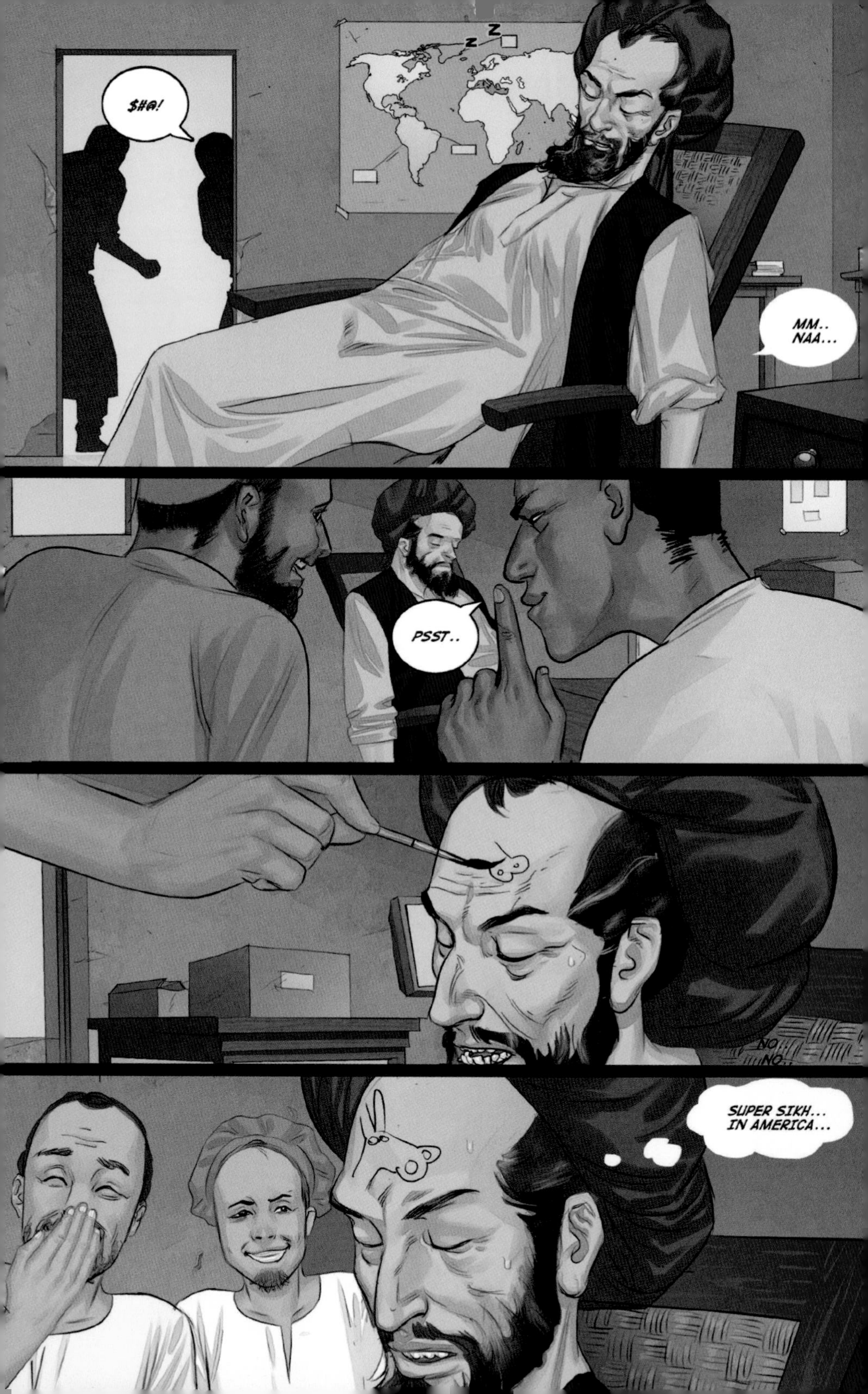

$#@!
Z Z
MM.. NAA...
PSST..
NO...
NO..
SUPER SIKH... IN AMERICA...

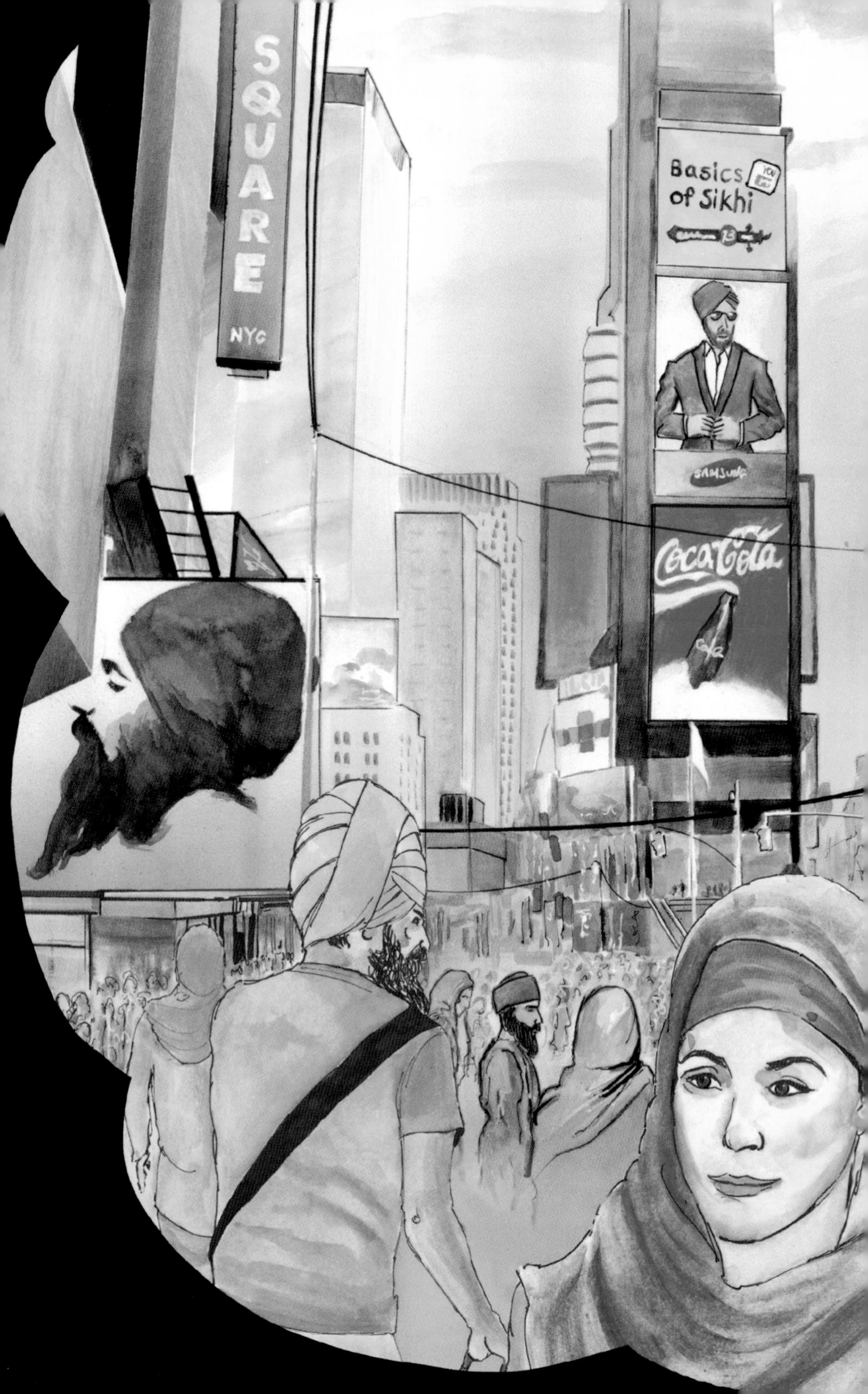
SQUARE
NYC
Basics of Sikhi
Coca-Cola

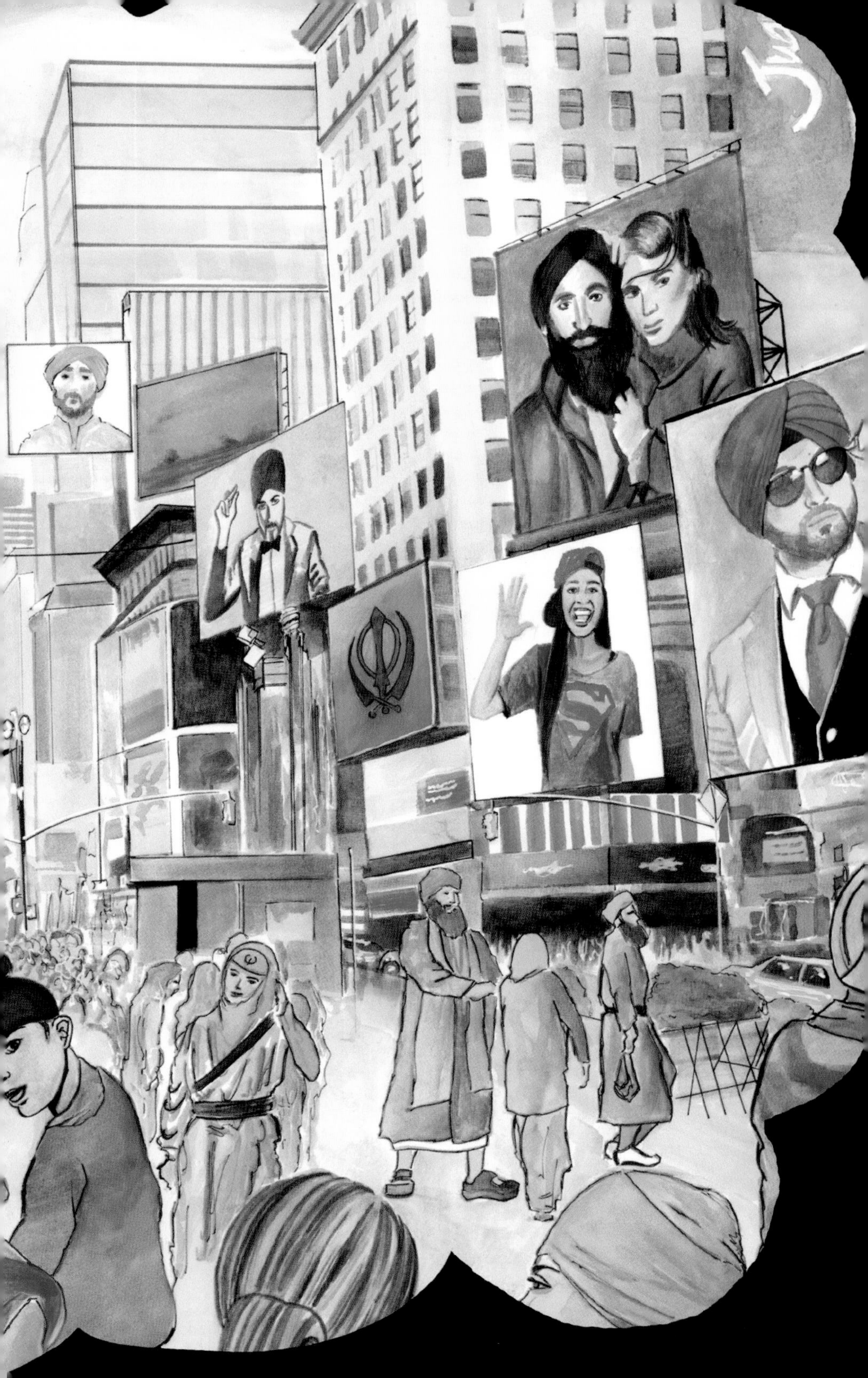

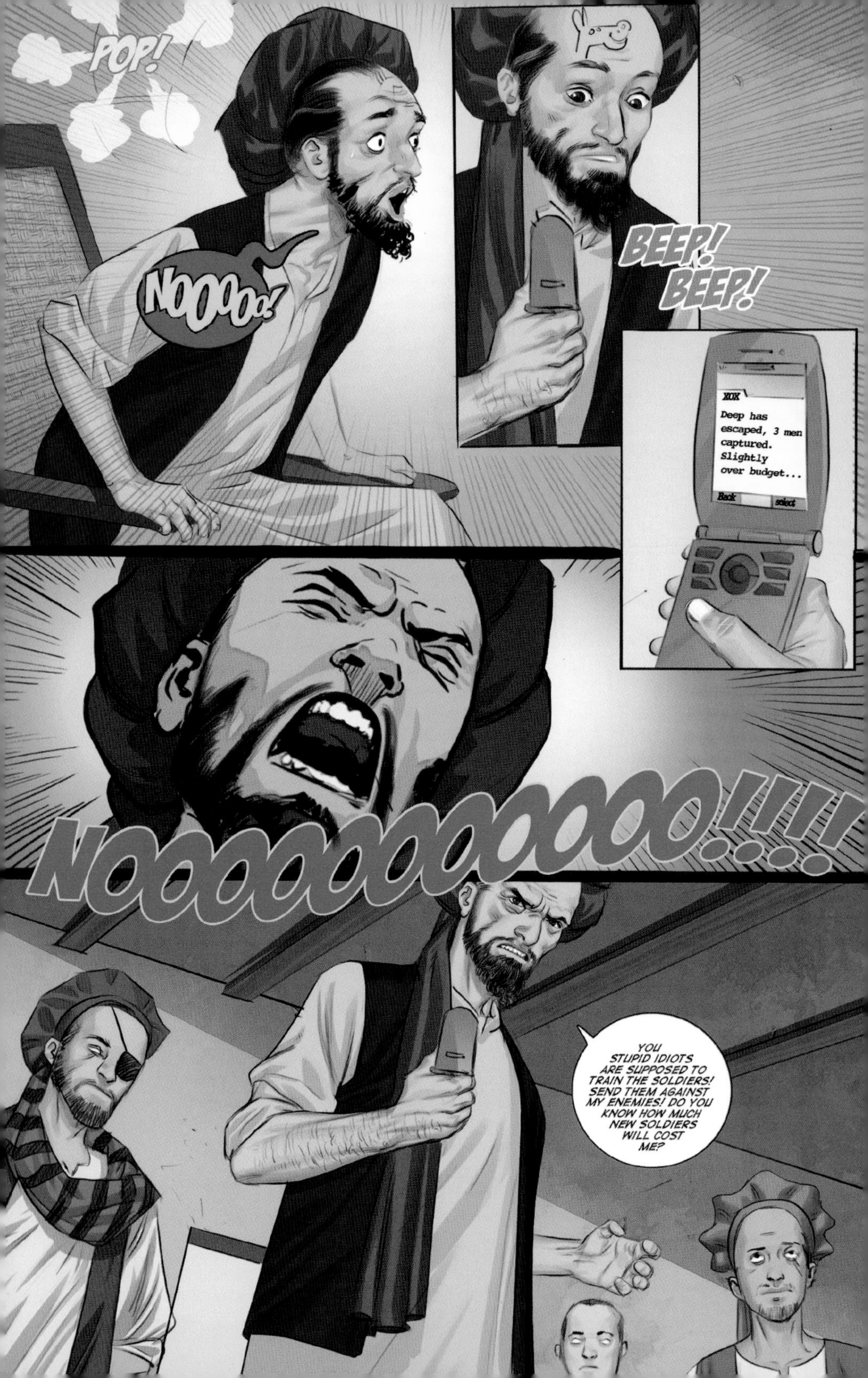
POP!
NOOOOo!
BEEP! BEEP!
XOX
Deep has escaped, 3 men captured. Slightly over budget...
Back
select
NOOOOOOOOOOO!!!!
YOU STUPID IDIOTS ARE SUPPOSED TO TRAIN THE SOLDIERS! SEND THEM AGAINST MY ENEMIES! DO YOU KNOW HOW MUCH NEW SOLDIERS WILL COST ME?

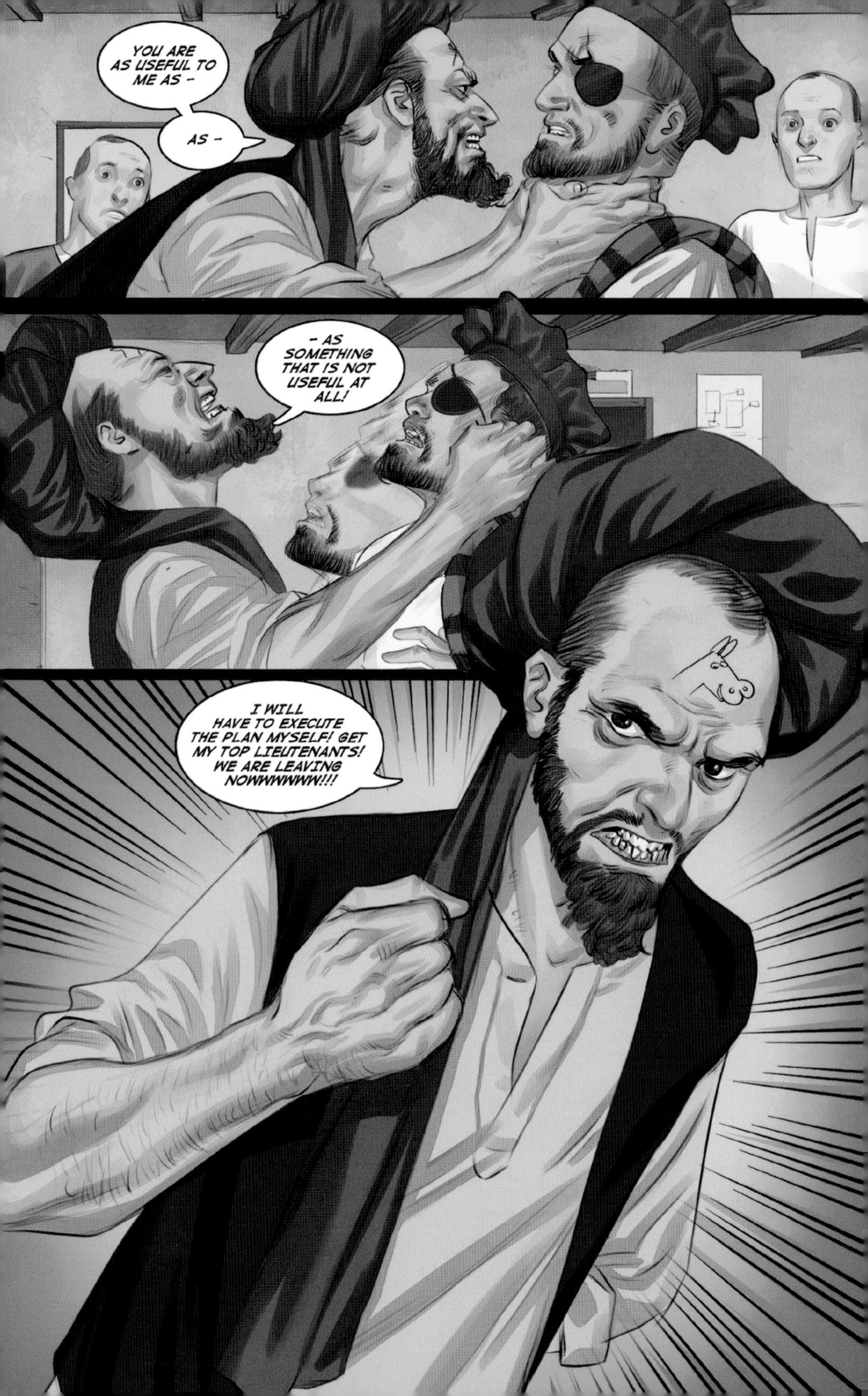
YOU ARE AS USEFUL TO ME AS -
AS -
- AS SOMETHING THAT IS NOT USEFUL AT ALL!
I WILL HAVE TO EXECUTE THE PLAN MYSELF! GET MY TOP LIEUTENANTS! WE ARE LEAVING NOWWWWWW!!!

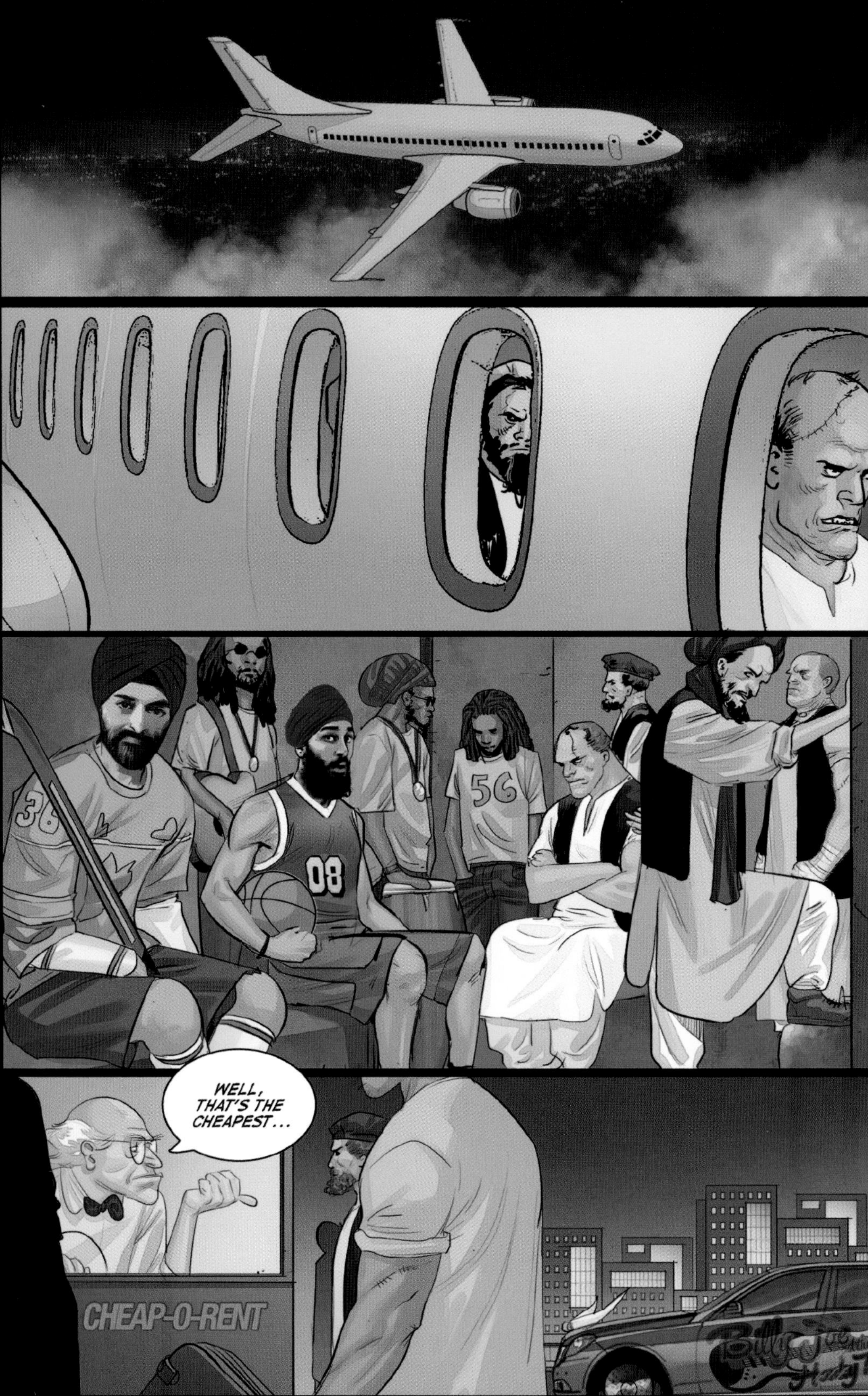
WELL, THAT'S THE CHEAPEST...
CHEAP-O-RENT

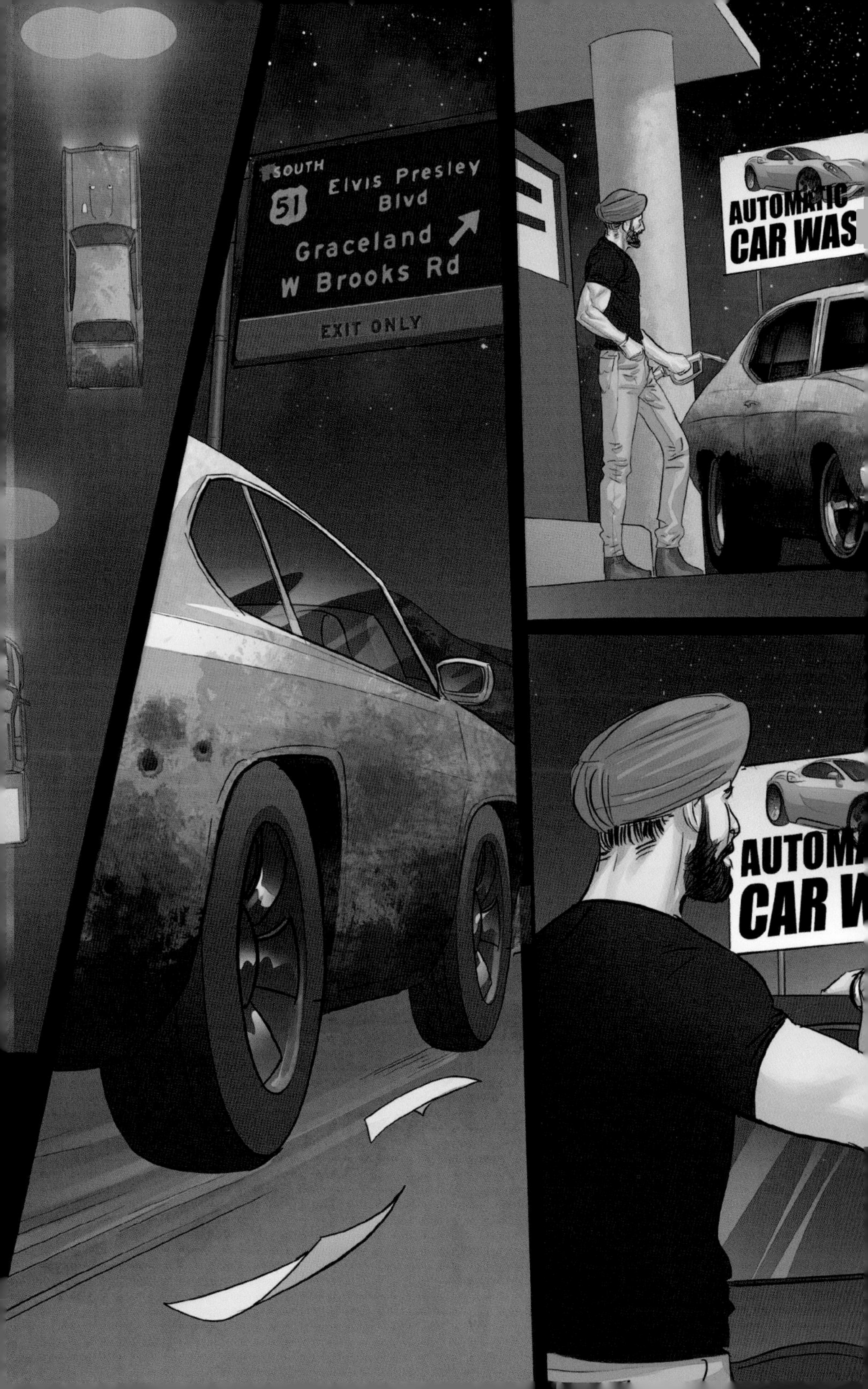
SOUTH
51
Elvis Presley
Blvd
Graceland
W Brooks Rd
EXIT ONLY
AUTOMATIC
CAR WAS
AUTOMA
CAR W

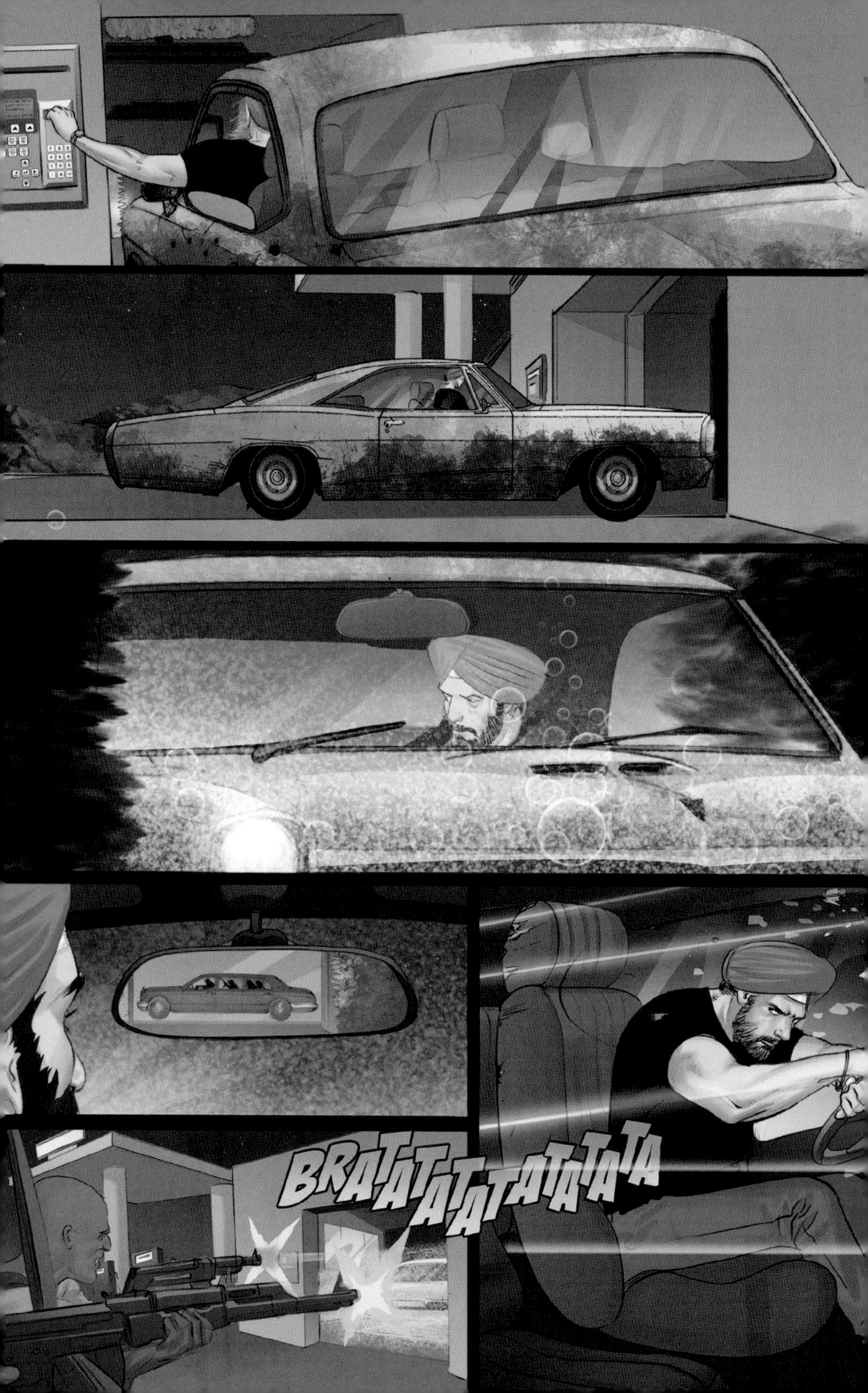
BRATATATATATATATA

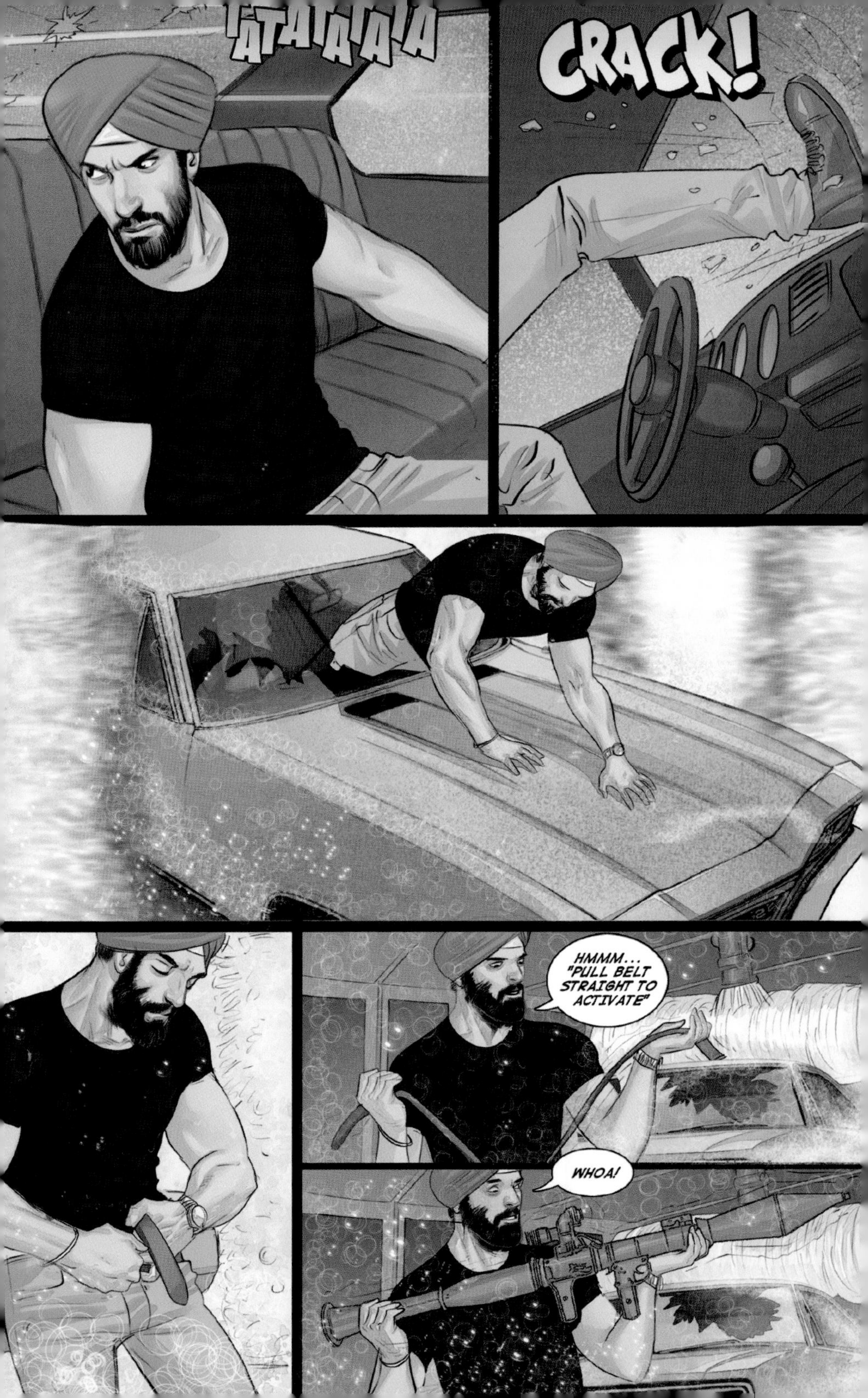
TATATATATA
CRACK!
HMMM... "PULL BELT STRAIGHT TO ACTIVATE"
WHOA!

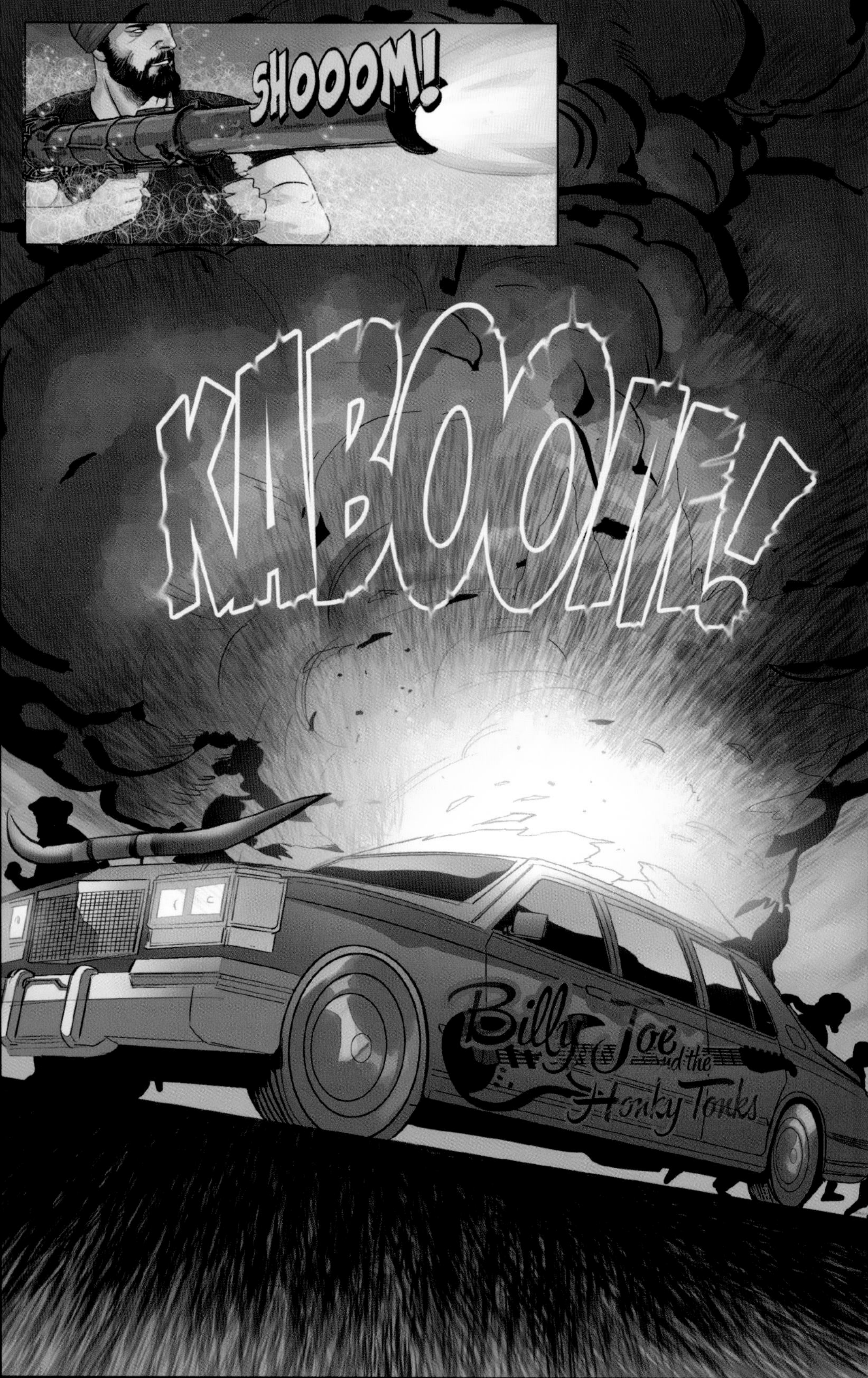
SHOOOM!
KABOOM!
Billy Joe and the Honky Tonks

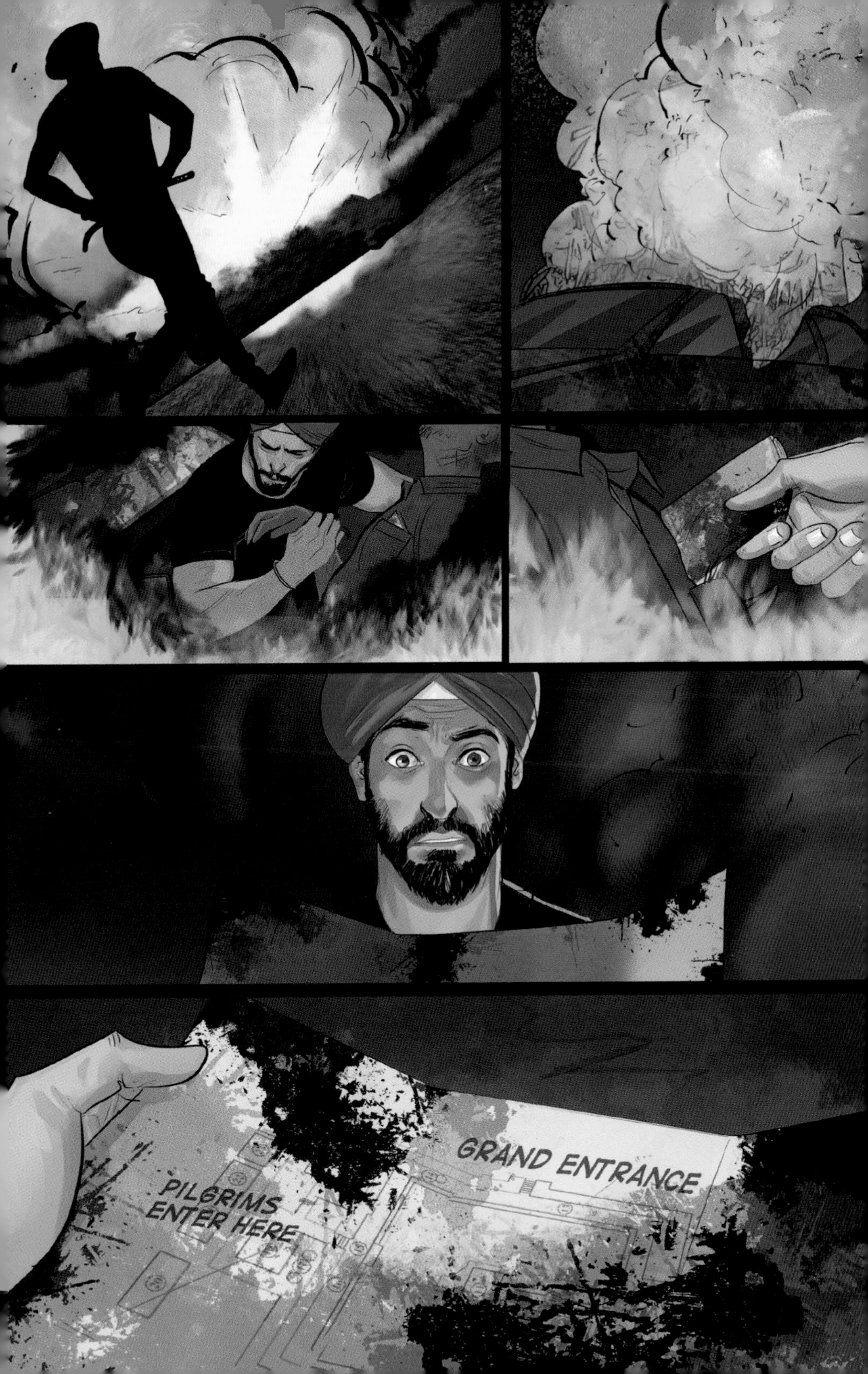
GRAND ENTRANCE
PILGRIMS ENTER HERE

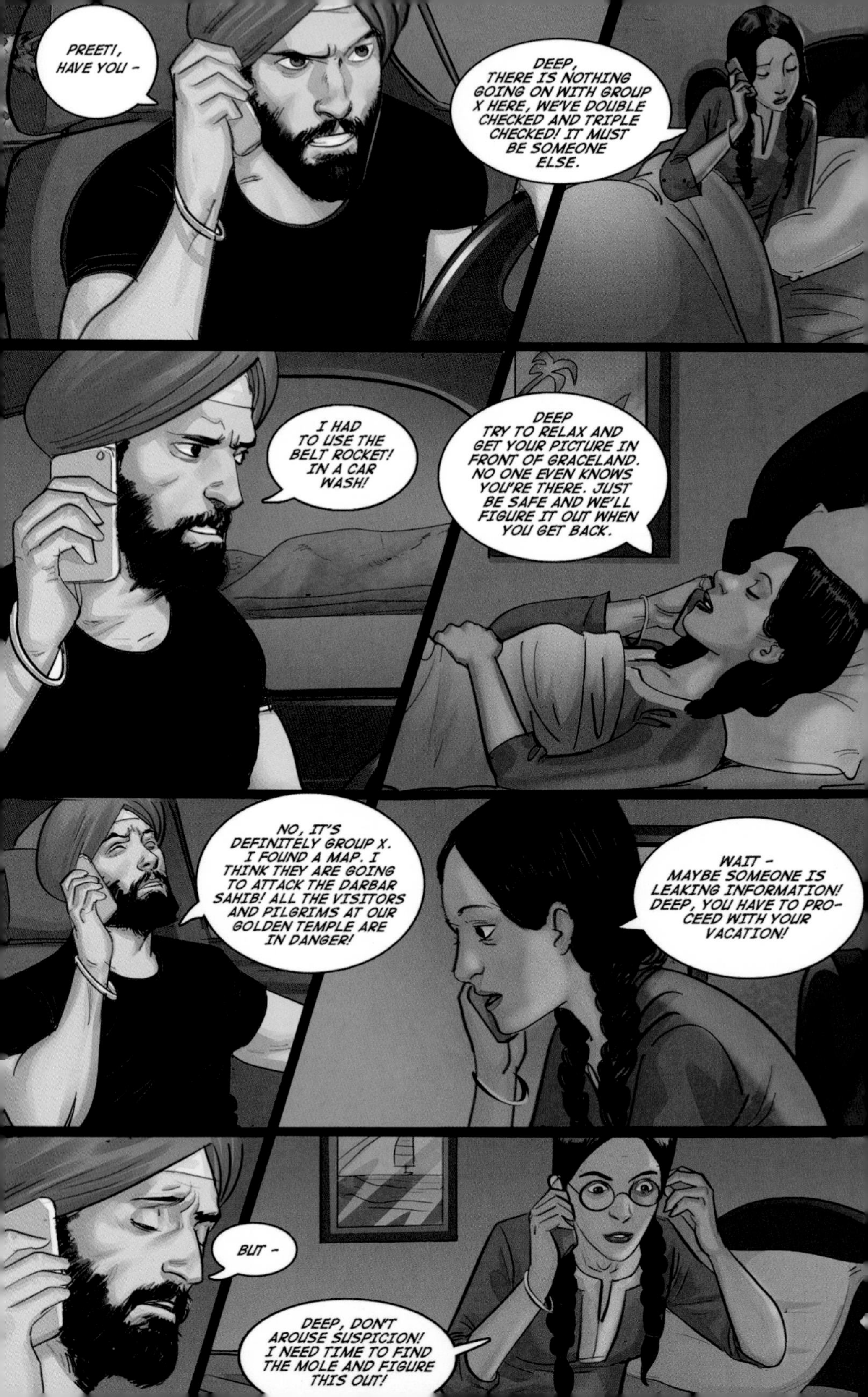
PREETI, HAVE YOU -
DEEP, THERE IS NOTHING GOING ON WITH GROUP X HERE, WE'VE DOUBLE CHECKED AND TRIPLE CHECKED! IT MUST BE SOMEONE ELSE.
I HAD TO USE THE BELT ROCKET! IN A CAR WASH!
DEEP TRY TO RELAX AND GET YOUR PICTURE IN FRONT OF GRACELAND. NO ONE EVEN KNOWS YOU'RE THERE. JUST BE SAFE AND WE'LL FIGURE IT OUT WHEN YOU GET BACK.
NO, IT'S DEFINITELY GROUP X. I FOUND A MAP. I THINK THEY ARE GOING TO ATTACK THE DARBAR SAHIB! ALL THE VISITORS AND PILGRIMS AT OUR GOLDEN TEMPLE ARE IN DANGER!
WAIT - MAYBE SOMEONE IS LEAKING INFORMATION! DEEP, YOU HAVE TO PROCEED WITH YOUR VACATION!
BUT -
DEEP, DON'T AROUSE SUSPICION! I NEED TIME TO FIND THE MOLE AND FIGURE THIS OUT!

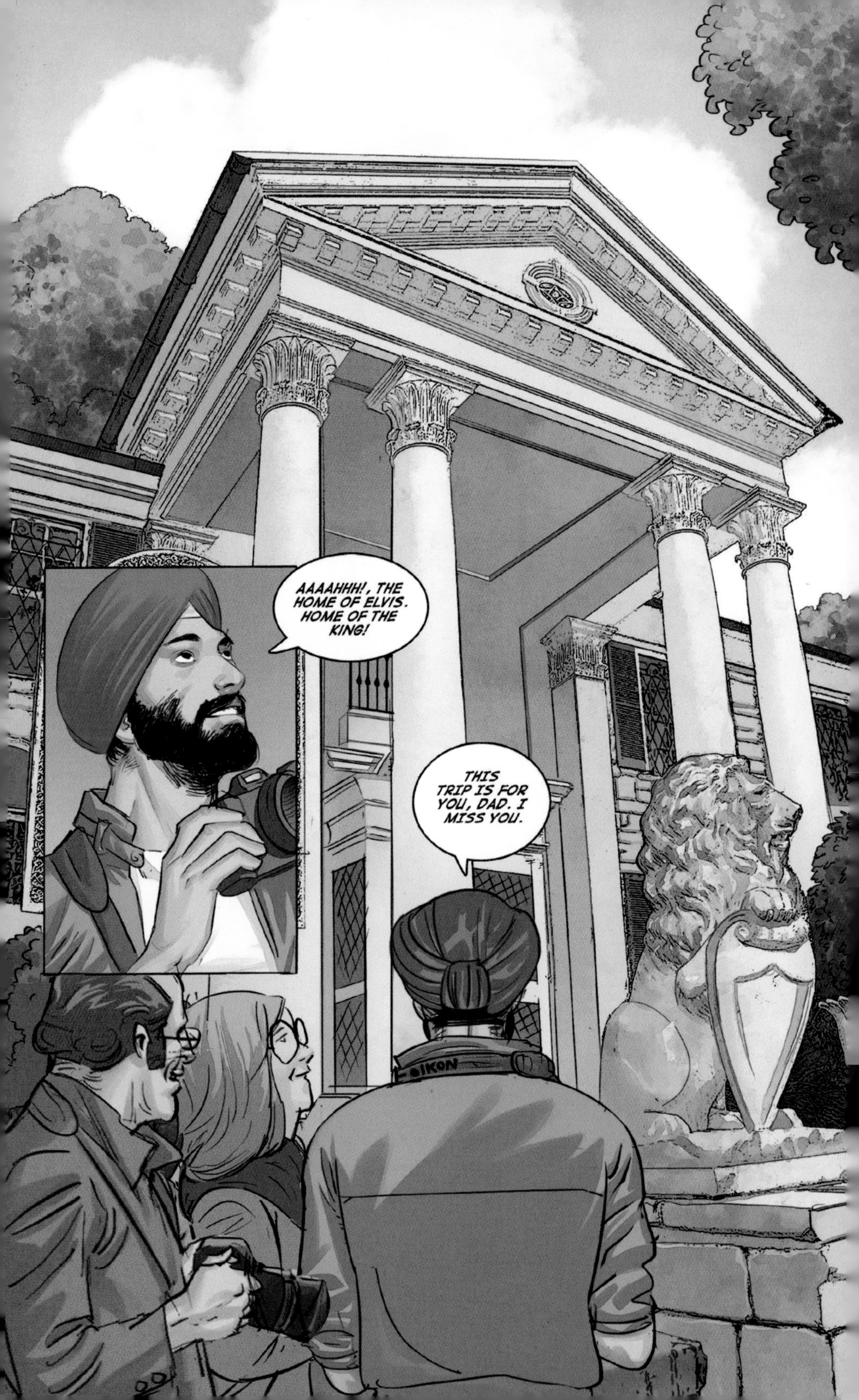
AAAAHHH!, THE HOME OF ELVIS. HOME OF THE KING!
THIS TRIP IS FOR YOU, DAD. I MISS YOU.

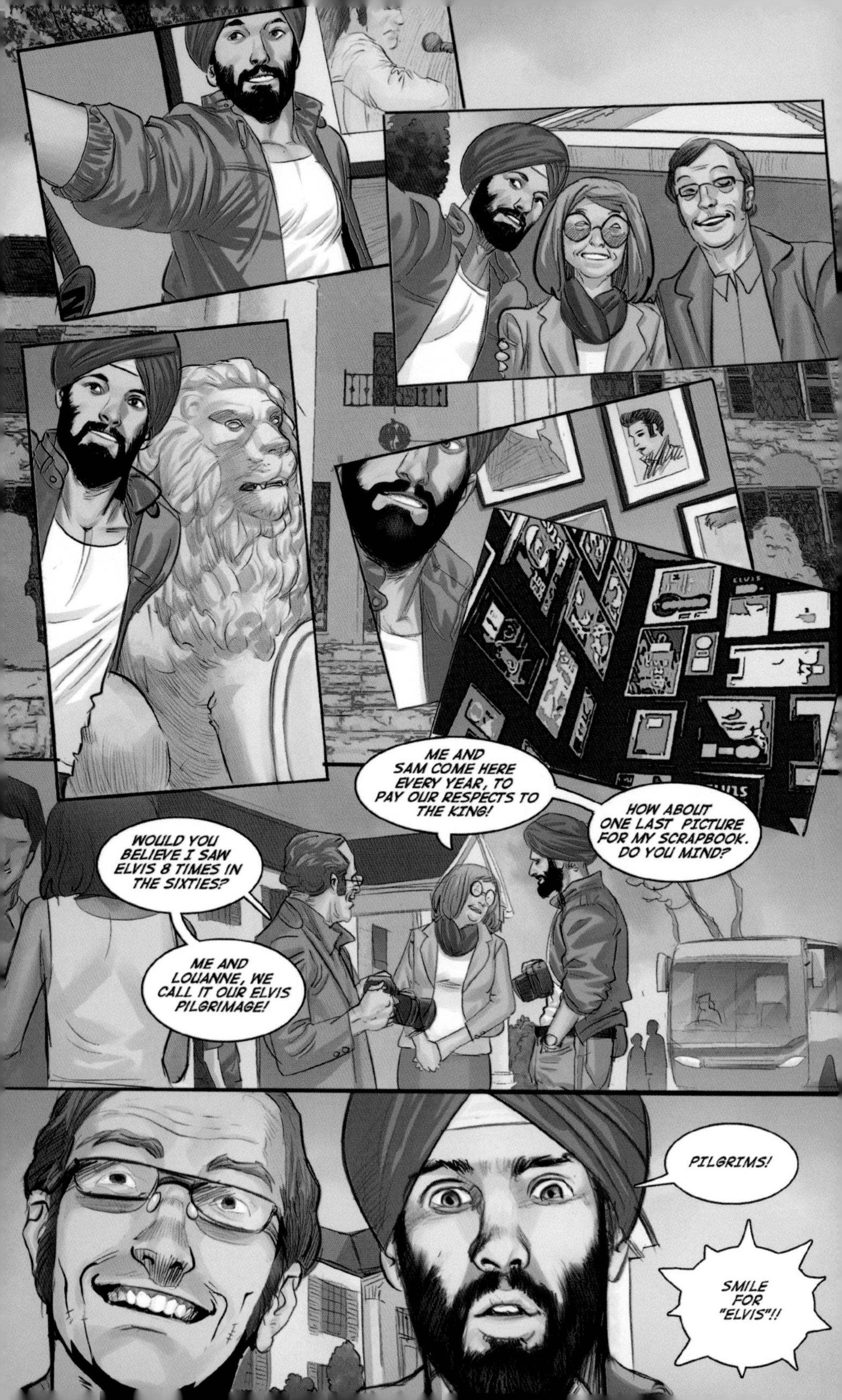
ME AND SAM COME HERE EVERY YEAR, TO PAY OUR RESPECTS TO THE KING!
HOW ABOUT ONE LAST PICTURE FOR MY SCRAPBOOK. DO YOU MIND?
WOULD YOU BELIEVE I SAW ELVIS 8 TIMES IN THE SIXTIES?
ME AND LOUANNE, WE CALL IT OUR ELVIS PILGRIMAGE!
PILGRIMS!
SMILE FOR "ELVIS"!!

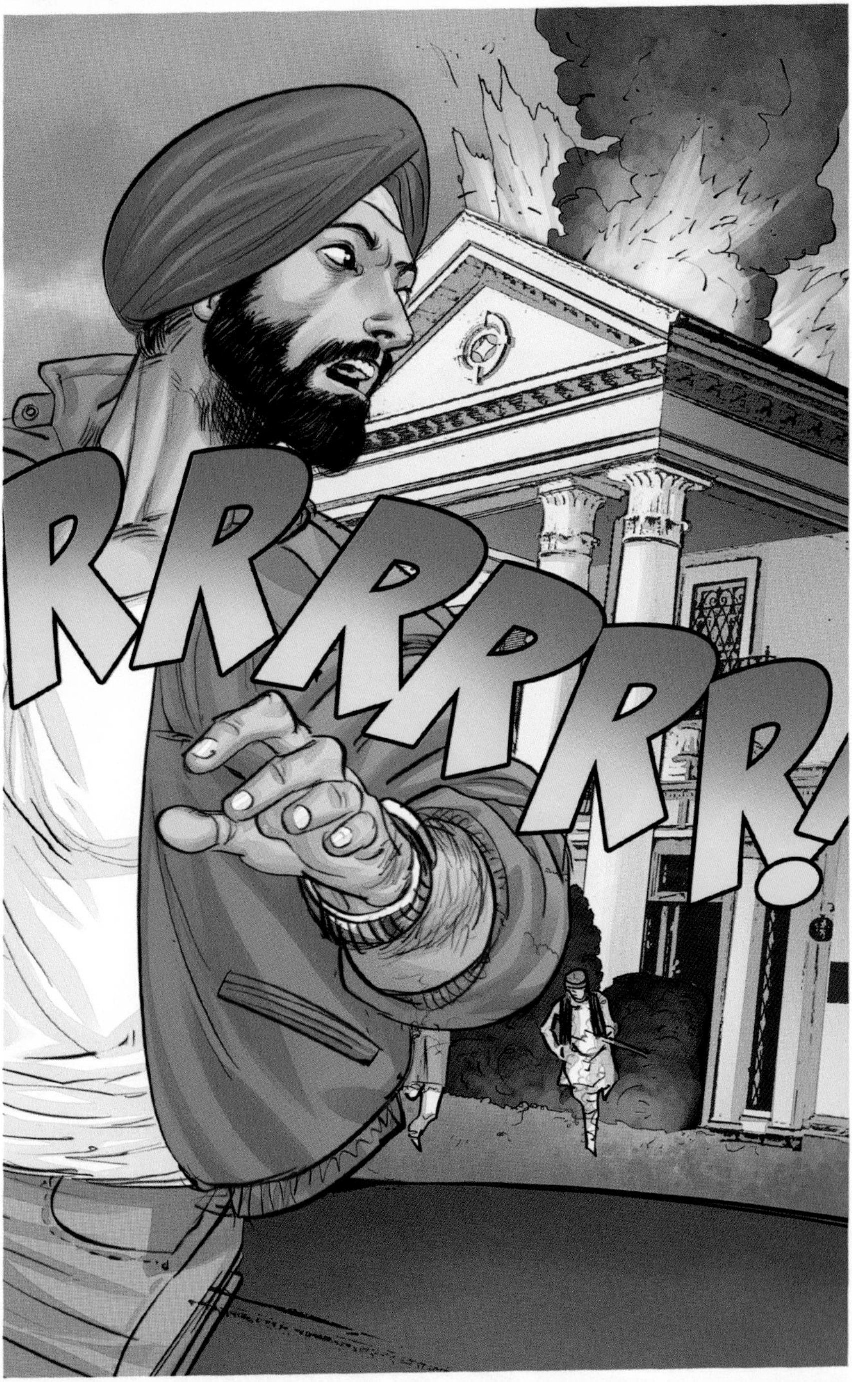
RRRRRRR!

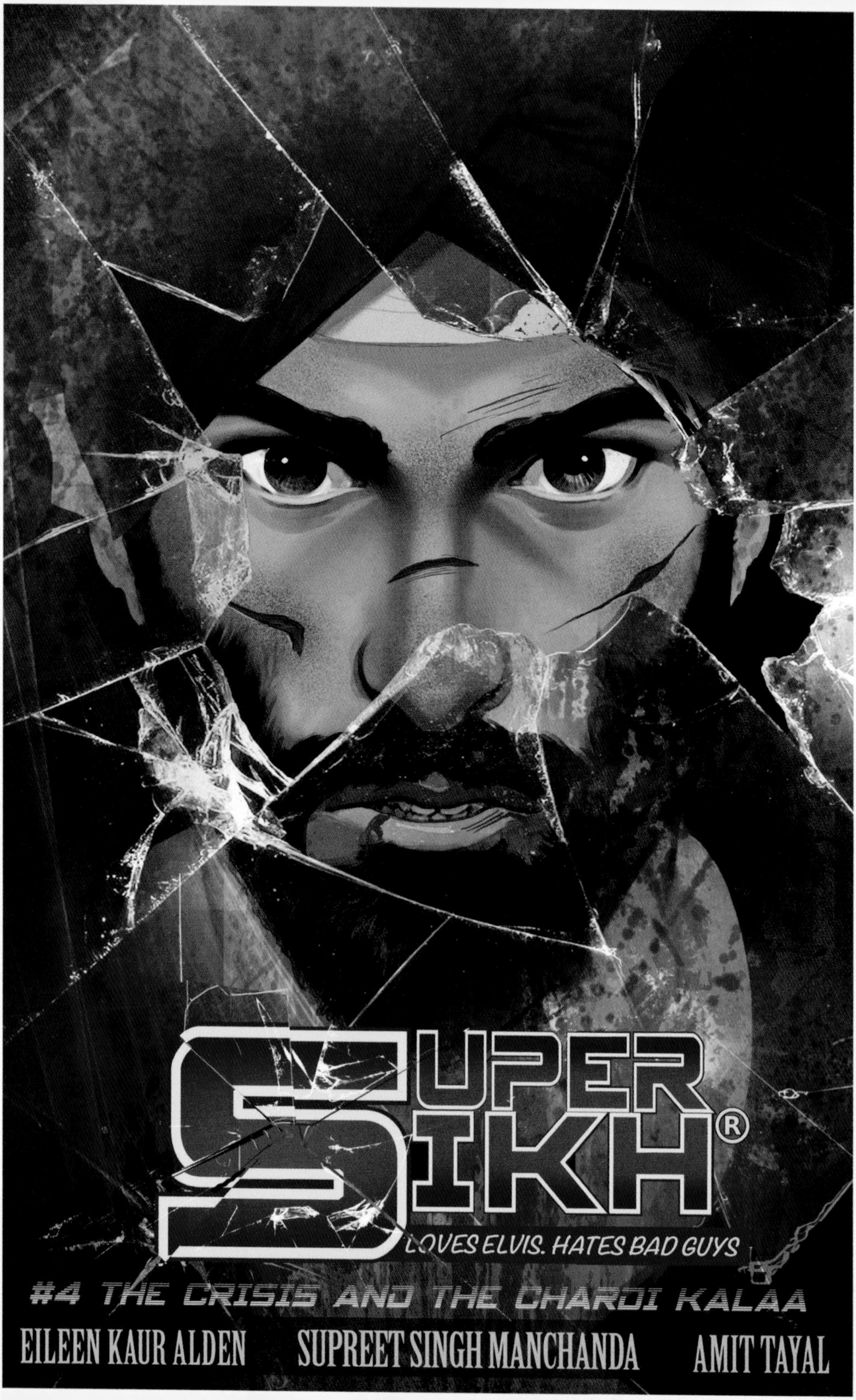
SUPER SIKH®
LOVES ELVIS. HATES BAD GUYS
#4 THE CRISIS AND THE CHARDI KALAA
EILEEN KAUR ALDEN
SUPREET SINGH MANCHANDA
AMIT TAYAL

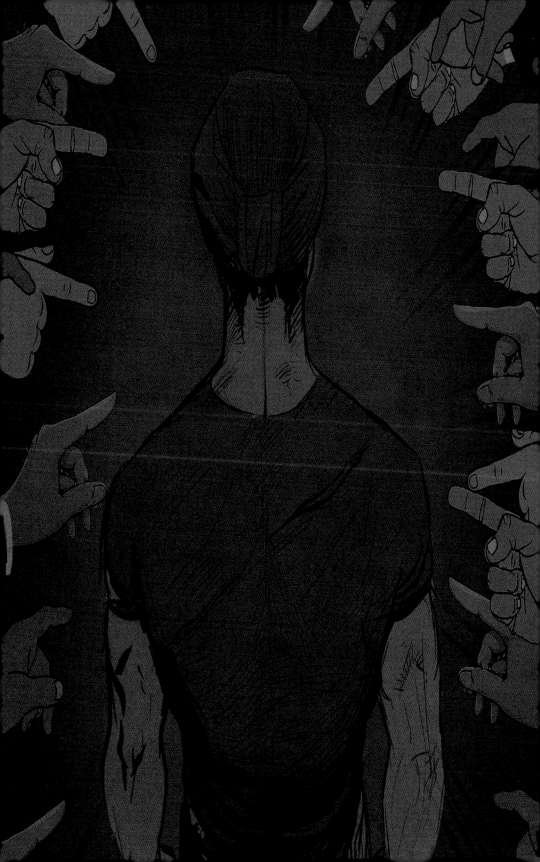

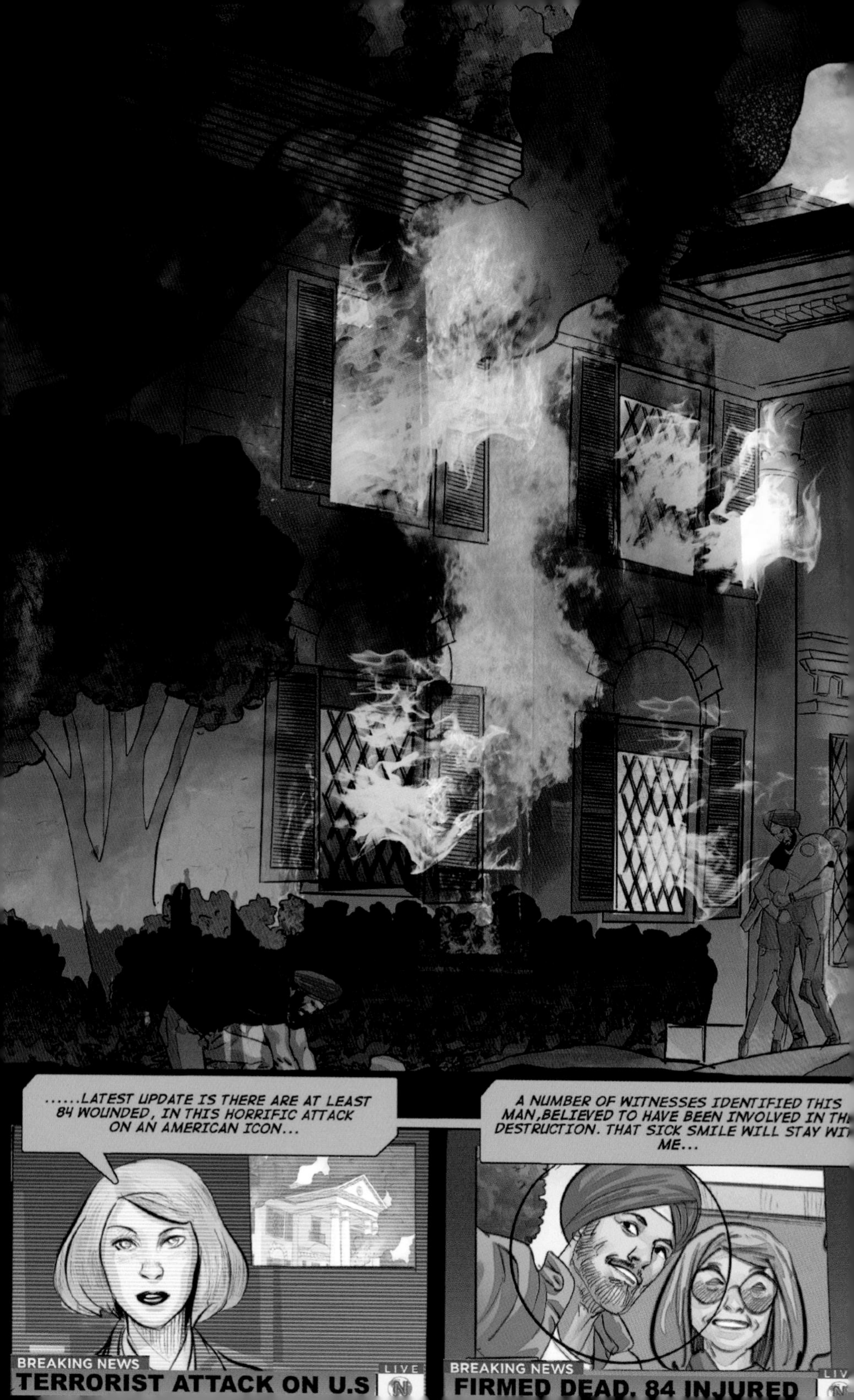
......LATEST UPDATE IS THERE ARE AT LEAST 84 WOUNDED, IN THIS HORRIFIC ATTACK ON AN AMERICAN ICON...
BREAKING NEWS
TERRORIST ATTACK ON U.S
LIVE
A NUMBER OF WITNESSES IDENTIFIED THIS MAN, BELIEVED TO HAVE BEEN INVOLVED IN TH DESTRUCTION. THAT SICK SMILE WILL STAY WI ME...
BREAKING NEWS
FIRMED DEAD. 84 INJURED
LIV

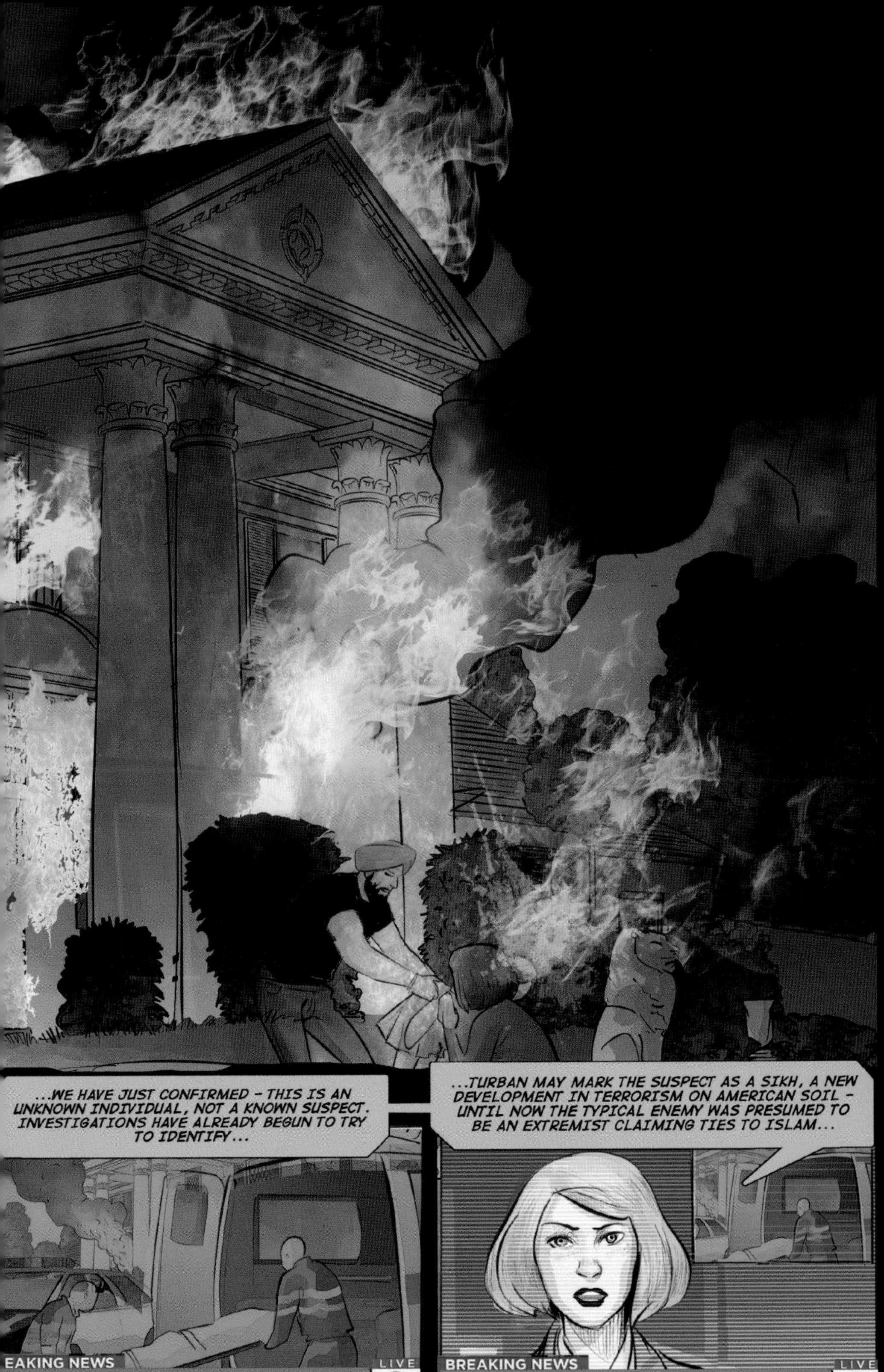
...WE HAVE JUST CONFIRMED - THIS IS AN UNKNOWN INDIVIDUAL, NOT A KNOWN SUSPECT. INVESTIGATIONS HAVE ALREADY BEGUN TO TRY TO IDENTIFY...
EAKING NEWS
LIVE
NO GROUP YET CLAIMING
...TURBAN MAY MARK THE SUSPECT AS A SIKH, A NEW DEVELOPMENT IN TERRORISM ON AMERICAN SOIL - UNTIL NOW THE TYPICAL ENEMY WAS PRESUMED TO BE AN EXTREMIST CLAIMING TIES TO ISLAM...
BREAKING NEWS
LIVE
TENNESSEE GOVERNOR DECL

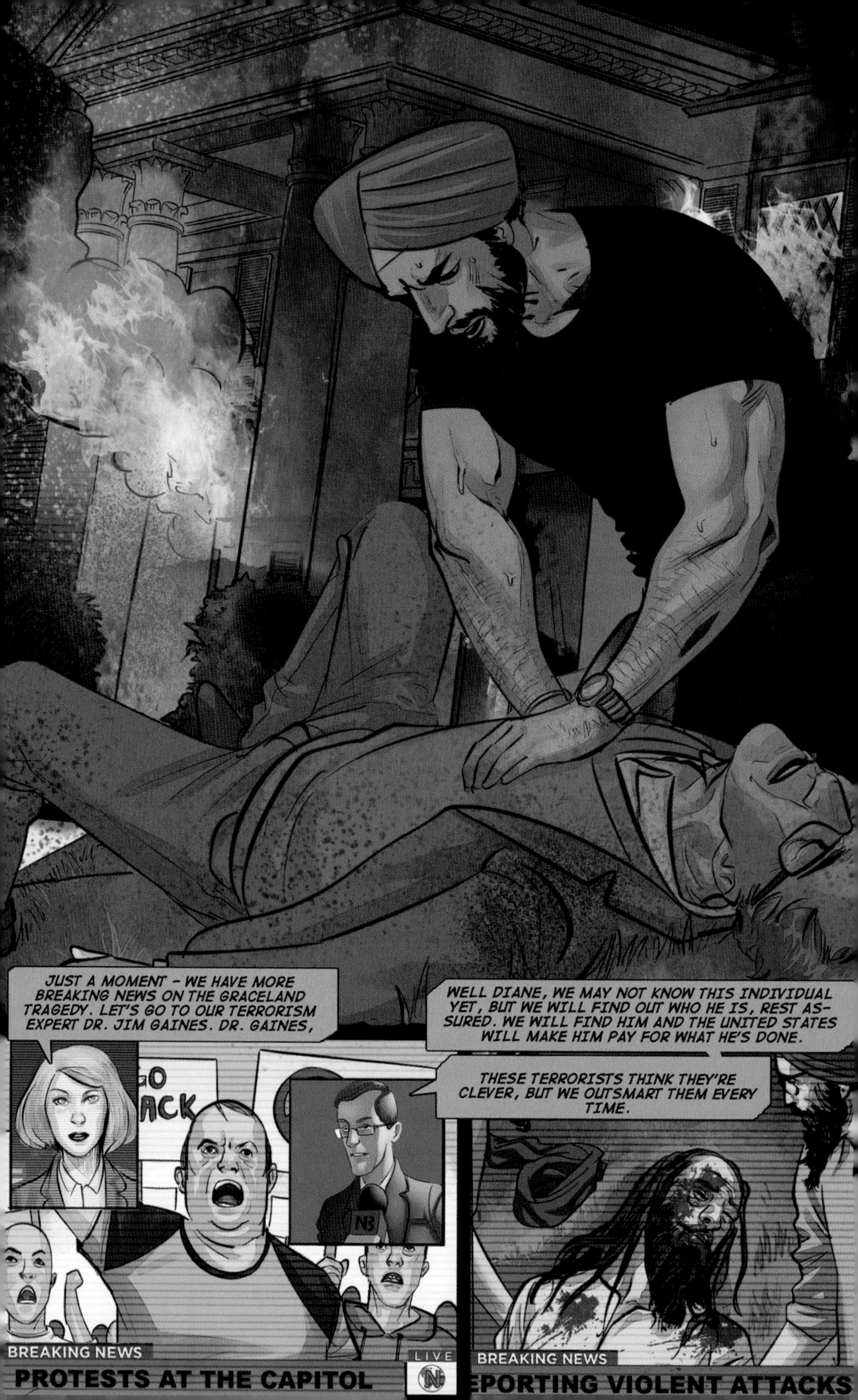
JUST A MOMENT - WE HAVE MORE BREAKING NEWS ON THE GRACELAND TRAGEDY. LET'S GO TO OUR TERRORISM EXPERT DR. JIM GAINES. DR. GAINES,
WELL DIANE, WE MAY NOT KNOW THIS INDIVIDUAL YET, BUT WE WILL FIND OUT WHO HE IS, REST ASSURED. WE WILL FIND HIM AND THE UNITED STATES WILL MAKE HIM PAY FOR WHAT HE'S DONE.
THESE TERRORISTS THINK THEY'RE CLEVER, BUT WE OUTSMART THEM EVERY TIME.
GO
ACK
NB
BREAKING NEWS
PROTESTS AT THE CAPITOL
LIVE
N
BREAKING NEWS
EPORTING VIOLENT ATTACKS

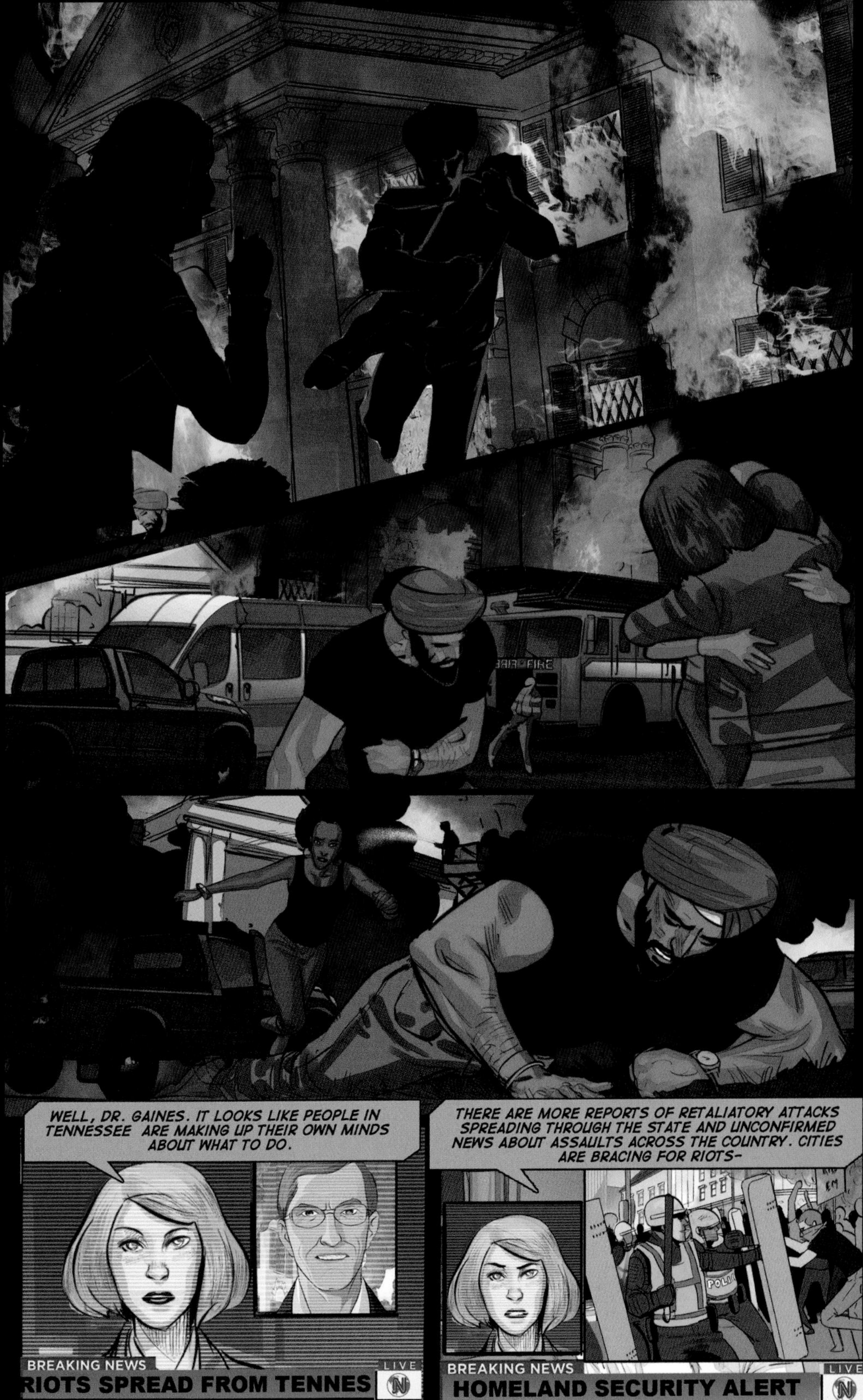
WELL, DR. GAINES. IT LOOKS LIKE PEOPLE IN TENNESSEE ARE MAKING UP THEIR OWN MINDS ABOUT WHAT TO DO.
BREAKING NEWS
LIVE
RIOTS SPREAD FROM TENNES
THERE ARE MORE REPORTS OF RETALIATORY ATTACKS SPREADING THROUGH THE STATE AND UNCONFIRMED NEWS ABOUT ASSAULTS ACROSS THE COUNTRY. CITIES ARE BRACING FOR RIOTS-
BREAKING NEWS
LIVE
HOMELAND SECURITY ALERT

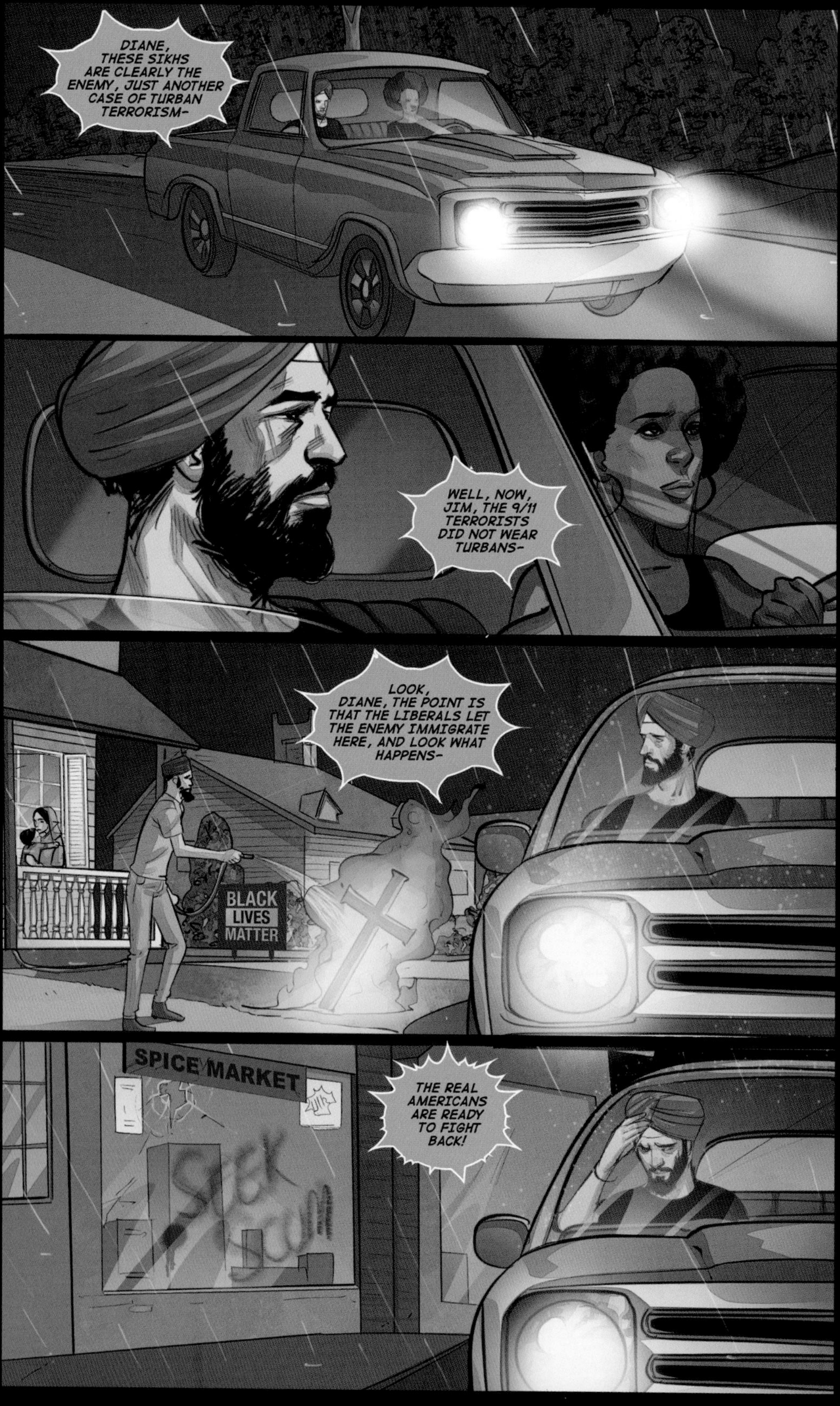
DIANE, THESE SIKHS ARE CLEARLY THE ENEMY, JUST ANOTHER CASE OF TURBAN TERRORISM-
WELL, NOW, JIM, THE 9/11 TERRORISTS DID NOT WEAR TURBANS-
LOOK, DIANE, THE POINT IS THAT THE LIBERALS LET THE ENEMY IMMIGRATE HERE, AND LOOK WHAT HAPPENS-
BLACK LIVES MATTER
SPICE MARKET
THE REAL AMERICANS ARE READY TO FIGHT BACK!

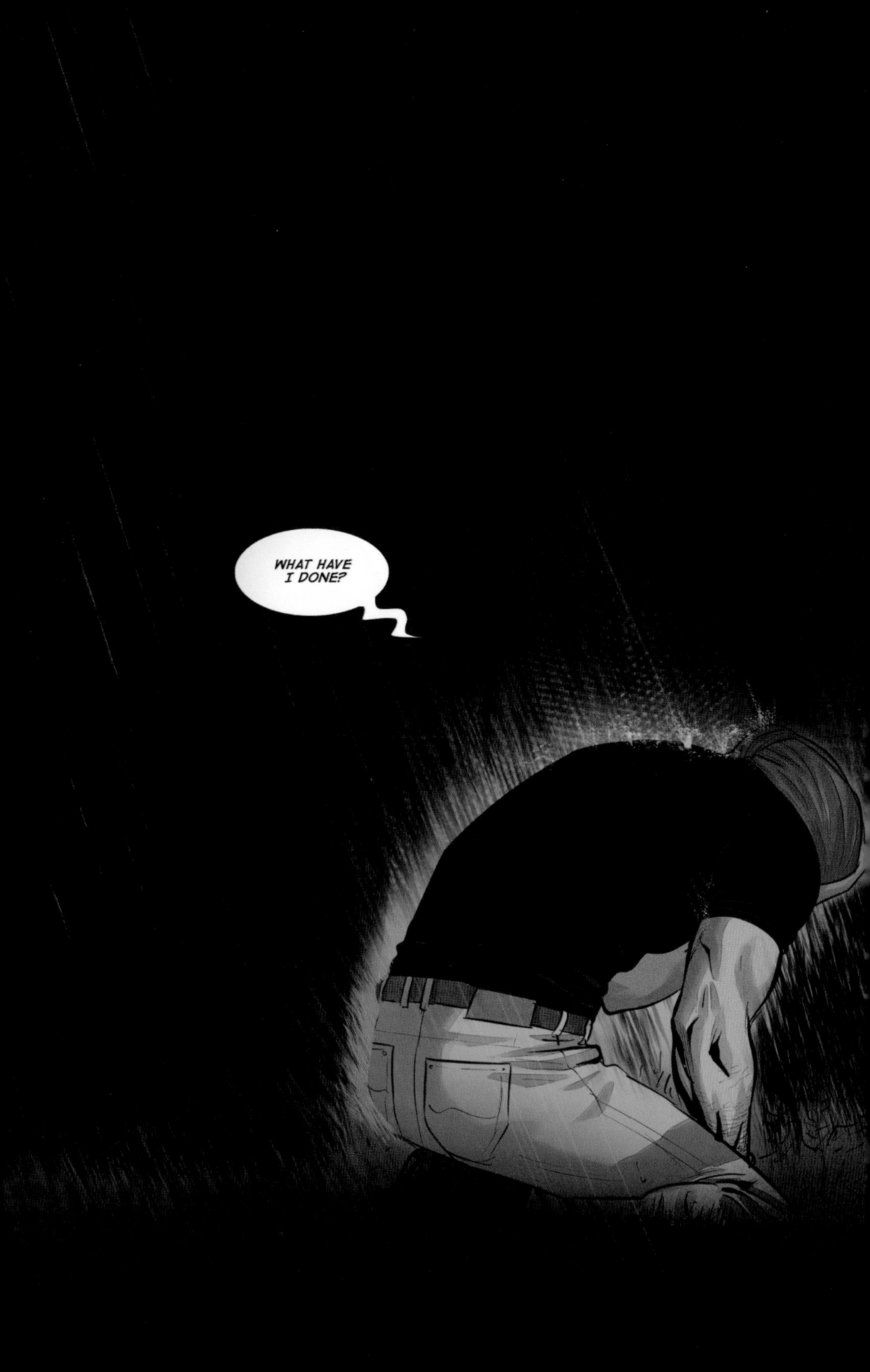
WHAT HAVE I DONE?

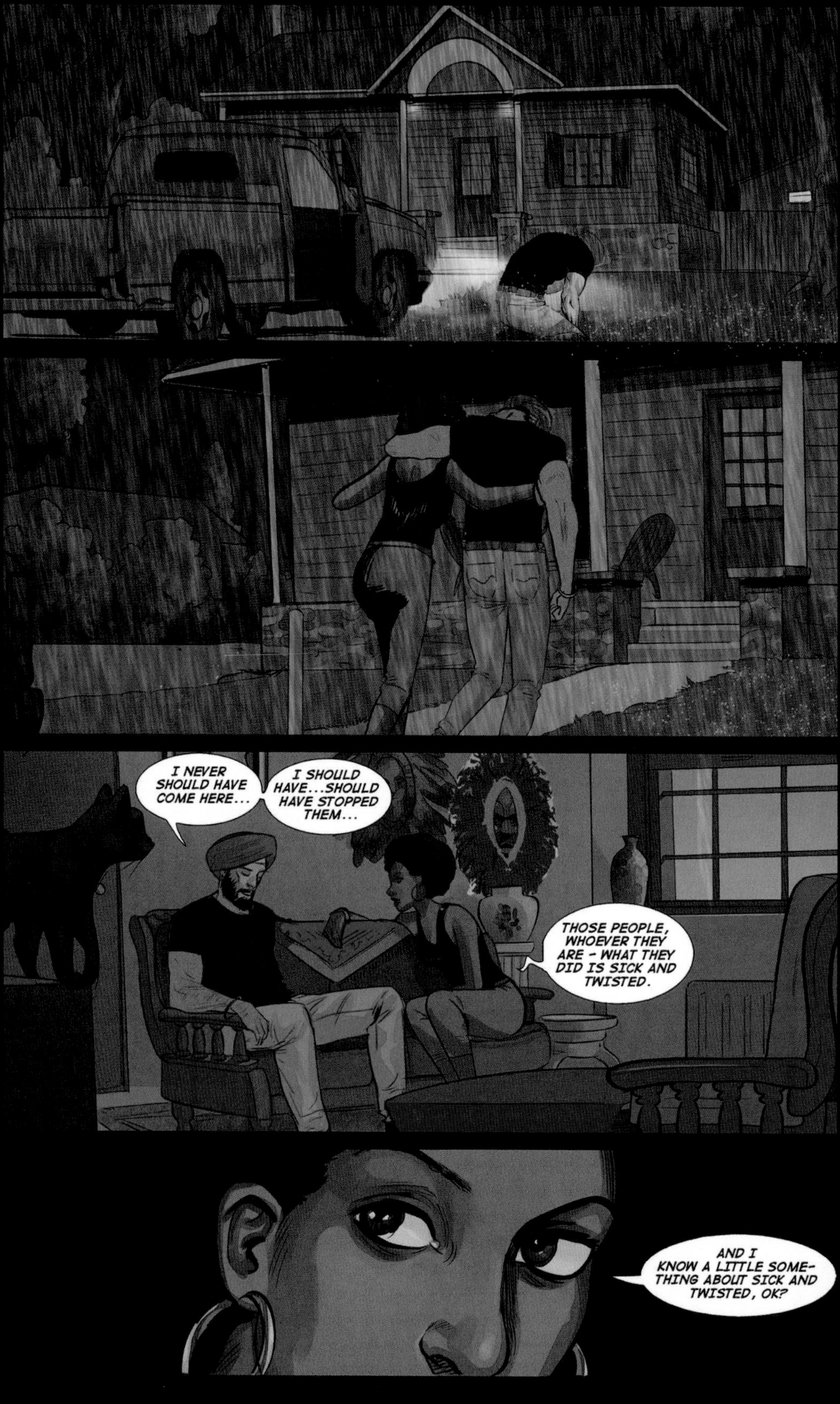
I NEVER SHOULD HAVE COME HERE...
I SHOULD HAVE...SHOULD HAVE STOPPED THEM...
THOSE PEOPLE, WHOEVER THEY ARE - WHAT THEY DID IS SICK AND TWISTED.
AND I KNOW A LITTLE SOME-THING ABOUT SICK AND TWISTED, OK?

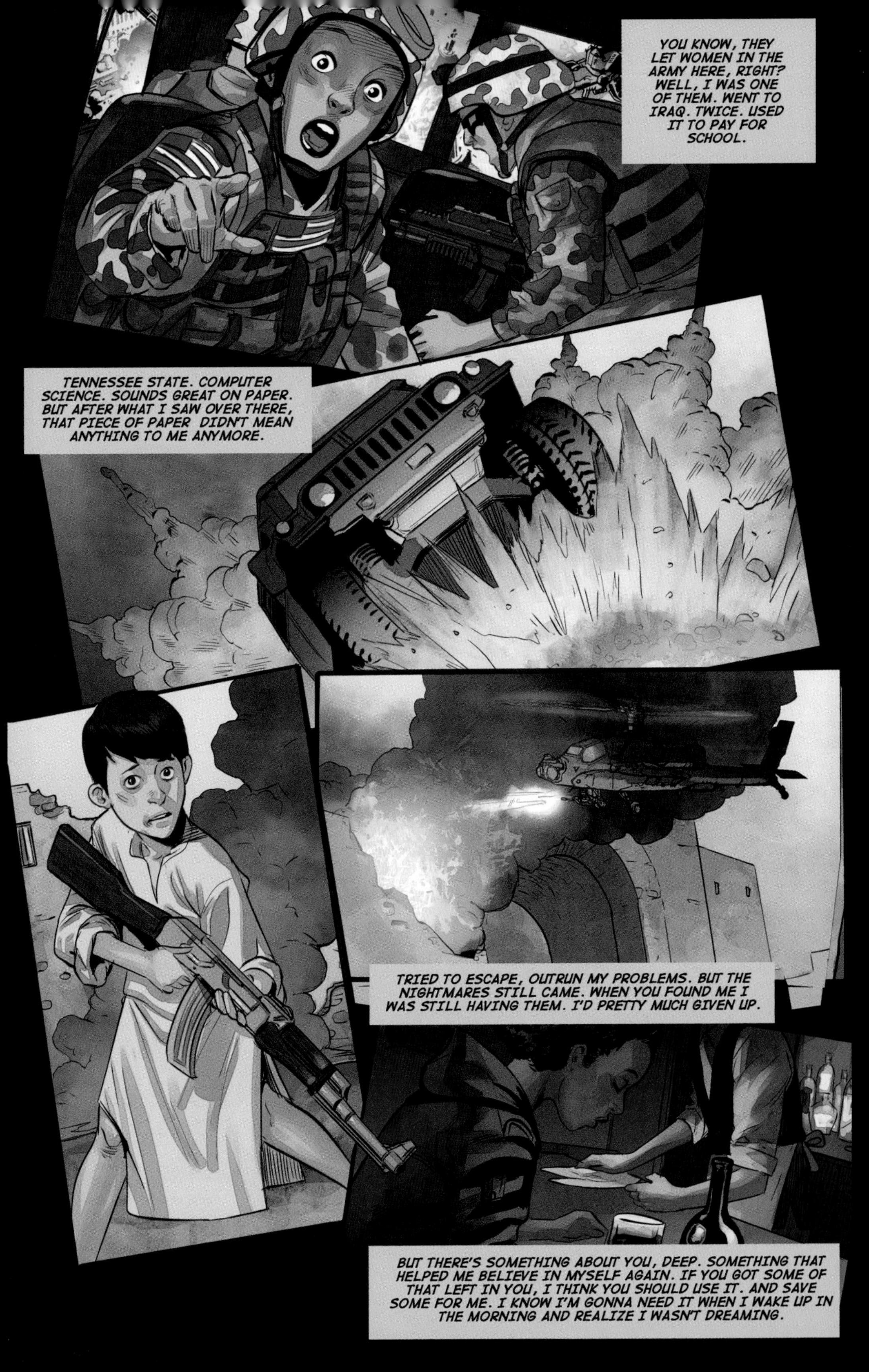

YOU KNOW, THEY LET WOMEN IN THE ARMY HERE, RIGHT? WELL, I WAS ONE OF THEM. WENT TO IRAQ. TWICE. USED IT TO PAY FOR SCHOOL.
TENNESSEE STATE. COMPUTER SCIENCE. SOUNDS GREAT ON PAPER. BUT AFTER WHAT I SAW OVER THERE, THAT PIECE OF PAPER DIDN'T MEAN ANYTHING TO ME ANYMORE.
TRIED TO ESCAPE, OUTRUN MY PROBLEMS. BUT THE NIGHTMARES STILL CAME. WHEN YOU FOUND ME I WAS STILL HAVING THEM. I'D PRETTY MUCH GIVEN UP.
BUT THERE'S SOMETHING ABOUT YOU, DEEP. SOMETHING THAT HELPED ME BELIEVE IN MYSELF AGAIN. IF YOU GOT SOME OF THAT LEFT IN YOU, I THINK YOU SHOULD USE IT. AND SAVE SOME FOR ME. I KNOW I'M GONNA NEED IT WHEN I WAKE UP IN THE MORNING AND REALIZE I WASN'T DREAMING.

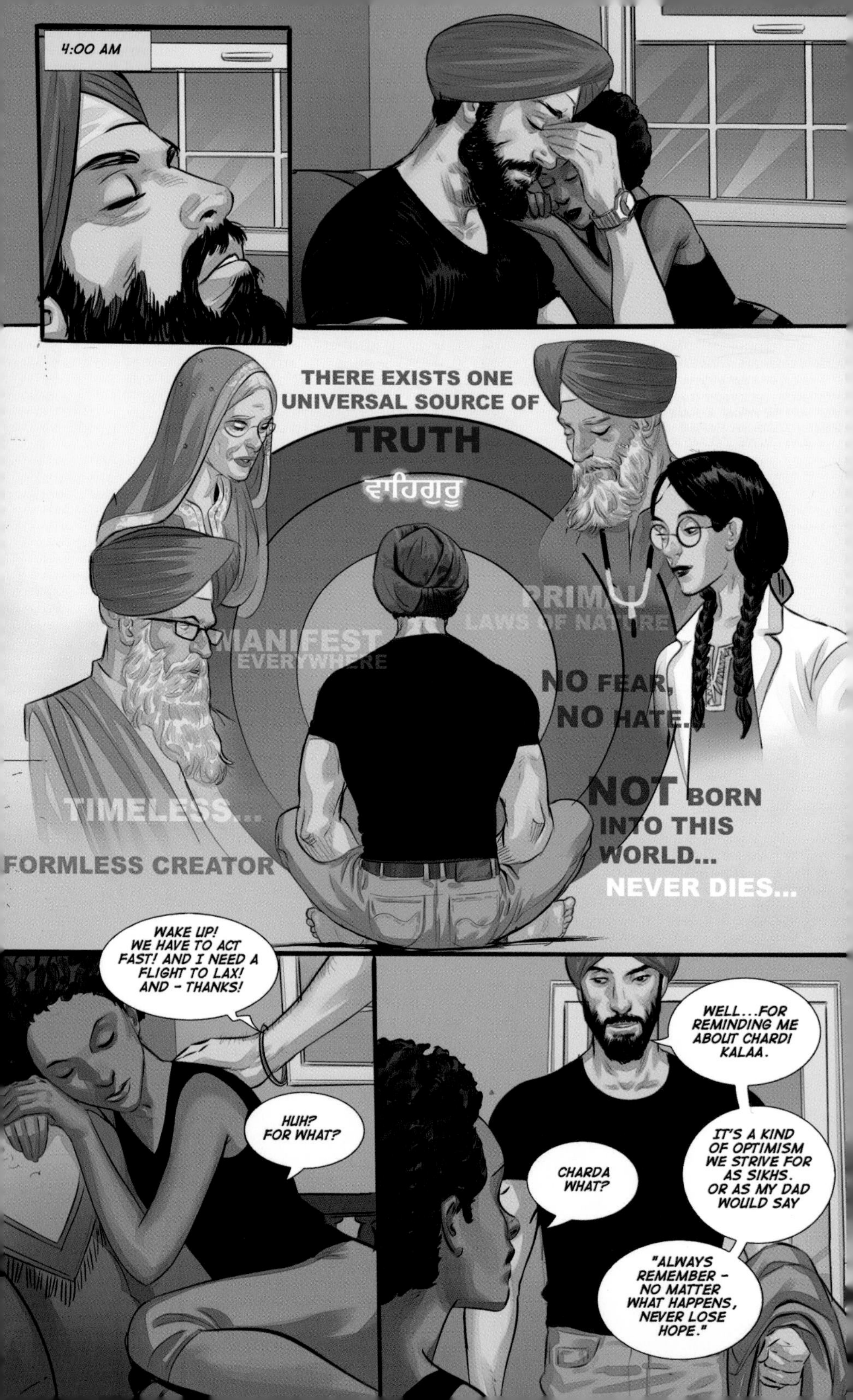
4:00 AM
THERE EXISTS ONE UNIVERSAL SOURCE OF
TRUTH
ਵਾਹਿਗੁਰੂ
PRIMAL
LAWS OF NATURE
MANIFEST
EVERYWHERE
NO FEAR, NO HATE...
TIMELESS...
FORMLESS CREATOR
NOT BORN INTO THIS WORLD...
NEVER DIES...
WAKE UP! WE HAVE TO ACT FAST! AND I NEED A FLIGHT TO LAX! AND - THANKS!
HUH? FOR WHAT?
WELL...FOR REMINDING ME ABOUT CHARDI KALAA.
CHARDA WHAT?
IT'S A KIND OF OPTIMISM WE STRIVE FOR AS SIKHS. OR AS MY DAD WOULD SAY
"ALWAYS REMEMBER - NO MATTER WHAT HAPPENS, NEVER LOSE HOPE."

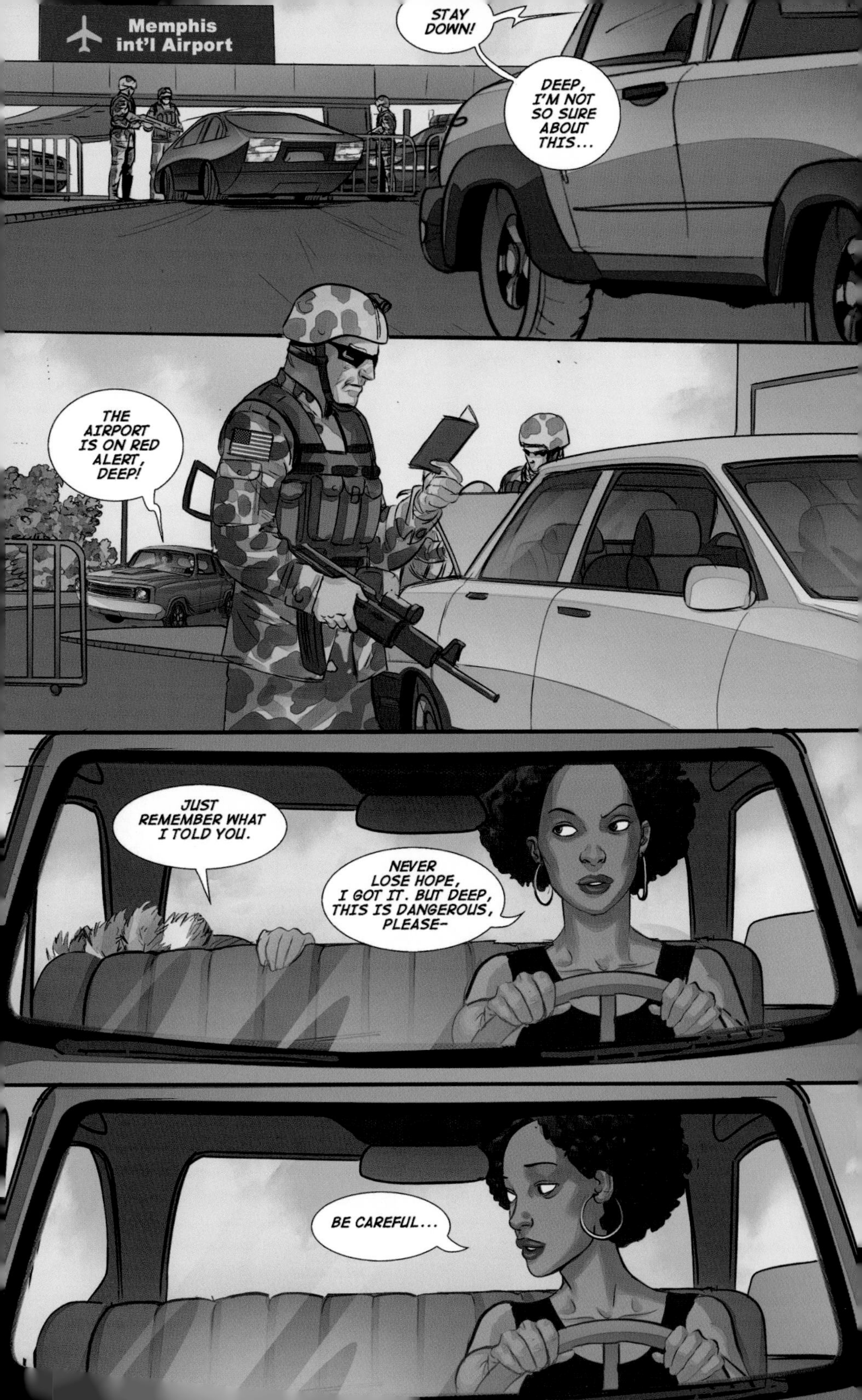
Memphis int'l Airport
STAY DOWN!
DEEP, I'M NOT SO SURE ABOUT THIS...
THE AIRPORT IS ON RED ALERT, DEEP!
JUST REMEMBER WHAT I TOLD YOU.
NEVER LOSE HOPE, I GOT IT. BUT DEEP, THIS IS DANGEROUS, PLEASE-
BE CAREFUL...

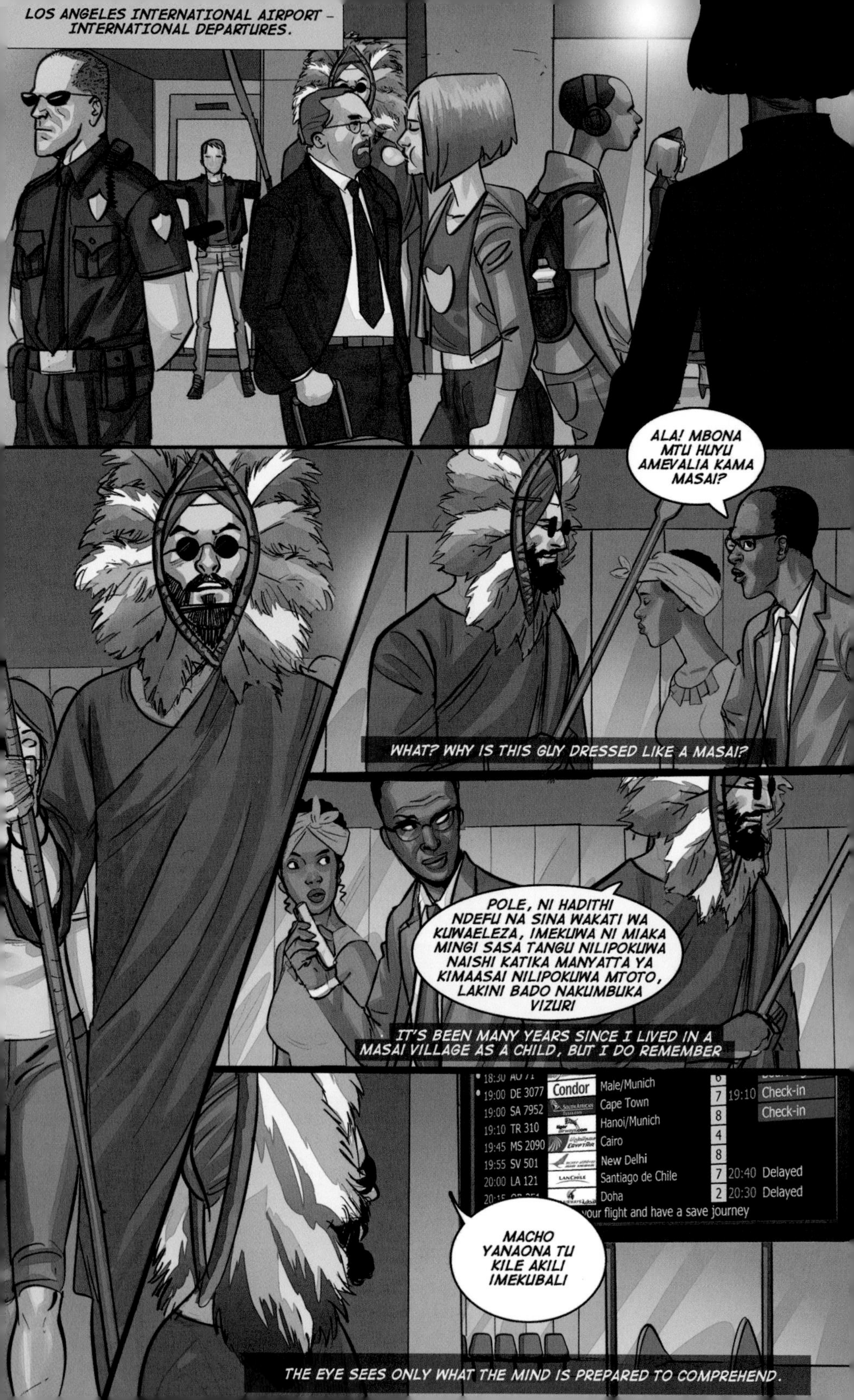
LOS ANGELES INTERNATIONAL AIRPORT – INTERNATIONAL DEPARTURES.
ALA! MBONA MTU HUYU AMEVALIA KAMA MASAI?
WHAT? WHY IS THIS GUY DRESSED LIKE A MASAI?
POLE, NI HADITHI NDEFU NA SINA WAKATI WA KUWAELEZA, IMEKUWA NI MIAKA MINGI SASA TANGU NILIPOKUWA NAISHI KATIKA MANYATTA YA KIMAASAI NILIPOKUWA MTOTO, LAKINI BADO NAKUMBUKA VIZURI
IT'S BEEN MANY YEARS SINCE I LIVED IN A MASAI VILLAGE AS A CHILD, BUT I DO REMEMBER
19:00 DE 3077 Condor Male/Munich 7 19:10 Check-in
19:00 SA 7952 Cape Town 8 Check-in
19:10 TR 310 Hanoi/Munich 8
19:45 MS 2090 Cairo 4
19:55 SV 501 New Delhi 8
20:00 LA 121 Santiago de Chile 7 20:40 Delayed
Doha 2 20:30 Delayed
your flight and have a save journey
MACHO YANAONA TU KILE AKILI IMEKUBALI
THE EYE SEES ONLY WHAT THE MIND IS PREPARED TO COMPREHEND.

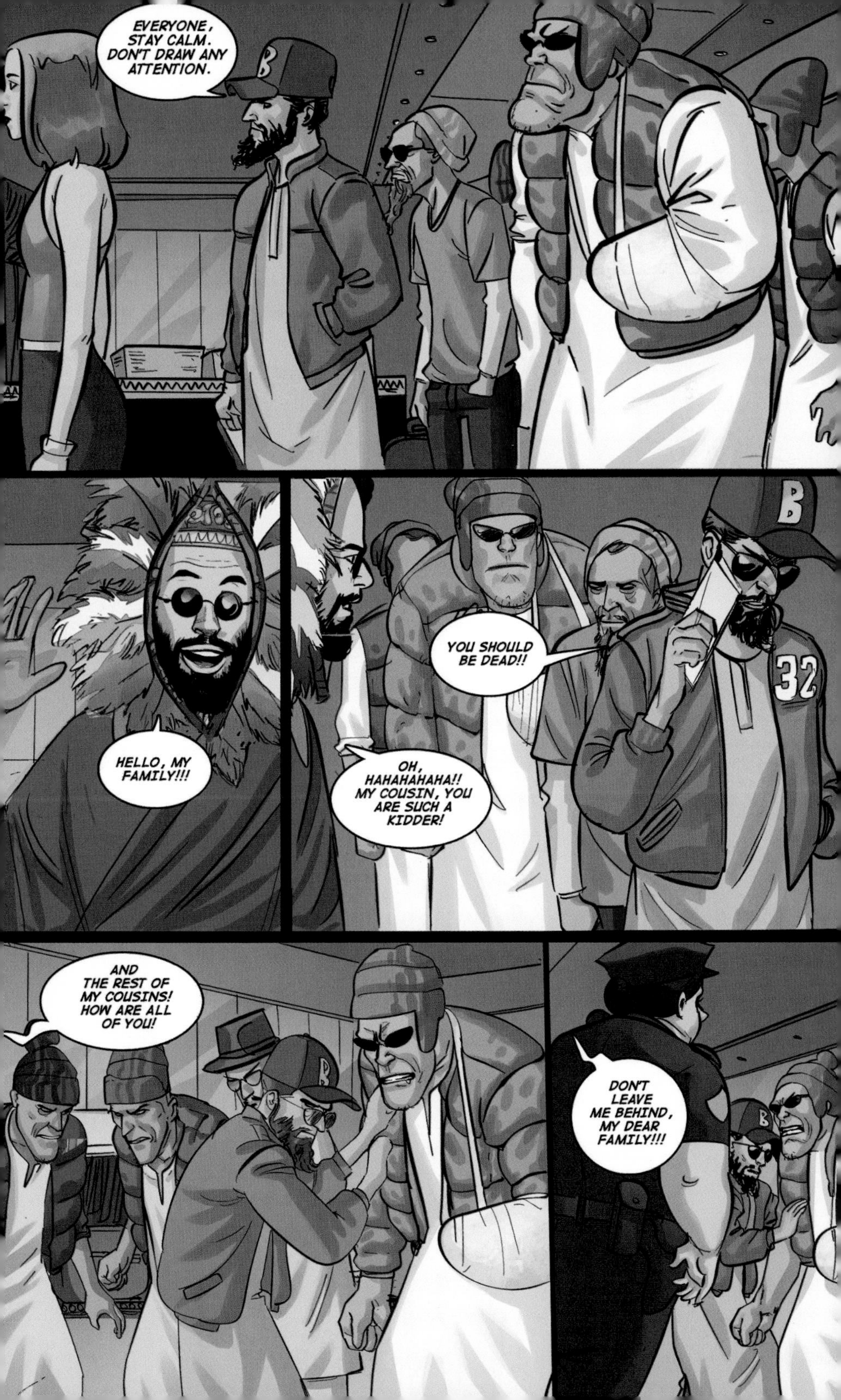
EVERYONE, STAY CALM. DON'T DRAW ANY ATTENTION.
HELLO, MY FAMILY!!!
YOU SHOULD BE DEAD!!
OH, HAHAHAHAHA!! MY COUSIN, YOU ARE SUCH A KIDDER!
AND THE REST OF MY COUSINS! HOW ARE ALL OF YOU!
DON'T LEAVE ME BEHIND, MY DEAR FAMILY!!!

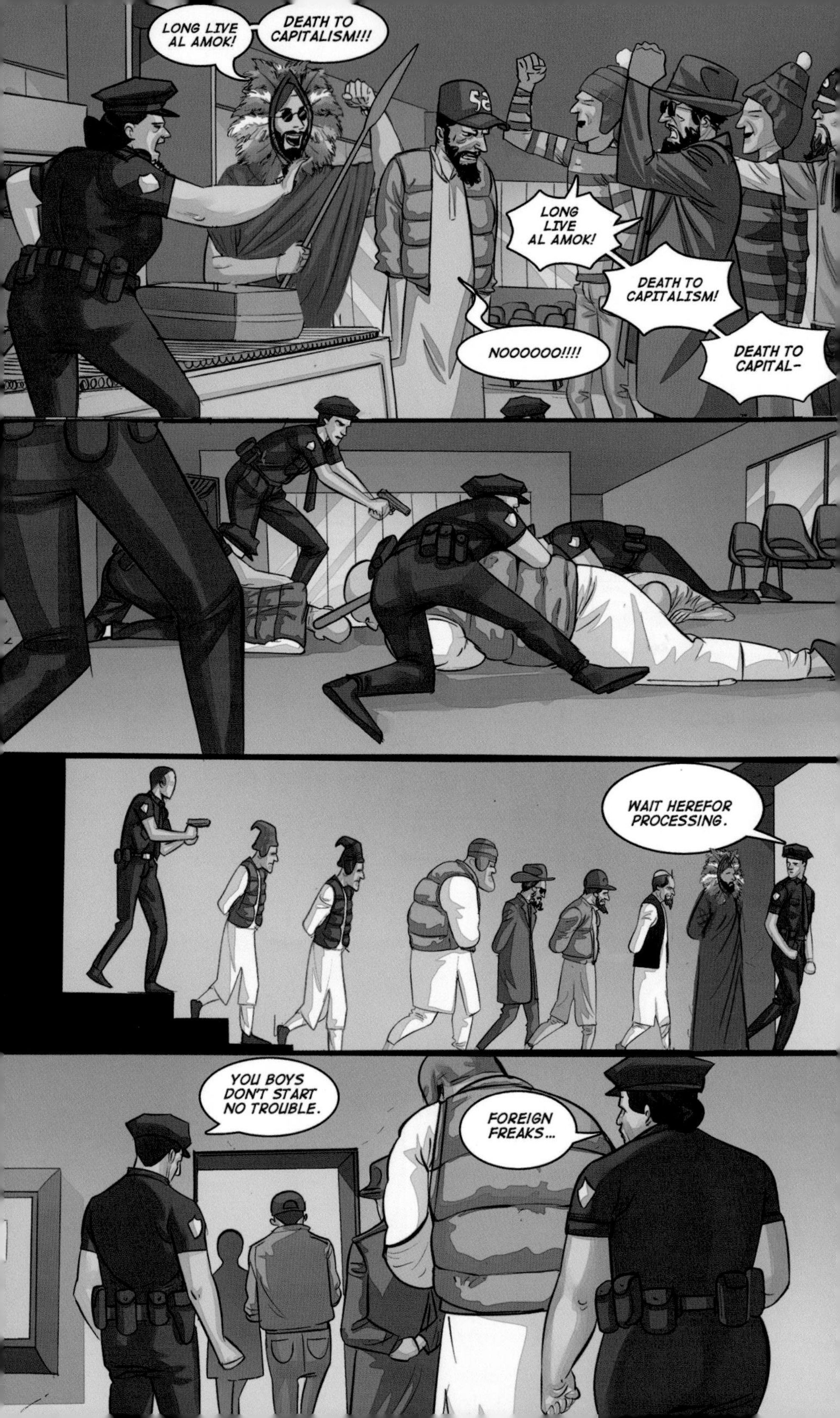
LONG LIVE AL AMOK!
DEATH TO CAPITALISM!!!
LONG LIVE AL AMOK!
DEATH TO CAPITALISM!
NOOOOOO!!!!
DEATH TO CAPITAL-
WAIT HEREFOR PROCESSING.
YOU BOYS DON'T START NO TROUBLE.
FOREIGN FREAKS...

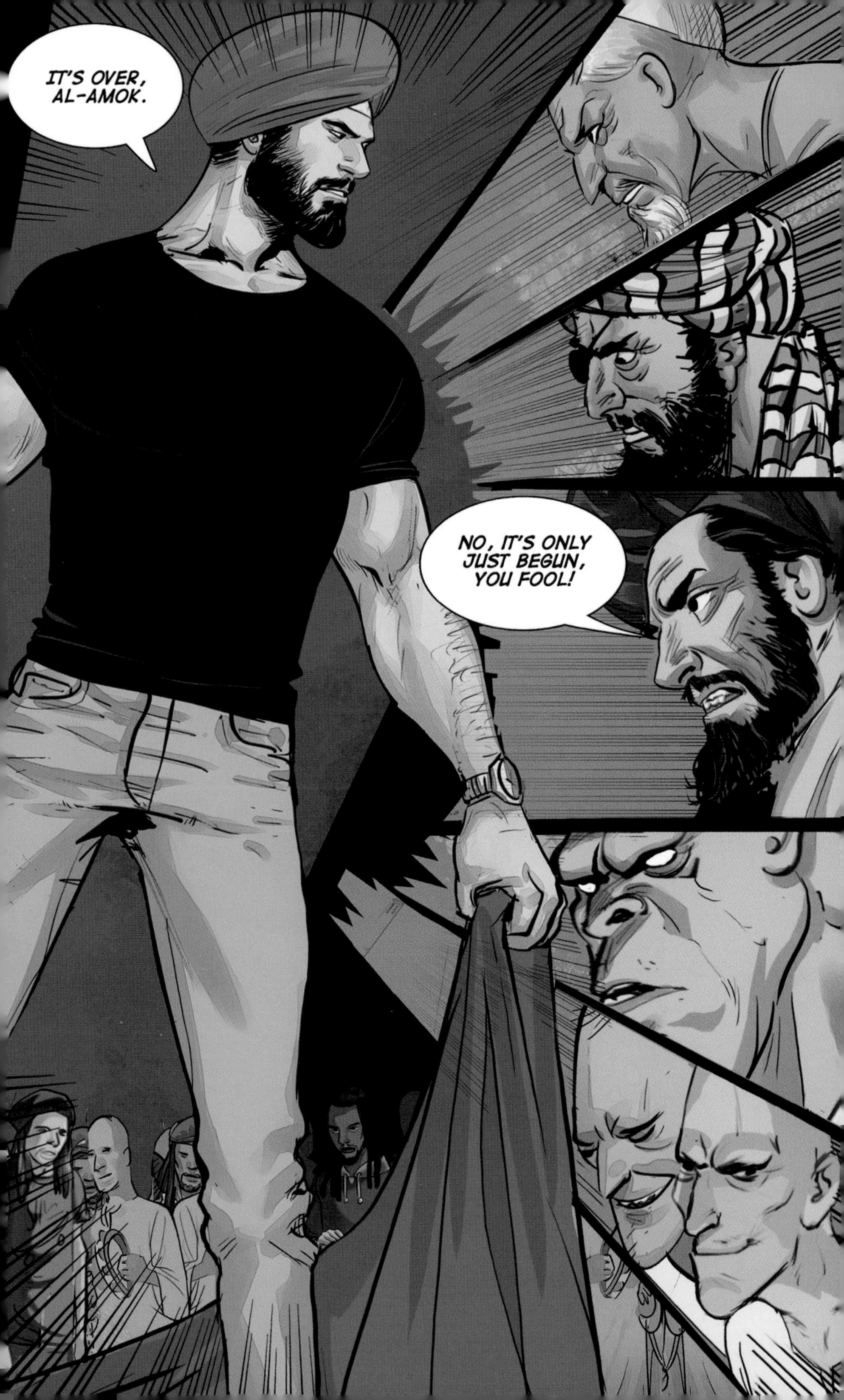
IT'S OVER, AL-AMOK.
NO, IT'S ONLY JUST BEGUN, YOU FOOL!

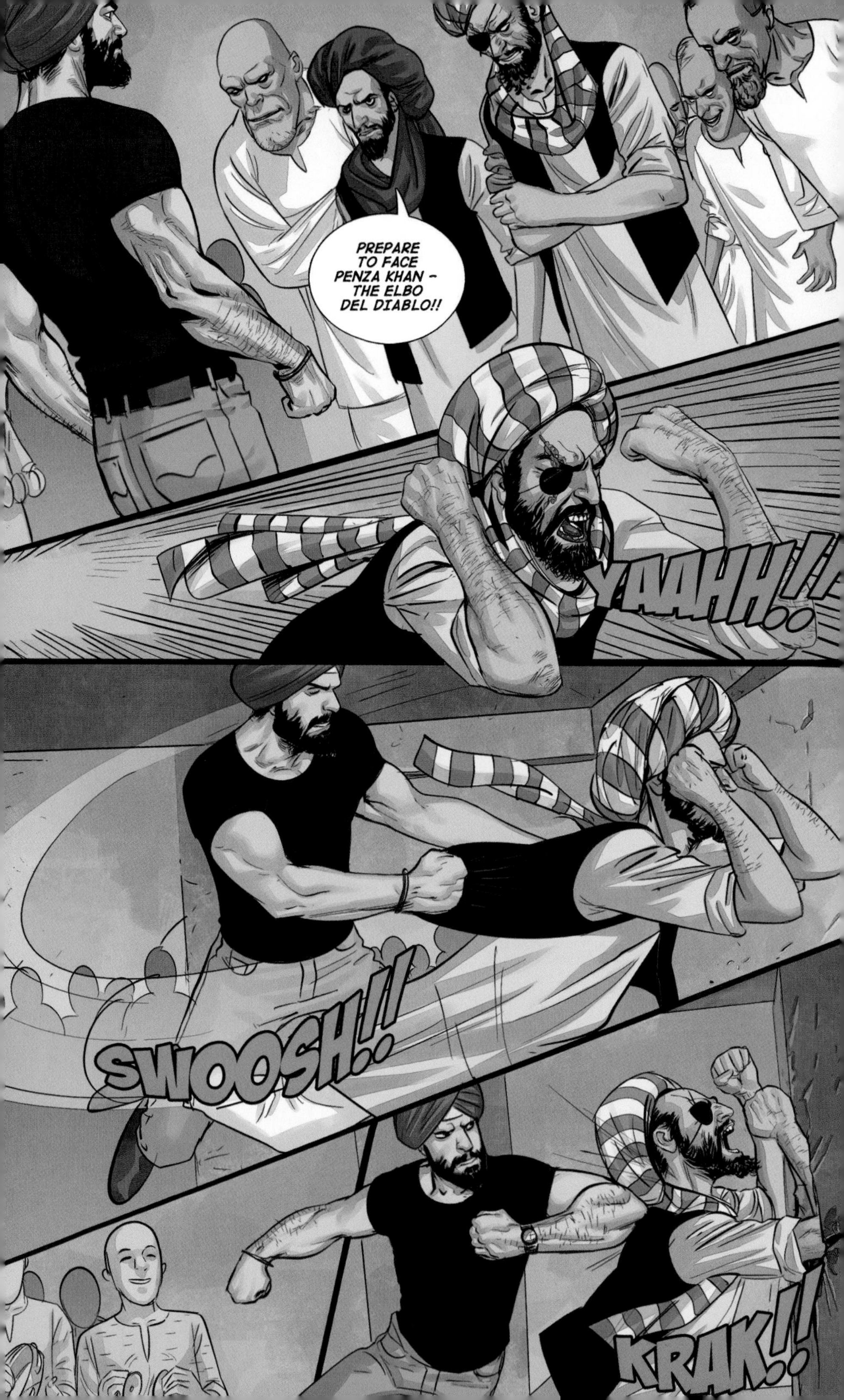
PREPARE TO FACE PENZA KHAN – THE ELBO DEL DIABLO!!
YAAHH!!
SWOOSH!!
KRAK!!

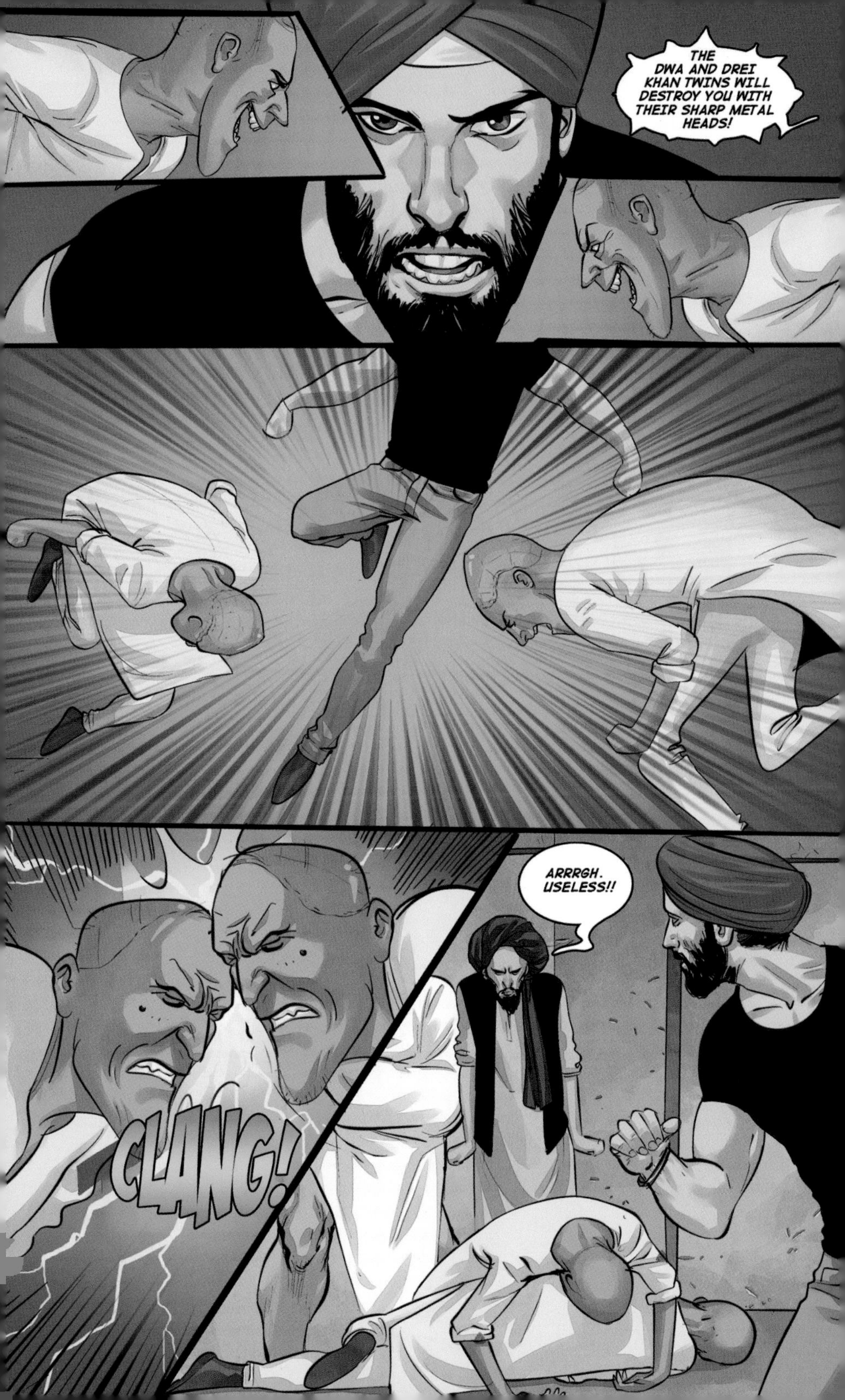
THE DWA AND DREI KHAN TWINS WILL DESTROY YOU WITH THEIR SHARP METAL HEADS!
CLANG!
ARRRGH. USELESS!!

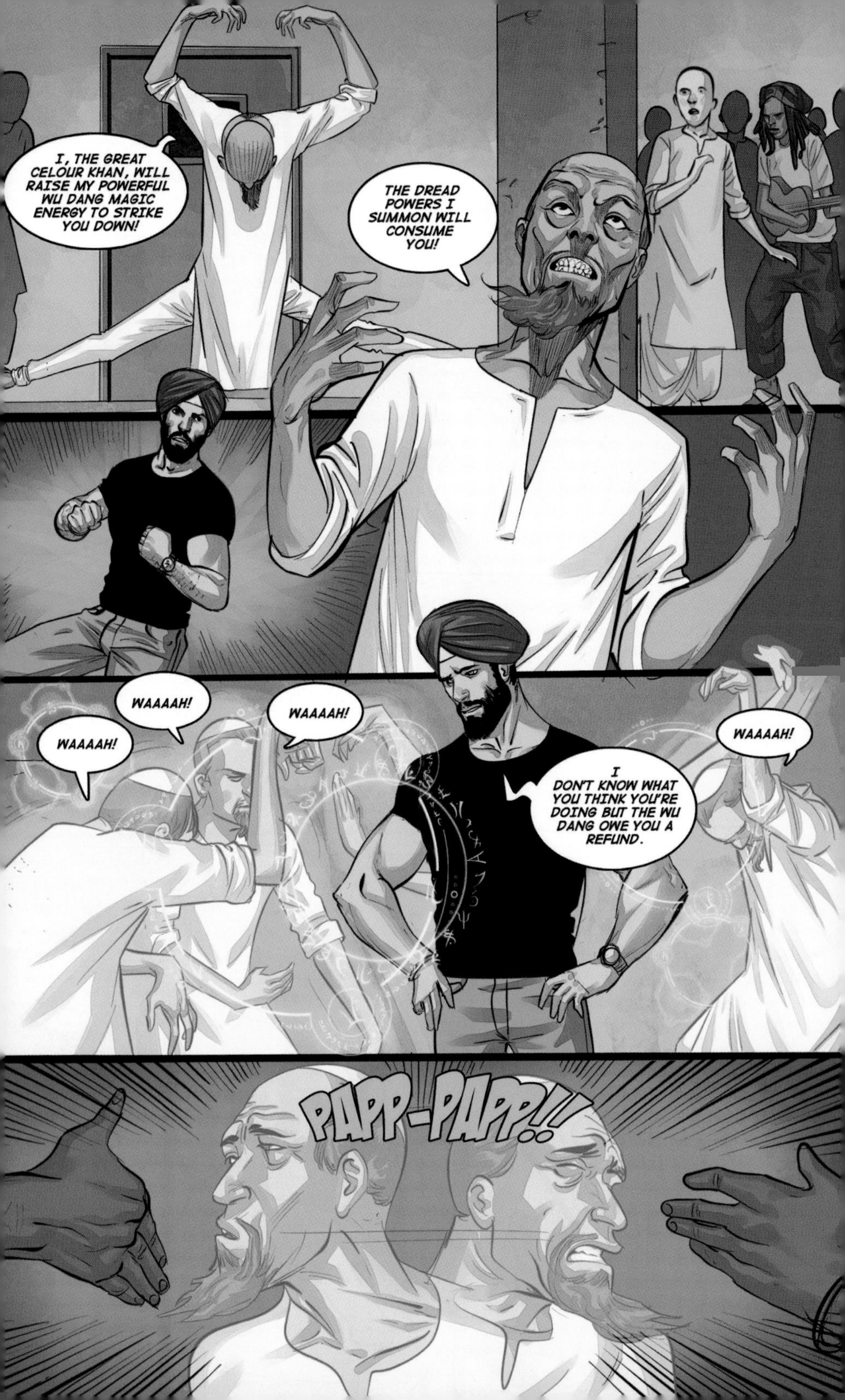
I, THE GREAT CELOUR KHAN, WILL RAISE MY POWERFUL WU DANG MAGIC ENERGY TO STRIKE YOU DOWN!
THE DREAD POWERS I SUMMON WILL CONSUME YOU!
WAAAAH!
WAAAAH!
WAAAAH!
WAAAAH!
I DON'T KNOW WHAT YOU THINK YOU'RE DOING BUT THE WU DANG OWE YOU A REFUND.
PAPP-PAPP!!

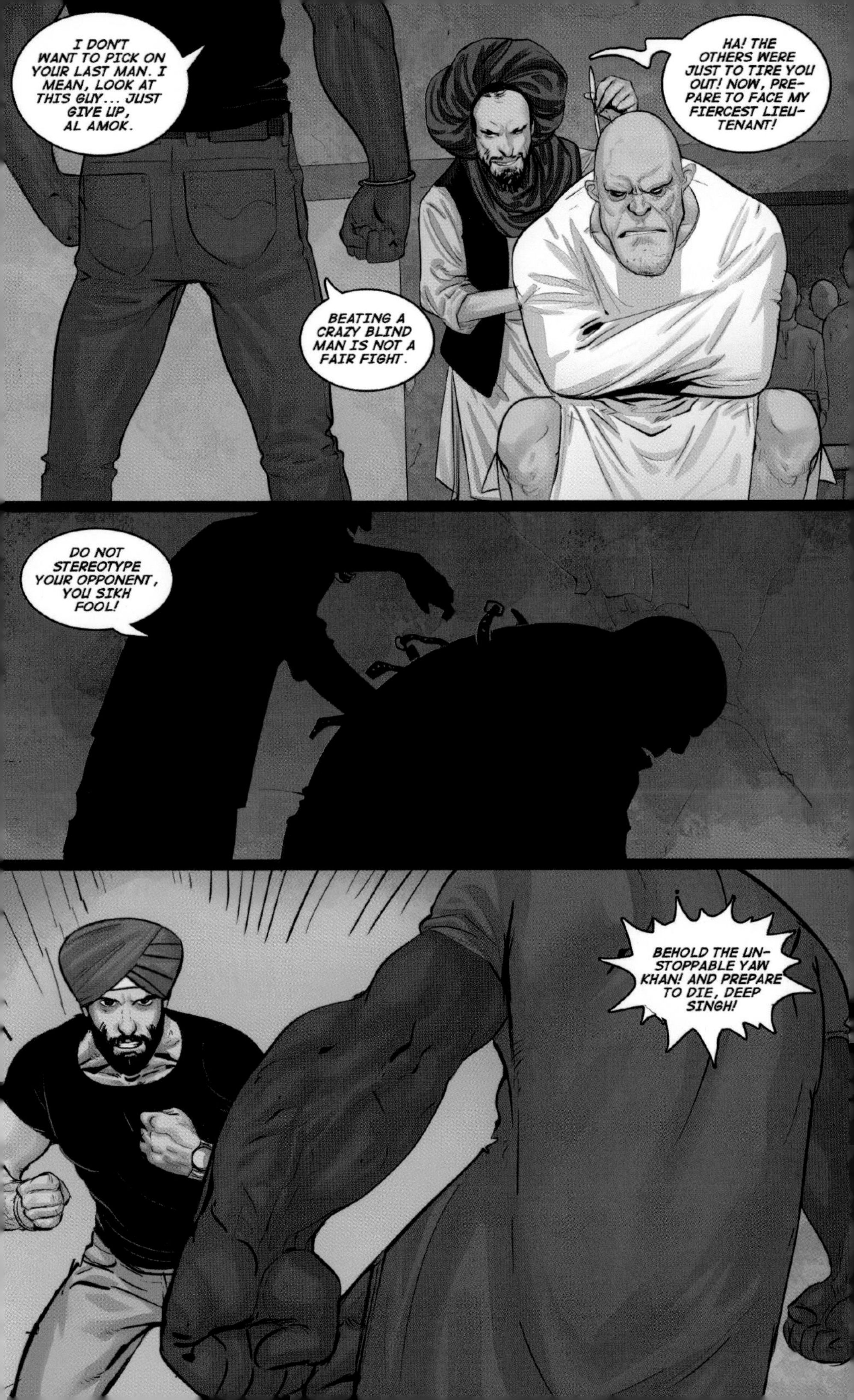
I DON'T WANT TO PICK ON YOUR LAST MAN. I MEAN, LOOK AT THIS GUY... JUST GIVE UP, AL AMOK.
HA! THE OTHERS WERE JUST TO TIRE YOU OUT! NOW, PREPARE TO FACE MY FIERCEST LIEUTENANT!
BEATING A CRAZY BLIND MAN IS NOT A FAIR FIGHT.
DO NOT STEREOTYPE YOUR OPPONENT, YOU SIKH FOOL!
BEHOLD THE UNSTOPPABLE YAW KHAN! AND PREPARE TO DIE, DEEP SINGH!

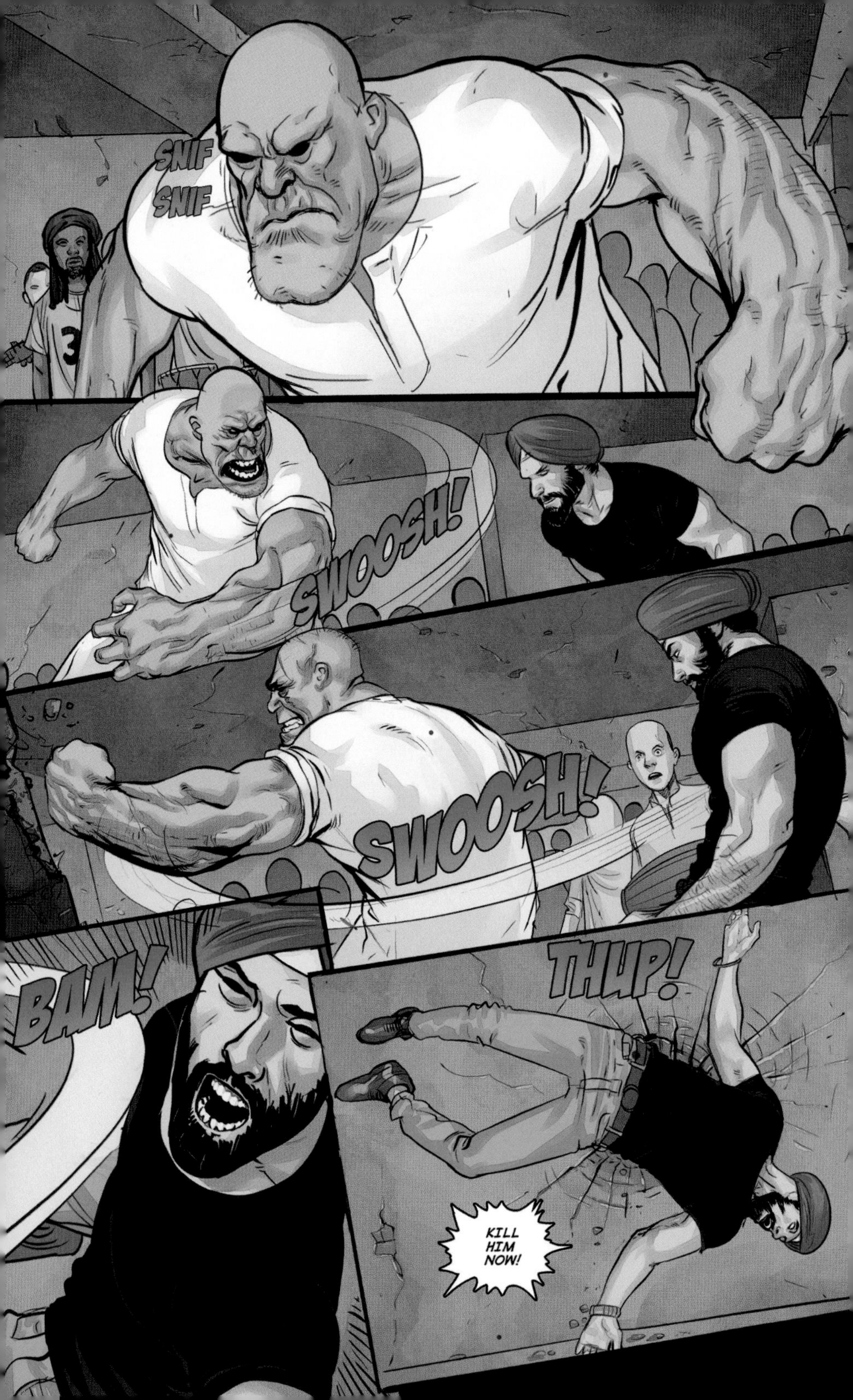
SNIF
SNIF
SWOOSH!
SWOOSH!
BAM!
THUP!
KILL HIM NOW!

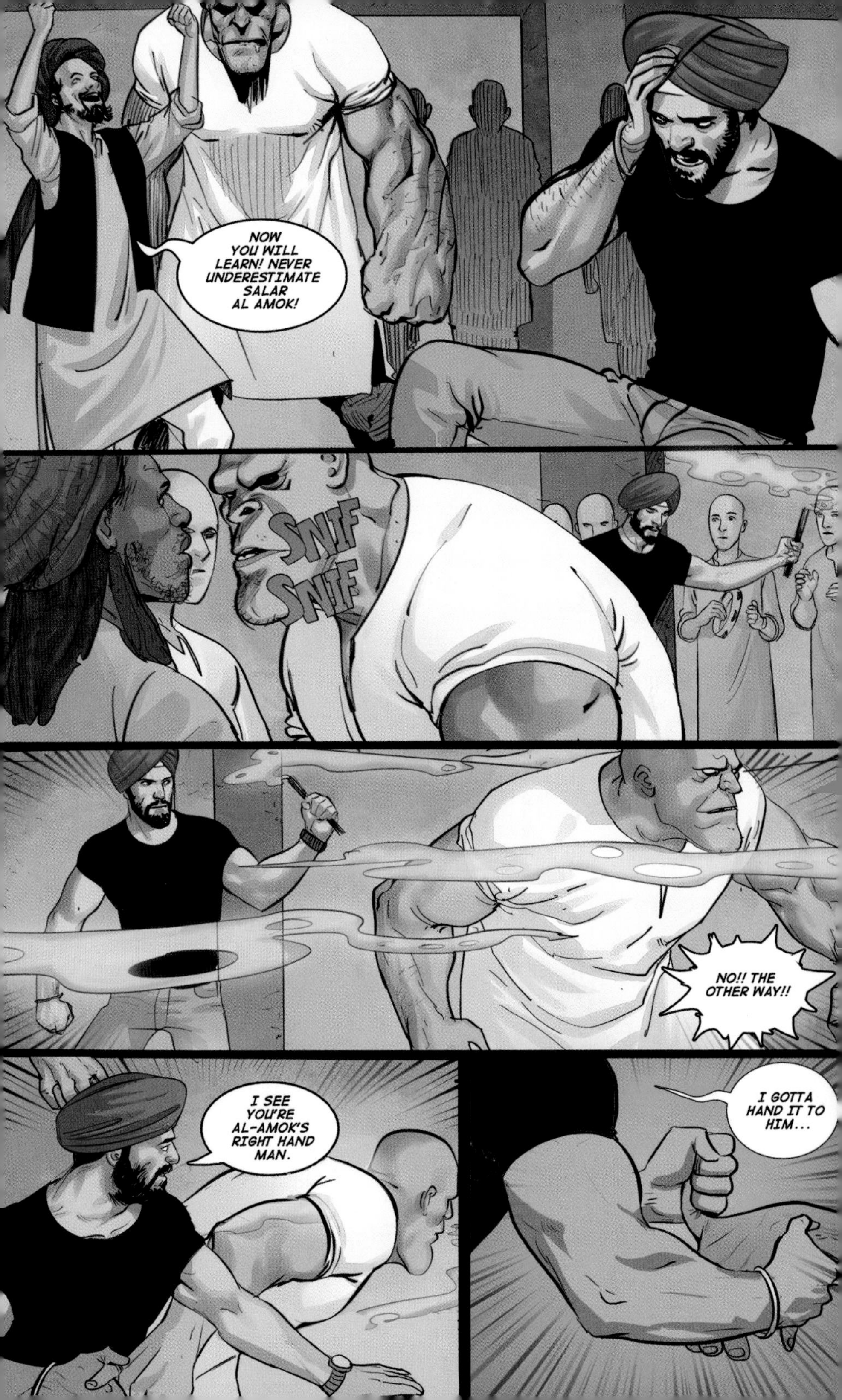
NOW YOU WILL LEARN! NEVER UNDERESTIMATE SALAR AL AMOK!
SNIF SNIF
NO!! THE OTHER WAY!!
I SEE YOU'RE AL-AMOK'S RIGHT HAND MAN.
I GOTTA HAND IT TO HIM...

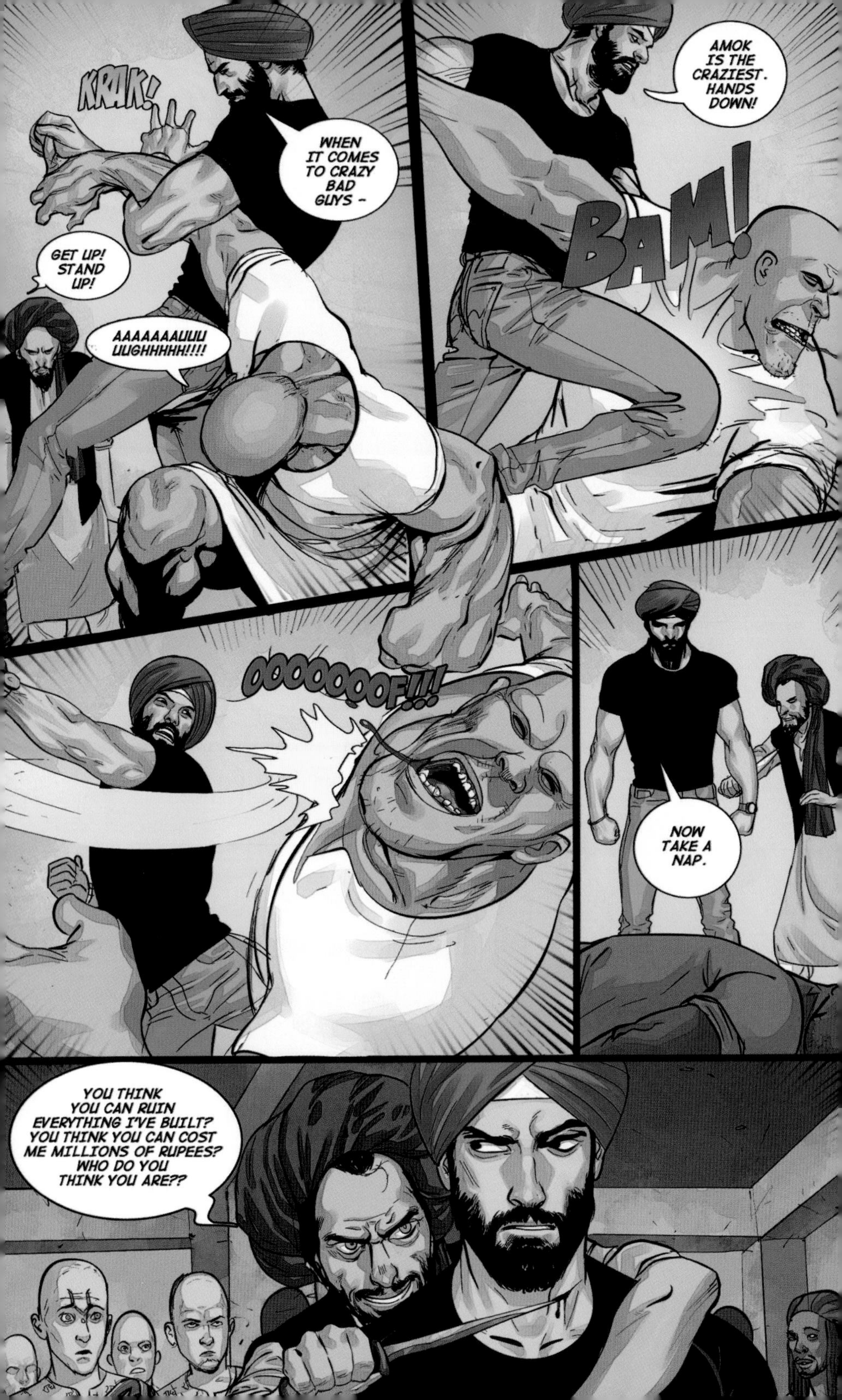
KRAK!
WHEN IT COMES TO CRAZY BAD GUYS -
GET UP! STAND UP!
AAAAAAAUUU UUGHHHHH!!!!
AMOK IS THE CRAZIEST. HANDS DOWN!
BAM!
OOOOOOOOF!!!
NOW TAKE A NAP.
YOU THINK YOU CAN RUIN EVERYTHING I'VE BUILT? YOU THINK YOU CAN COST ME MILLIONS OF RUPEES? WHO DO YOU THINK YOU ARE??

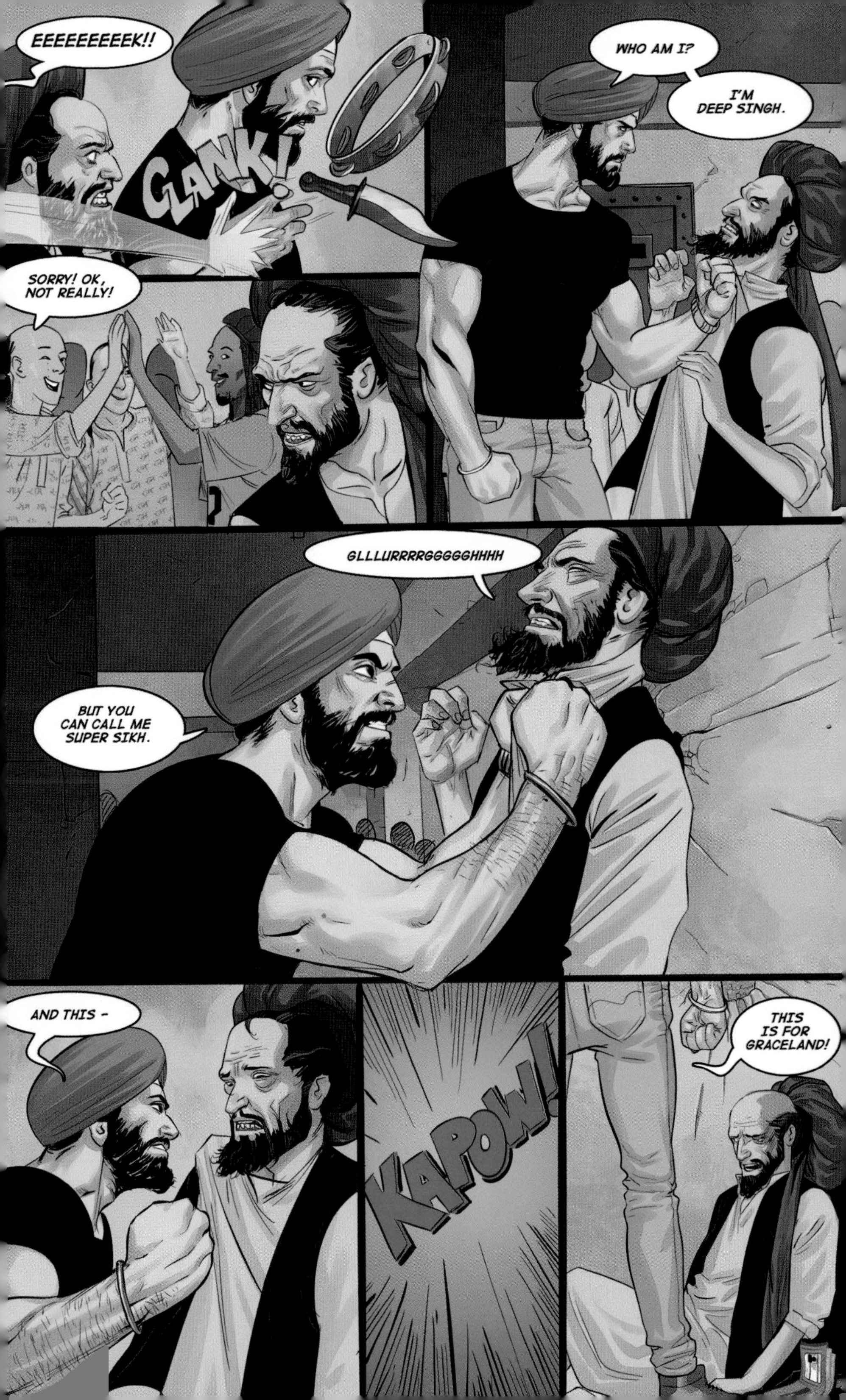
EEEEEEEEEK!!
CLANK!
WHO AM I?
I'M DEEP SINGH.
SORRY! OK, NOT REALLY!
GLLLURRRRGGGGGHHHH
BUT YOU CAN CALL ME SUPER SIKH.
AND THIS -
KAPOW!
THIS IS FOR GRACELAND!

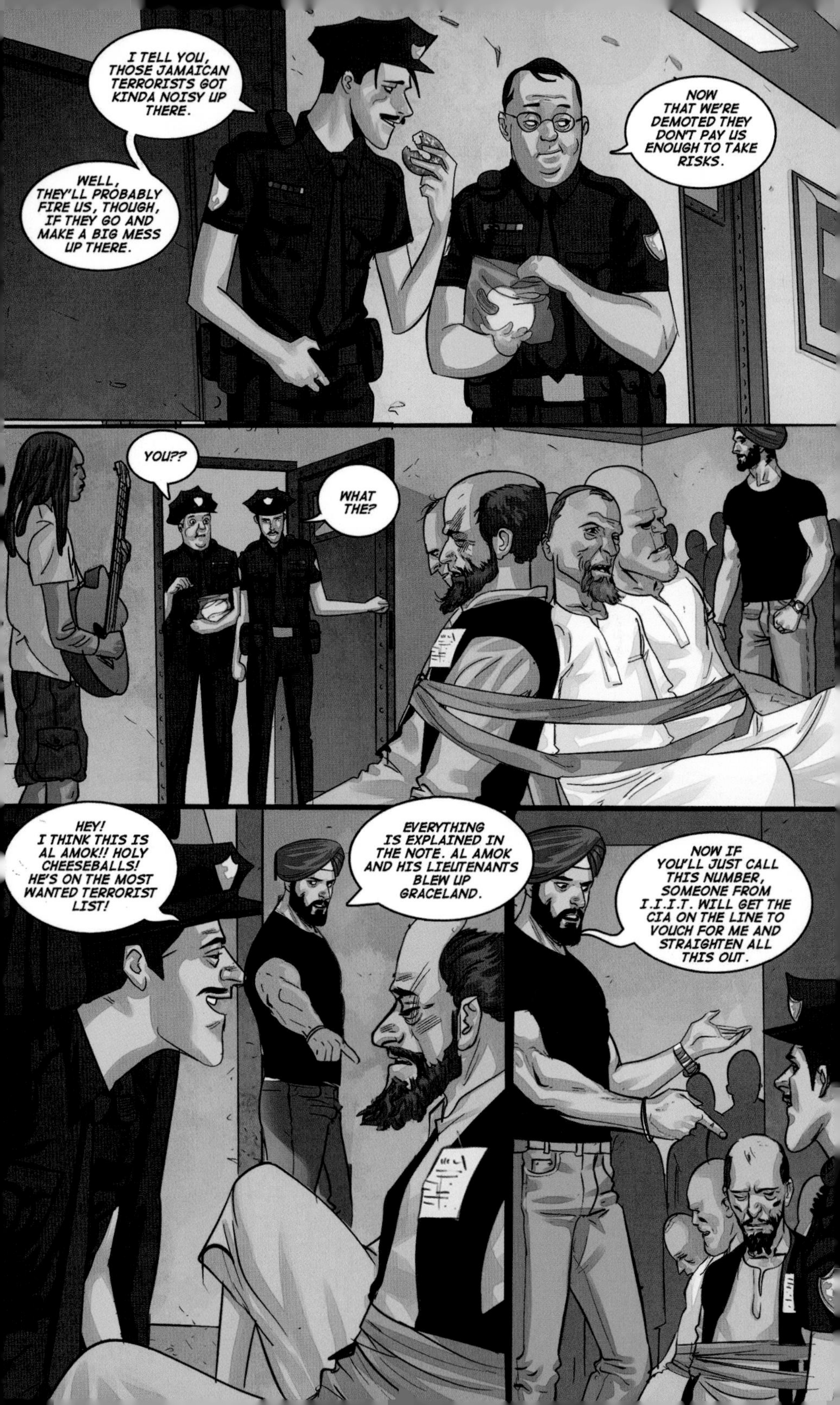
I TELL YOU, THOSE JAMAICAN TERRORISTS GOT KINDA NOISY UP THERE.
WELL, THEY'LL PROBABLY FIRE US, THOUGH, IF THEY GO AND MAKE A BIG MESS UP THERE.
NOW THAT WE'RE DEMOTED THEY DON'T PAY US ENOUGH TO TAKE RISKS.
YOU??
WHAT THE?
HEY! I THINK THIS IS AL AMOK!! HOLY CHEESEBALLS! HE'S ON THE MOST WANTED TERRORIST LIST!
EVERYTHING IS EXPLAINED IN THE NOTE. AL AMOK AND HIS LIEUTENANTS BLEW UP GRACELAND.
NOW IF YOU'LL JUST CALL THIS NUMBER, SOMEONE FROM I.I.I.T. WILL GET THE CIA ON THE LINE TO VOUCH FOR ME AND STRAIGHTEN ALL THIS OUT.

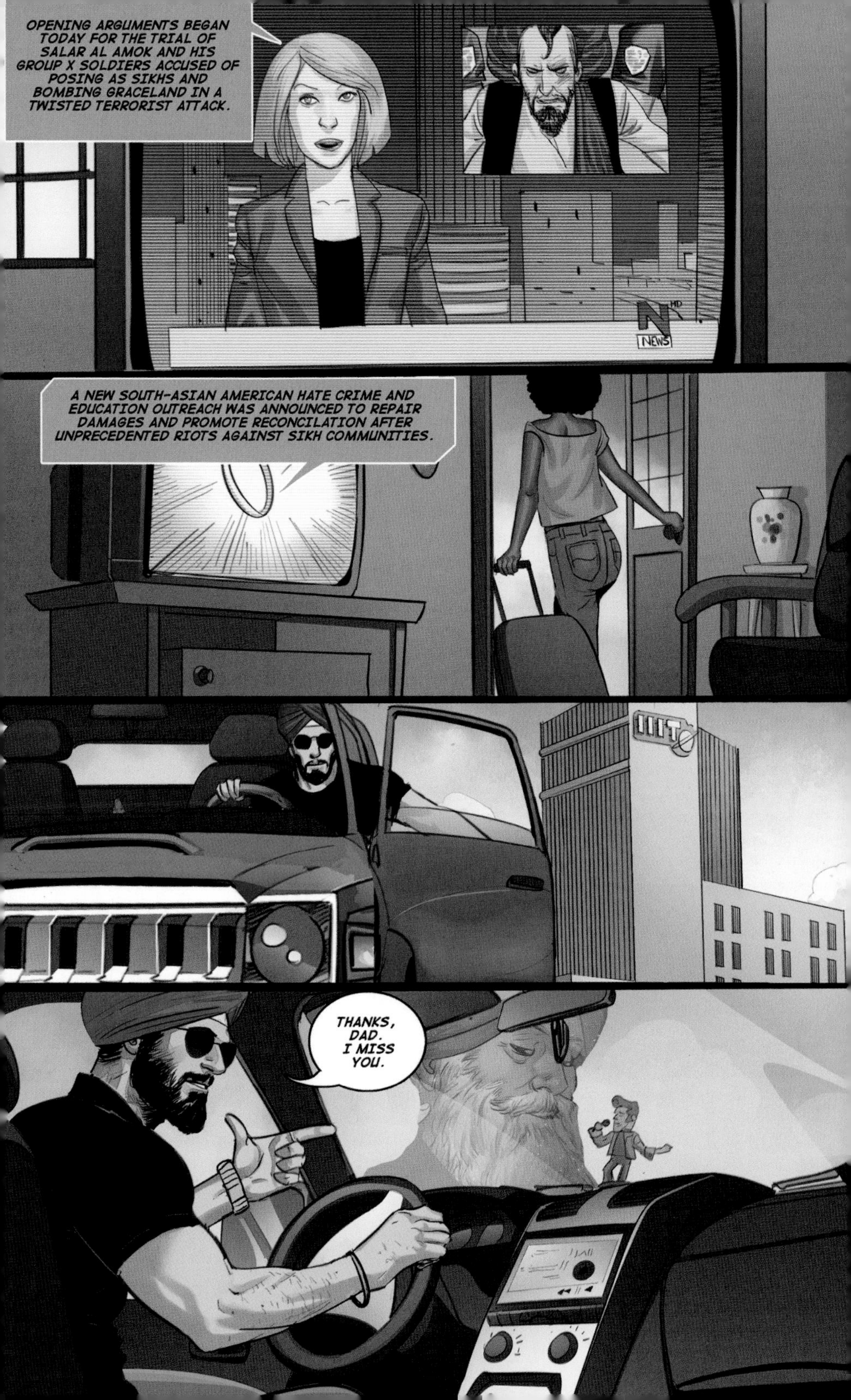
OPENING ARGUMENTS BEGAN TODAY FOR THE TRIAL OF SALAR AL AMOK AND HIS GROUP X SOLDIERS ACCUSED OF POSING AS SIKHS AND BOMBING GRACELAND IN A TWISTED TERRORIST ATTACK.
NEWS
A NEW SOUTH-ASIAN AMERICAN HATE CRIME AND EDUCATION OUTREACH WAS ANNOUNCED TO REPAIR DAMAGES AND PROMOTE RECONCILATION AFTER UNPRECEDENTED RIOTS AGAINST SIKH COMMUNITIES.
THANKS, DAD. I MISS YOU.

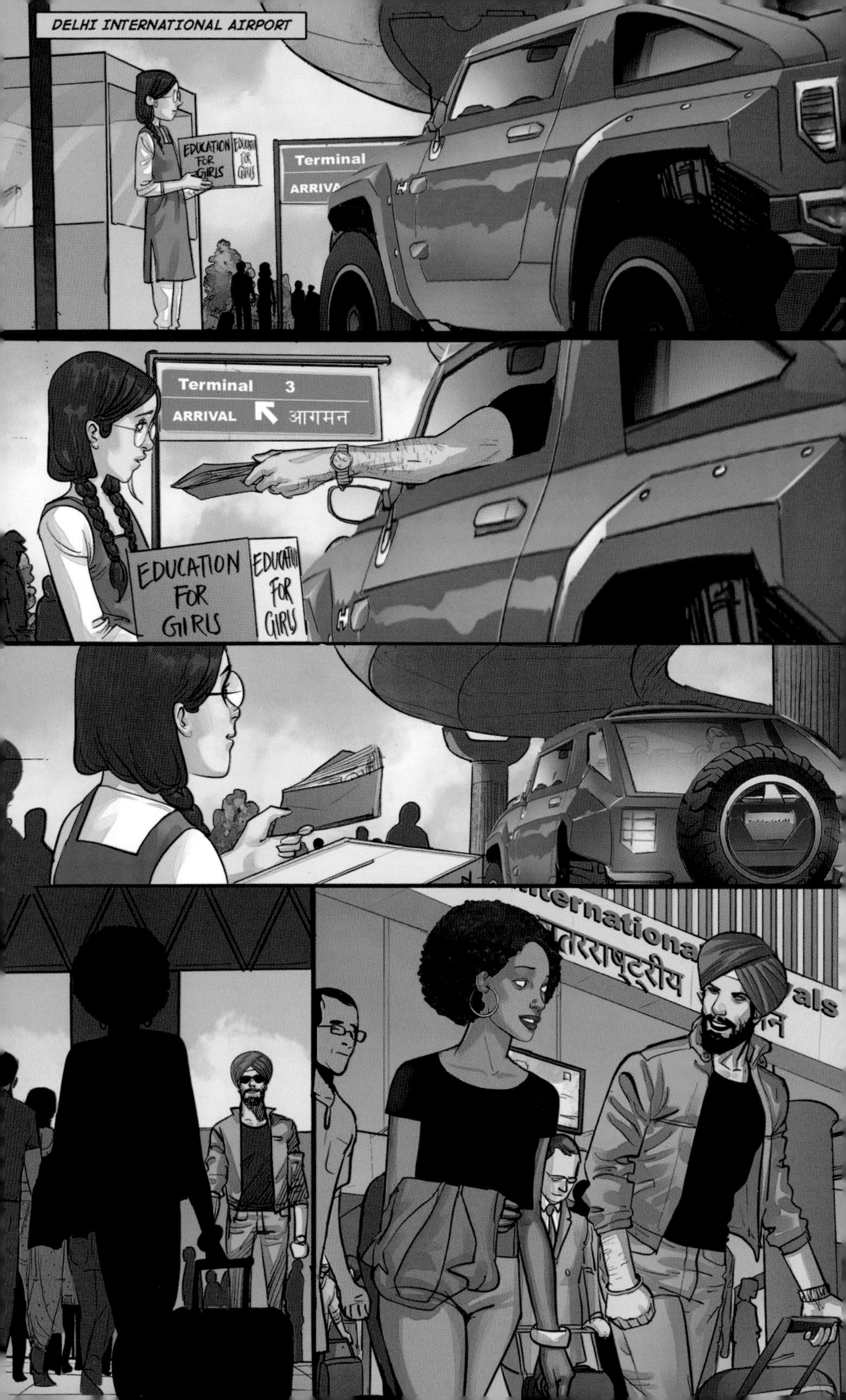
DELHI INTERNATIONAL AIRPORT
EDUCATION FOR GIRLS
Terminal 3
ARRIVAL आगमन
EDUCATION FOR GIRLS

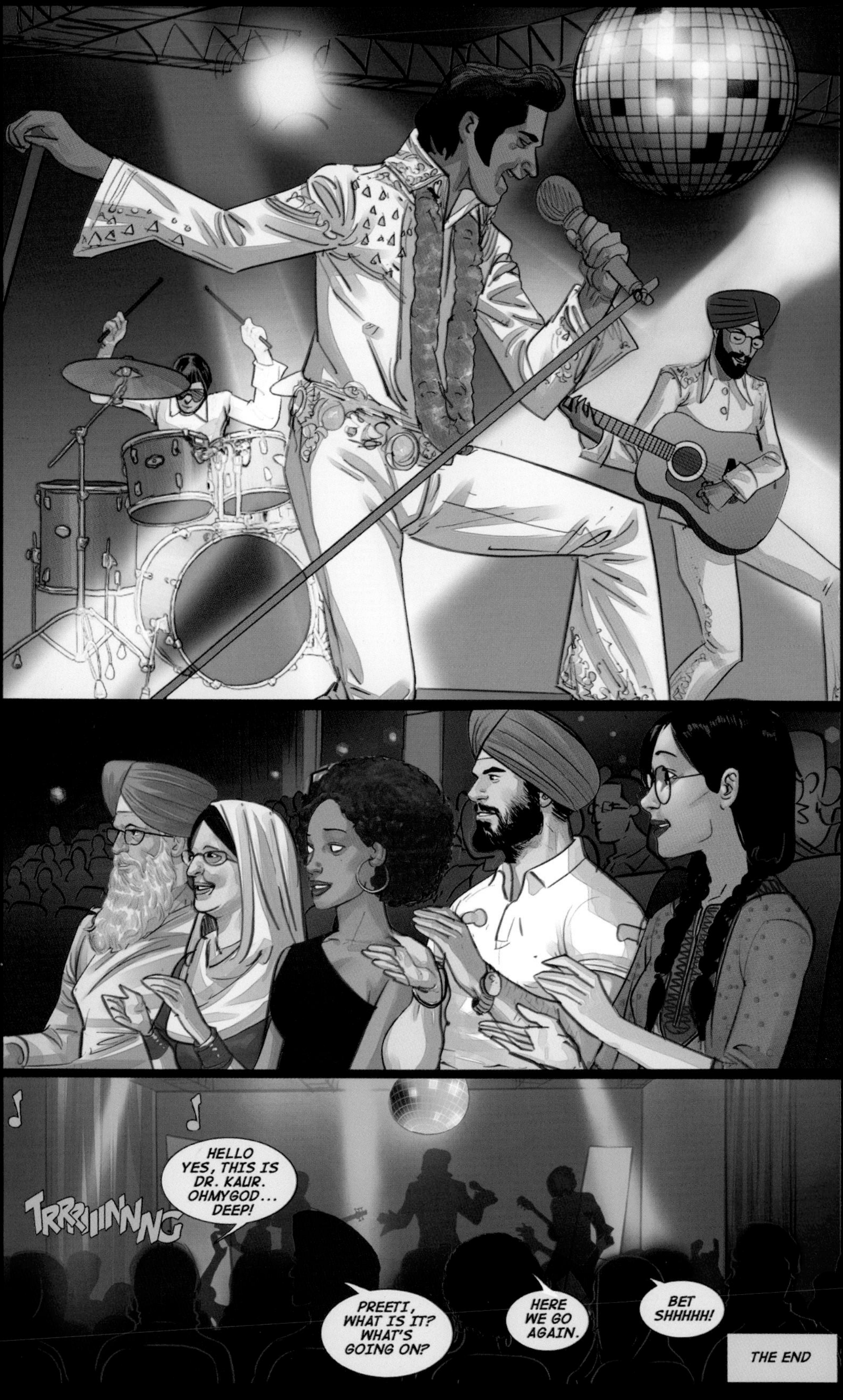

TRRRIINNNG
HELLO YES, THIS IS DR. KAUR. OHMYGOD... DEEP!
PREETI, WHAT IS IT? WHAT'S GOING ON?
HERE WE GO AGAIN.
BET SHHHHH!
THE END